Communications
in Computer and Information Science 2272

Series Editors

Gang Li , *School of Information Technology, Deakin University, Burwood, VIC, Australia*
Joaquim Filipe , *Polytechnic Institute of Setúbal, Setúbal, Portugal*
Zhiwei Xu, *Chinese Academy of Sciences, Beijing, China*

Rationale
The CCIS series is devoted to the publication of proceedings of computer science conferences. Its aim is to efficiently disseminate original research results in informatics in printed and electronic form. While the focus is on publication of peer-reviewed full papers presenting mature work, inclusion of reviewed short papers reporting on work in progress is welcome, too. Besides globally relevant meetings with internationally representative program committees guaranteeing a strict peer-reviewing and paper selection process, conferences run by societies or of high regional or national relevance are also considered for publication.

Topics
The topical scope of CCIS spans the entire spectrum of informatics ranging from foundational topics in the theory of computing to information and communications science and technology and a broad variety of interdisciplinary application fields.

Information for Volume Editors and Authors
Publication in CCIS is free of charge. No royalties are paid, however, we offer registered conference participants temporary free access to the online version of the conference proceedings on SpringerLink (http://link.springer.com) by means of an http referrer from the conference website and/or a number of complimentary printed copies, as specified in the official acceptance email of the event.

CCIS proceedings can be published in time for distribution at conferences or as post-proceedings, and delivered in the form of printed books and/or electronically as USBs and/or e-content licenses for accessing proceedings at SpringerLink. Furthermore, CCIS proceedings are included in the CCIS electronic book series hosted in the SpringerLink digital library at http://link.springer.com/bookseries/7899. Conferences publishing in CCIS are allowed to use Online Conference Service (OCS) for managing the whole proceedings lifecycle (from submission and reviewing to preparing for publication) free of charge.

Publication process
The language of publication is exclusively English. Authors publishing in CCIS have to sign the Springer CCIS copyright transfer form, however, they are free to use their material published in CCIS for substantially changed, more elaborate subsequent publications elsewhere. For the preparation of the camera-ready papers/files, authors have to strictly adhere to the Springer CCIS Authors' Instructions and are strongly encouraged to use the CCIS LaTeX style files or templates.

Abstracting/Indexing
CCIS is abstracted/indexed in DBLP, Google Scholar, EI-Compendex, Mathematical Reviews, SCImago, Scopus. CCIS volumes are also submitted for the inclusion in ISI Proceedings.

How to start
To start the evaluation of your proposal for inclusion in the CCIS series, please send an e-mail to ccis@springer.com.

Jule M. Krüger · Daniela Pedrosa · Dennis Beck ·
Marie-Luce Bourguet · Andreas Dengel ·
Rami Ghannam · Alan Miller ·
Anasol Peña-Rios · Jonathon Richter
Editors

Immersive Learning Research Network

10th International Conference on Immersive Learning, iLRN 2024
Glasgow, UK, June 10–13, 2024
Revised Selected Papers, Part II

Editors
Jule M. Krüger
University of Potsdam
Potsdam, Germany

Dennis Beck
University of Arkansas
Arkansas, AR, USA

Andreas Dengel
Goethe-Universität Frankfurt am Main
Frankfurt, Germany

Alan Miller
University of St Andrews
St Andrews, UK

Jonathon Richter
University of Montana
Missoula, MT, USA

Daniela Pedrosa
Polytechnic Institute of Santarém
Santarém, Portugal

Marie-Luce Bourguet
Queen Mary University of London
London, UK

Rami Ghannam
University of Glasgow
Glasgow, UK

Anasol Peña-Rios
BT Research Labs
Ipswich, UK

ISSN 1865-0929 ISSN 1865-0937 (electronic)
Communications in Computer and Information Science
ISBN 978-3-031-80471-7 ISBN 978-3-031-80472-4 (eBook)
https://doi.org/10.1007/978-3-031-80472-4

© The Editor(s) (if applicable) and The Author(s), under exclusive license
to Springer Nature Switzerland AG 2025

This work is subject to copyright. All rights are solely and exclusively licensed by the Publisher, whether the whole or part of the material is concerned, specifically the rights of translation, reprinting, reuse of illustrations, recitation, broadcasting, reproduction on microfilms or in any other physical way, and transmission or information storage and retrieval, electronic adaptation, computer software, or by similar or dissimilar methodology now known or hereafter developed.
The use of general descriptive names, registered names, trademarks, service marks, etc. in this publication does not imply, even in the absence of a specific statement, that such names are exempt from the relevant protective laws and regulations and therefore free for general use.
The publisher, the authors and the editors are safe to assume that the advice and information in this book are believed to be true and accurate at the date of publication. Neither the publisher nor the authors or the editors give a warranty, expressed or implied, with respect to the material contained herein or for any errors or omissions that may have been made. The publisher remains neutral with regard to jurisdictional claims in published maps and institutional affiliations.

This Springer imprint is published by the registered company Springer Nature Switzerland AG
The registered company address is: Gewerbestrasse 11, 6330 Cham, Switzerland

If disposing of this product, please recycle the paper.

Preface

The 10th annual International Conference of the Immersive Learning Research Network (iLRN 2024) continued to push the boundaries of immersive learning, offering a hybrid experience that combined a virtual campus experience on the iLRN Virtual Campus (powered by ©FrameVR) and CVent meetings in June, followed by on-location events at the University of Glasgow and the University of St Andrews in Scotland, UK. This year's conference brought together an international community of scholars, practitioners, and innovators to explore the theme of Tech4Good!

Submissions to this year's iLRN conference truly leveraged the idea of using tech for good. The iLRN community's mission is reflected in diverse focus areas that drive positive educational and societal change. Learning innovation and educational technologies enhance personalized learning while upholding ethics and privacy. Inclusive design, educational equity, and digital inclusion ensure access for all. Ubiquitous learning and digital twins create immersive environments, and our emphasis on health, well-being, and climate change education prepares learners for a sustainable future. We support lifelong learning through museums, libraries, heritage education, and community engagement. Special education, K-12 STEM, language learning, and workforce training address diverse needs, while data analytics and assessment drive continuous improvement. By integrating these domains, iLRN embodies "Tech for Good," fostering meaningful educational and societal impacts.

Building on the success of our past conferences, iLRN 2024 showcased cutting-edge research that explores the transformative potential of immersive learning to create more inclusive, engaging, and effective learning experiences for diverse populations. The conference also provided a platform for attendees to network, connect, and contribute to the growing area of immersive learning. In addition, the iLRN 2024 keynote and featured speakers represented diverse backgrounds and perspectives, including experts worldwide, contributing to the discussion of applications of Immersive Learning in different domains. In keeping with our commitment to innovation and inclusion, iLRN 2024 featured various exciting events, including Guided Virtual Adventures and iLRN-Fuser Game Jams. We hosted thirteen academic tracks, including three special tracks: Immersive Learning across Latin America, which explored state-of-the-art research, use cases, and projects specifically for the Latin America region; Sustainable Development and Immersive Learning in the Climate Emergency; and Literacy Equity and Immersive Learning.

Four hundred seventy-three authors from 189 academic institutions, research centers and companies in 38 countries submitted publications to the Academic and iLEAD (immersive Learning Education and Design) tracks. Countries included Albania, Australia, Austria, Belgium, Brazil, Canada, China, Colombia, Estonia, Finland, France, Germany, Greece, Honduras, India, Ireland, Italy, Japan, North Korea, Latvia, Malaysia, Mexico, Morocco, Netherlands, New Zealand, Norway, Philippines, Portugal, South Korea, Spain, Sweden, Switzerland, Tanzania, Turkey, Ukraine, the UK, and the USA.

One hundred forty-four submissions were received for the Academic track, 129 of which were submitted for publication. These include full and short papers, work-in-progress (WiP) poster papers, and submissions to the Doctoral Colloquium (DC). Every submission underwent a rigorous review by at least three members of the Program Committee to maintain high scientific and quality standards, including meta-reviews for each full and short paper. This thorough review process, which included a double-anonymized review and plagiarism check, ensured the originality and quality of all contributions. After the peer-review process, all authors were given meaningful feedback on their submissions, further enhancing the quality of the conference.

We are pleased to partner with Springer's Communications in Computer and Information Science (CCIS) series to publish all accepted and registered best full and short papers in the Academic Stream presented at iLRN2024. Forty-three full and short papers (30 full papers and 13 short papers) were accepted in their initial submission category for the Springer proceedings (29.8% acceptance rate).

We celebrated outstanding contributions through our Best Academic Paper awards. These awards, which include categories for student papers, recognize the highest quality of research presented at the conference. The Program Chairs chose final nominees from those that received the best reviews and were nominated for awards by reviewers. The winners were selected by an independent jury panel, which was asked to review the nominated papers based on contribution, methodology, and clarity.

Reviewers provided feedback on submitted papers, suggested improvements, and recommended to the Program Chairs whether to accept, reject, or request paper changes. Reviewing is a volunteer and time-intensive process, and we are grateful to all our reviewers for contributing to our community. We implemented the Best Academic Reviewer award as a small way to recognize them for their service. An independent jury panel chose the winning reviews. The jury panel made a meta-review of the nominated reviews based on the study's rigor and contribution to improving a paper and developing the conference. In addition, we recognized the service our conference organizing committee provided by volunteering their time to make this event happen. We acknowledged their significant contribution via the Service awards. The list of winners is available in the Awards section of this volume. We sincerely thank those involved who volunteered their time to make this such a great event and the attendees for joining us and sharing their excellent work with the iLRN community. Their dedication and hard work were instrumental in the success of iLRN2024.

July 2024

Andreas Dengel
Marie-Luce Bourguet
Rami Ghannam
Alan Miller

Organization

Steering Committee

Dennis Beck	University of Arkansas, USA, Chair of the Steering Committee, iLRN Knowledge Tree
Leonel Morgado	Universidade Aberta, Portugal & INESC TEC, Portugal, iLRN Director of Scientific Quality
Daphne Economou	University of Westminster, UK, iLRN Director of Conferences
Christian Gütl	Graz University of Technology, Austria, iLRN Scientific Advisory Board Chair
Anasol Peña-Rios	BT Research Labs, UK, iLRN Director of Publications
Andreas Dengel	Goethe University Frankfurt, Germany, IEEE TC on Immersive Learning Environments
Jonathon Richter	iLRN President and Chief Executive Officer
Michael Hamaoka	OMAX Corporation, USA, iLRN Chief Technical Officer

General Chairs

Andreas Dengel	GoetheUniversität Frankfurt am Main, Germany
Marie-Luce Bourguet	Queen Mary University of London, UK
Rami Ghannam	University of Glasgow, UK
Alan Miller	University of St Andrews, UK

Academic Stream Lead Program Chairs

Jule Krüger	University of Potsdam, Germany
Eliane Schlemmer	Universidade do Vale do Rio dos Sinos, Brazil

Education and Design (iLEAD) Stream Chairs

Paula MacDowell	University of Saskatchewan, Canada
Jewoong Moon	University of Alabama, USA
Douglas Wilson	George Mason University, USA

Publication Chairs

Daniela Pedrosa Santarém Polytechnic University, Portugal
Dennis Beck University of Arkansas, USA

Publication Co-editor Assistants

Diana Almeida University of Aveiro, Portugal
Jonas Maurer Goethe Universität Frankfurt am Main, Germany
Maria Castelhano University of Porto, Portugal

Academic Full and Short Paper Program Chairs

Alexander Steinmaurer Graz University of Technology, Austria
Junjie Gavin Wu Macao Polytechnic University, China

Doctoral Colloquium Chairs and Work-in-Progress Program Chairs

Noah Glaser University of Missouri, USA
Matthew Schmidt University of Georgia, USA
Carl Boel Thomas More University of Applied Sciences, Belgium

Local Chairs

Rami Ghannam University of Glasgow, UK

Local Committee and Event Coordination

Lavinia Hirsu University of Glasgow, UK
Gabriella Rodolico University of Glasgow, UK
Marco Gilardi University of the West of Scotland, UK

Administration and Operations Chairs

Jonathon Richter iLRN President and Chief Executive Officer
Michael Hamaoka OMAX Corporation, USA; iLRN Chief Technical Officer

Virtual Campus and Technical Chairs

Genevieve Smith-Nunes University of Cambridge, UK
Michael Hamaoka OMAX Corporation, USA
Marco Gilardi University of the West of Scotland, UK

Videos, Posters, and Exhibitions Chair

Aliane Krassmann Instituto Federal Farroupilha, Brazil

Registration Chairs

Alec Bodzin Lehigh University, USA
Muhammad Zahid Iqbal Teesside University, UK

Finance Chair

Patrick O'Shea Appalachian State University, USA

Session Chair Director

Laurissa Tokarchuk Queen Mary University of London, UK
Daniel Livingstone Glasgow School of Arts, UK

Awards Chairs

Daphne Economou University of Westminster, UK
Filippo Gabriele Prattico Politecnico di Torino, Italy

Evaluation Chair

Sarah Ramaiah   University of Alabama, USA

iLRNFuser Game Jam Series Chair

Markos Mentzelopoulos   University of Westminster, UK

Guided Virtual Adventure Chair

Amany Alkhayat   Teachers College, Columbia University, USA

Opportunity and Inclusion Chair

Sarune Savickaite   University of Glasgow, UK

Community UX Engagement Chair

Arathi Suresh   Hitcher Encounters, UK

Sponsorships and Partnerships

Tim Scapin   Appalachian State University, USA
Fredrica Higgs   Appalachian State University, USA

Special Track LATAM Chairs

Jorge Bacca-Acosta   Fundación Universitaria Konrad Lorenz, Colombia
Cecilia Avila-Garzon   Fundación Universitaria Konrad Lorenz, Colombia
Jennifer Samaniego   Universidad Técnica Particular de Loja, Ecuador

Special Track: Literacy Equity and Immersive Learning Chairs

Ken Bigger   Barbara Bush Foundation for Family Literacy, USA
Stephanie Moore   University of New Mexico, USA
Dennis Beck   University of Arkansas, USA

Special Track: Sustainable Development and Immersive Learning in the Climate Emergency Chairs

Alan Miller   University of St Andrews, UK
Joan Condell   University of Ulster, UK
Gozde Yildiz   University of Siena, Italy

Volunteer Coordinator

Charlene Hardin   Embry-Riddle Aeronautical University, USA

International and Publicity Chairs Coordinators

Stylianos Mystakidis   Hellenic Open University, Greece
Mengjie Huang   Xi'an Jiaotong-Liverpool University, China
Jorge Bacca-Acosta   Fundación Universitaria Konrad Lorenz, Colombia

International Co-chairs (The Americas)

Minjuan Wang   San Diego State University, IEEE-TLT EiC, USA
Romero Tori   University of São Paulo, Brazil
Eliane Schlemmer   Universidade do Vale do Rio dos Sinos, Brazil
Jorge Bacca-Acosta   Fundación Universitaria Konrad Lorenz, Colombia

International Co-chairs (Europe)

Mikhail Fominykh	Norwegian University of Science and Technology, Norway
Sébastien George	Le Mans University - LIUM, France
Andri Ioannou	Cyprus University of Technology and CYENS CoE, Cyprus
Ioannis Kazanidis	International Hellenic University, Kavala, Greece
Michael D. Kickmeier-Rust	St.Gallen University of Teacher Education, Switzerland
Fabrizio Lamberti	Politecnico di Torino, Italy
Fotis Liarokapis	Cyprus University of Technology and CYENS CoE, Cyprus
Daniel Livingstone	Glasgow School of Art, Scotland
Eleni Mangina	University College Dublin, Ireland
Tassos Anastasios Mikropoulos	University of Ioannina, Greece
Ekaterina Prasolova-Førland	Norwegian University of Science and Technology, Norway
Mohamed Yassine Zarouk	University of Potsdam, Germany
Krzysztof Walczak	Poznań University of Economics and Business, Poland
Ioana-Andreea Stefan	Advanced Technology Systems, Romania

International Co-chairs (Middle East)

Malek Alrashidi	University of Tabuk, Saudi Arabia
Mohammad AL-Smadi	Qatar University, Qatar
Elhanan Gazit	Ono Academic College & Tel-Aviv University, Israel

International Co-chairs (Africa)

Koos de Beer	University of Pretoria, South Africa

International Co-chairs (Asia)

Noor Dayana Abd Halim	Universiti Teknologi Malaysia, Malaysia
Su Cai	Beijing Normal University, China
Yiyu Cai	Nanyang Technological University, Singapore

Morris Siu-Yung Jong	Chinese University of Hong Kong, China
Fengfeng Ke	Florida State University, USA
Kenneth Y T Lim	National Institute of Education, Singapore
Jeeheon Ryu	Chonnam National University, South Korea
Jolanda G. Tromp	Duy Tan University, Da Nang, Vietnam
Ramesh C Sharma	Dr. B. R. Ambedkar University Delhi, India

International Co-chairs (Oceania)

Erica Southgate	University of Newcastle, Australia

Program Committee (Reviewers and Meta-Reviewers)

Alan Miller	University of St Andrews, Scotland
Alec Bodzin	Lehigh University, USA
Alessandro Visconti	Politecnico di Torino, Italy
Alexander Mikroyannidis	Open University, UK
Alexander Steinmaurer	IT:U Institute of Digital Sciences, Austria
Aliane Krassmann	Federal Institute of Education, Science and Technology Farroupilha, Brazil
Alvaro Pistono	Universidade de Tras-os-Montes e Alto Douro/Uab, Portugal
Alvaro Uribe Quevedo	University of Ontario Institute of Technology, Canada
Amany Alkhayat	Columbia University, USA
Amelia Ijiri	Kyoto Institute of Technology, Japan
Amy Kuntz	Penn State, USA
Anastasija Nikiforova	University of Tartu, Estonia
Andreas Dengel	Goethe University Frankfurt, Germany
Anthi Karatrandu	University of Patras, Greece
Anthony Scavarelli	Carleton University, Canada
Antonio Coelho	University of Porto, Portugal
Antonis Natsis	University of Ioannina, Greece
Aolin Ding	Accenture Labs, USA
Ashley Etemadi	Harvard Graduate School of Education, USA
Aymeric Bouchereau	Université Paris-Est Créteil, France
Bárbara Cleto	ESMAD/uniMAD, Portugal
Benedikt Hensen	RWTH Aachen University, Germany
Birte Heinemann	RWTH Aachen University, Germany

Carl Boel	Thomas More University of Applied Sciences, Belgium
Cecilia Avila	Fundación Universitaria Konrad Lorenz, Colombia
Charlene Hardin	Freelance UX Designer & Artist, USA
Cheng Ye	Vanderbilt University Medical Center, USA
Chenwi Neba Cyril	Austin Peay State University, USA
Christine Moore	Arizona State University, USA
Cinthia Spricigo	Pontifical Catholic University of Paraná, Brazil
Claudio Schapsis	Sacred Heart University, USA
Corinne Brenner	Killer Snails, USA
Craig Frehlich	Independent Consultant, Canada
Daniela Pedrosa	Santarém Polytechnic University & CIDTFF, Portugal
David Fernes	Goethe University Frankfurt, Germany
Deepak Marahatta	Tribhuvan University, Nepal
Dennis Beck	University of Arkansas, USA
Doug Wilson	George Mason University, USA
Drew Davidson	Carnegie Mellon University, USA
Edicio Faller	Ateneo de Davao University, Philippines
Eleni Mangina	University College Dublin, Ireland
Elisa Serrano-Ausejo	Umeå University, Sweden
Elliot Hu-Au	Montclair State University, USA
Emily Johnson	University of Central Florida, USA
Evelyn Vovou	University of Athens, Greece
Fabian Froehlich	New York University, USA
Fabrício Soares	Federal University of Rio Grande do Sul, Brazil
Fahima Djelil	IMT Atlantique, France
Farzan Baradaran Rahimi	MacEwan University, Canada
Federico De Lorenzis	Politecnico di Torino, Italy
Filipe Fernandes	COPPE/UFRJ, Brazil
Frederick Bigrat	Université Paris-Panthéon-Assas, France
Fridolin Wild	Open University, UK
Gabriella Rodolico	University of Glasgow, UK
Gary Burnett	Loughborough University, UK
Genevieve Smith-Nunes	Cambridge University, UK
George Koutromanos	National and Kapodistrian University of Athens, Greece
George Peter Swift	Durham University, UK
Gigi Johnson	Maremel Institute, USA
Gozde Yildiz	University of Siena, Italy
Hamida Khatri	University of Texas at Dallas, USA

Hao He	Emporia State University, USA
Helen Geng	Lingnan University, China
Houda Mouttalib	UH2C - EMSI, Morocco
Hubert Cecotti	Fresno State, USA
Hugo Leon-Garza	British Telecom Research Labs, UK
Iain Oliver	University of St Andrews, UK
Inês Messias	Polytechnic Institute of Santarém, Portugal
Ivan Kaštelan	University of Novi Sad, Serbia
Jan Waligórski	AGH University of Kraków, Poland
Jasmin Cowin	Touro University, USA
Jasmine Aavaranta Hansén	National Historical Museums of Sweden, Sweden
Jeff Kim	Auburn University, USA
Jennifer Nester	Lehigh University, USA
Jennifer Samaniego	Universidad Técnica Particular de Loja, Ecuador
Jeonghun Lee	Dankook University, South Korea
Jewoong Moon	University of Alabama, USA
Ji Eun Ha	Yong-In Art & Science University, South Korea
Joao Luis de Miranda	ESTG/IPP, CERENA/IST, Portugal
João Piedade	Universidade de Lisboa, Portugal
Jorge Luis Bacca Acosta	Fundación Universitaria Konrad Lorenz, Colombia
José Joaquim de Moura Ramos	Universidade da Coruña, Spain
Josef Buchner	St. Gallen University of Teacher Education, Switzerland
Joseph Bertelsen	Missouri Valley Community Schools, USA
Judith Okonkwo	Imìsí 3D, Nigeria
Judy Jaunzems-Fernuk	University of Saskatchewan, Canada
Jule M. Krüger	University of Potsdam, Germany
Julia Sebastien	Cornell University, USA
Juliana Hernandez	Universidad de Medellín - Universidad Nacional de Colombia, Colombia
Junjie Gavin Wu	City University of Hong Kong, China
Karla Alvarado	Instituto Superior Tecnológico del Austro, Ecuador
Kayoko Nakamura	Keio University, Japan
Ken Bigger	Barbara Bush Foundation for Family Literacy, USA
Laura Sheerman	Swansea University, UK
Laurissa Tokarchuk	Queen Mary University of London, UK
Lavinia Hirsu	University of Glasgow, UK
Lee Ackerman	TEKsystems Global Services, UK
Leonel Morgado	INESC TEC / Universidade Aberta, Portugal

Leticia Neira Tovar	University Autónoma de Nuevo León, Mexico
Liane Tarouco	UFRGS, Brazil
Lidia Yatluk	University of Groningen, Netherlands
Lili Yan	Michigan State University, USA
Long Cheng	ETH Zurich, Switzerland
Lorenzo Valente	Politecnico di Torino, Italy
Ludovic Hamon	Univérsité du Maine, France
Manuel Gericota	ISEP, Portugal
Marco Gilardi	University of the West of Scotland, UK
Marie-Luce Bourguet	Queen Mary University of London, UK
Mário Madureira Fontes	PUCSP, Brazil
Mark Childs	Durham University, UK
Marlon Carrión	UTPL, Ecuador
Martha Mendez	Independent Researcher, Colombia
Masturah Sabri	Universiti Malaysia Perlis, Malaysia
Matt Glowatz	University College Dublin, Ireland
May Kristine Jonson Carlon	RIKEN Center for Brain Science, Japan
Meryem Yilmaz Soylu	Georgia Institute of Technology, USA
Michael Cowling	CQUniversity, Australia
Michael Holly	Graz University of Technology, Austria
Michael Vallance	Future University Hakodate, Japan
Ming Chen	University of Bristol, UK
Minjie Hu	Wellington Institute of Technology, New Zealand
Miriam Mulders	Universität Duisburg-Essen, Germany
Mohammad Al Bukhari Marzuki	Sultan Azlan Shah Polytechnic, Malaysia
Mohammad Lorgat	Universidade Católica de Moçambique, Mozambique
Mohan Yang	Old Dominion University, USA
Nestor Duque	Universidad Nacional de Colombia, Colombia
Nikolaos Pellas	University of Western Macedonia, Greece
Noah Glaser	University of Missouri, USA
Nor Sanak Mohd Nabil	Universiti Utara Malaysia, Malaysia
Nuodi Zhang	Florida State University, USA
Paula MacDowell	University of Saskatchewan, Canada
Pedro Cardoso	University of Aveiro / DigiMedia, Portugal
Pedro Neves Rito	Instituto Politécnico de Viseu, Portugal
Pelissier Chrysta	LHUMAIN - Université de Montpellier 3, France
Petrina Vasileiou	National Historical Museums, Sweden
Pia Spangenberger	University of Potsdam, Germany
Pratama Atmaja	University of Pembangunan Nasional "Veteran" Jawa Timur, Indonesia
Quincy Wang	Simon Fraser University, Canada

Radu Comes	Technical University of Cluj-Napoca, Romania
Ramon Fabregat	Universitat de Girona, Spain
Raquel Becerril	University of Lille, France
Razeen Hussain	University of Genoa, Italy
Robson Araujo-Junior	Lehigh University, USA
Rohana J. Swihart	Prescott College, USA
Rolf Kruse	FH Erfurt, Germany
Ryo Toyoda	AKKODiS Ltd., Japan
Saba Saneinia	University of Science and Technology of China, China
Sai Gattupalli	University of Massachusetts Amherst, USA
Salah Ahmed	Shaanxi Normal University, China
Santhosh Sivasubramani	IIT Hyderabad, India
Sarah Barker	Fielding Graduate University, USA
Sarune Savickaite	University of Glasgow, UK
Scott Warren	University of North Texas, USA
Shari Metcalf	Harvard University, USA
Shweta Singh	CQU, Australia
Siti Noraisyah Abd Rahman	National Academy of Arts Culture and Heritage (ASWARA), Malaysia
Skuli Bjorn Gunnarsson	Gunnar Gunnarsson Institute, Iceland
Sree Kalyan Patiballa	University of Alabama, USA
Stavros Nikou	University of Strathclyde, UK
Stylianos Mystakidis	University of Patras, Greece
Susanna Nocchi	Technological University Dublin, Ireland
Tassos Mikropoulos	University of Ioannina, Greece
Teresa Crea	University of New South Wales, Australia
Tessa Forshaw	Harvard University, USA
Thayná Bertholini	Federal University of Espírito Santo, Brazil
Tobias Loetscher	University of South Australia, Australia
Toks Bakare	asktoks.com, USA
Tryfon Sivenas	National and Kapodistrian University of Athens, Greece
Valentina Tabares	Universidad Nacional de Colombia, Colombia
Victoria Abramenka-Lachheb	University of Michigan, USA
Vlasios Kasapakis	University of the Aegean, Greece
Wellington Villota	Universidad Católica de Santiago de Guayaquil, Ecuador
Wenyi Lu	University of Missouri, USA
Wiebke Sophie Ost	University of Kassel, Germany
Xiaomeng Huang	New York University, USA
Xichen Li	Columbia University, USA

Xingxing Xie	Pennsylvania State University, USA
Xinhang Hermione Hu	University of Maryland, USA
Yalun Zhou	Rensselaer Polytechnic Institute, USA
Yannick Prié	LINA - University of Nantes, France
Yao Huang	Sam Houston State University, USA
Yasuyuki Yukawa	Kiramex Corporation, Japan
Yuning Gao	New York University, USA
Zahrasadat Hosseini	Oklahoma State University, USA
Zeta Dooly	Waterford Institute of Technology, Ireland
Zeynep Piri	Kastamonu University, Turkey

Contents – Part II

Special Track 1: Immersive Learning Across Latin America: State of Research, Use Cases and Projects

Metaverse Education Research Across Latin America: A Systematic Mapping Study 3
   Filipe Fernandes and Cláudia Werner

Building Extended Reality Learning Communities in Universities: The CIRE-UNAH Case in Honduras 19
   Marcos E. Zúniga-Solórzano and Ramon Fabregat

Special Track 2: Sustainable Development and Immerse Learning in the Climate Emergency

Amplifying Immersive Climate Learning 37
   Maria Andrei, Sharon Pisani, Alan Miller, Iain Oliver,
   Catherine Anne Cassidy, Sonja Heinrich, and Richard Bates

Creating Authentic Historical Costumes to Augment Virtual Humans for Cultural Heritage 52
   Junyu Zhang, Alan Miller, and Perin Westerhof Nyman

What the Amazon Can't Deliver: Lessons Learned from Virtual Reality-Based Sustainability Education 68
   Kristian H. Träg and Miriam Mulders

Immersive Learning of Cerebral Visual Impairment: Understanding Vision Through Dynamic Immersive Simulations 81
   Catherine Anne Cassidy, Iain Oliver, Kamila Oles,
   Helen St Clair Tracy, Andrew Blaikie, and Alan Miller

Design and Development of XR-Based Data Problem-Solving Content for Sustainable Development in Education 96
   Suhyun Ki and Jeeheon Ryu

Special Track 3: Literacy Equity and Immersive Learning

Outline of a Theoretical and Technological Approach for Reducing Inequalities in the Design of a 360 Synchronous Interactive Telepresence System 109
   Andrea Garavaglia, Ilaria Terrenghi, and Maurizio De Nino

Mind Perception of Avatars: A Focus Group Study 123
   Komala Mazerant, Alexander P. Schouten, Sanne B. T. Smit, Zeph M. C. van Berlo, and Lotte M. Willemsen

Author Index 139

Contents – Part I

Foundations in Immersive Learning Research and Theory

The Vibrotactile Paradox: Corrective and Reenforcing Feedback in Educational VR 3
   Fabian Froehlich, Bruce D. Homer, and Jan L. Plass

Scent Box: Prototyping and Instructions for Olfactory Enhancement of VR-Experiences 18
   Pia Spangenberger, Kilian Sanchez-Holguin, and Sarah-Christin Freytag

Measuring Cognitive Load with Eye-Tracking During Mental Rotation with 2D and 3D Visualization in AR 34
   Yuko Suzuki, Fridolin Wild, and Eileen Scanlon

Augmented Didactic: Interacting with 3D Models to Enhance the Memory Systems 49
   Luna Lembo, Elèna Cipollone, Stefania Morsanuto, and Francesco Peluso Cassese

Complexity of Agency in VR Learning Environments: Exploring Associations with Interactivity, Learning Outcomes, and Affect 65
   Eileen McGivney, Anna C. M. Queiroz, Mark Roman Miller, Sunny Liu, Brian Beams, Eugy Han, Erika S. Woolsey, Kai Frazier, Xander Petersen, Jeff Hancock, and Jeremy Bailenson

Ready Student One: A Framework for Avatar Design in Higher Education 80
   Gary Burnett

A Literature Review and Taxonomy of In-VR Questionnaire User Interfaces ... 95
   Saeed Safikhani, Lennart Nacke, and Johanna Pirker

Describing and Interpreting an Immersive Learning Case with the Immersion Cube and the Immersive Learning Brain 112
   Dennis Beck and Leonel Morgado

Exploiting the TARC Framework: The Relations Between Educators' Attitudes Towards AR, Innovativeness, Digital Skills, and AR Skills in Education 130
   Stavros A. Nikou, Maria Perifanou, and Anastasios A. Economides

Perceptions of Higher Education Students on Immersive Virtual Reality
for Communication Skills Training. The Bodyswaps Case 142
   Carl Boel

Adaptive Learning and Instruction with Augmented Reality: A Scoping
Review 156
   Jule M. Krüger

An Evaluation of Headset vs Desktop Use for Accessing Virtual Worlds in
a Higher Education Context 167
   Gary Burnett

Design of Virtual Reality Environments to Support Learning in History
Education 177
   Elisa Serrano-Ausejo and Peter Mozelius

Perfecting the Interdisciplinary Storm: Immersive Narrative Development
Workflows in Context of Meteorology Labs 187
   Rachael Kaye, Austin Porter, Christine Moore, Neha Balamurugan,
   Hanieh Khaleghian, and Robert LiKamWa

Assessment and Evaluation (A&E)

Is Usability Always Productive in Learning Environments? 201
   David Panzoli, Judicaël Thivet, Eduarda Abrantes, Gustavo dos Reis,
   Michel Galaup, Pierre Lagarrigue, and Maria Gonzalez Martinez

Galleries, Libraries, Archives and Museums (GLAM)

The Application of Procedurally Generated Libraries in Immersive Virtual
Reality 217
   Saeed Safikhani, Benedikt Gross, and Johanna Pirker

Designing MetaHuman-Based Historical Characters in Virtual Exhibitions
and Scenes: A Case Study on St Andrews 232
   Victor Yuan, Alan Miller, Perin Joy Westerhof Nyman, and Iain Oliver

Inclusion, Diversity, Equity, Access, and Social Justice (IDEAS)

Preliminary Report: Innovations in Participatory Immersive XR Research
for Transition-Aged Autistic Adults 249
   Matthew Schmidt, Jie Lu, Noah Glaser, Shangman Li, and Yueqi Weng

Preliminary Analysis of Empathy-Driven Design and Inclusive
Cybersecurity Education: The Initial Phase of the uSucceed Project's
Virtual Reality Curriculum for Neurodiverse Adults in STEM 261
    Noah Glaser, Prasad Calyam, Yupei Duan, Shangman Li,
    Sai Shreya Nuguri, Cannon Ousley, Anirudh Kambhampati,
    Zeinab Parishani, Amogh Chetankumar Joshi, and Mohan Yang

Exploring the Inclusive Design and Use of Social Multi-platform Virtual
Reality for a Post-secondary Gender Diversity Workshop 272
    Anthony Scavarelli, Ali Arya, Robert J. Teather, Rebecca Wakelin,
    Sarah Gauen, and Julie McCann

STEM Education (STEM)

A Computer-Supported Collaborative Learning Environment for Computer
Science Education 287
    Michael Holly, Jannik Hildebrandt, and Johanna Pirker

AR for Science Education: Students' Behaviour Patterns
and the Relationship Between Cognitive Load, Knowledge
Acquisition and Performance 302
    Jessica Lizeth Domínguez Alfaro, Michaela Arztmann, and Johan Jeuring

Spatial Audio Cues in an Immersive Virtual Reality STEM Escape Room
Game: A Comparative Study 317
    Georgios Vontzalidis, Stylianos Mystakidis, Athanasios Christopoulos,
    and Konstantinos Moustakas

Lessons upon Dislikes: Educational Game Design Principles from Players'
Negative Feedback 329
    Wenyi Lu, Hao He, Fan Yu, James Laffey, Alex Urban, Joseph Griffin,
    Troy D. Sadler, and Sean Goggins

Exploring the Influence of Immersive Virtual Reality on Science Learning
– An Affordance Approach 348
    Fabian Froehlich, Jan L. Plass, and Bruce D. Homer

Immersive Learning in History Education: Exploring the Capabilities
of Virtual Avatars and Large Language Models 363
    Alexander Steinmaurer, Andreas Dengel, Mario Comanici,
    Josef Buchner, Josef Memminger, and Christian Gütl

The Potential of Virtual Reality for Immersive HCI Education: Insights
from an Empirical Study 375
    Tanmesh Shah and Andreas Riener

Promoting Science Identity Exploration: An Analysis of the Game Design Features in WaterWays 386
   TzuChin Chen, Hana Haddad, Corinne Brenner, Jessica Ochoa Hendrix, and Mandë Holford

Medical and Healthcare Education (MHE)

Learning from Immersive Augmented Reality on COVID-19 Transmission 399
   Ioannis Vrellis, Tassos Mikropoulos, and George Koutromanos

Workforce Development and Industry Training (WDIT)

Breaking Barriers in Getting to Yes: Using Immersive Media for Cross-Cultural Negotiation Training 417
   Ashley Etemadi

Self and Co-regulated Learning with Immersive Learning Environments (SCILE)

Creativo: Design and Evaluation of a Multi-user Collaborative Learning Environment in Virtual Reality 431
   Luca Schreiber, Markus Weißenberger, and Andreas Riener

The Impact of Cognitive, Affective, and Psychomotor Learning Perception on Learning Outcomes in the eXtended Reality Based Nursing Simulation 446
   Yuseon Jeong, Kukhyeon Kim, and Jeeheon Ryu

Immersive Virtual Learning Spaces for Emotional Engagement in Education with the Classroom-Ready Virtual Reality Device CLASS VR 460
   Celestino Magalhães, Marco Bento, and José Alberto Lencastre

Method for Evaluation and Classification of Self and Co-regulation of Learning in Immersive Narratives 471
   Cristiane Jorge Bonfim, Leonel Morgado, and Daniela Pedrosa

Author Index 483

Special Track 1: Immersive Learning Across Latin America: State of Research, Use Cases and Projects

Metaverse Education Research Across Latin America: A Systematic Mapping Study

Filipe Fernandes[1](✉) and Cláudia Werner[2]

[1] Federal Institute of Southeast Minas Gerais (IF Sudeste MG), Manhuaçu, Minas Gerais, Brazil
`filipe.fernandes@ifsudestemg.edu.br`
[2] Federal University of Rio de Janeiro (COPPE/UFRJ), Rio de Janeiro, Rio de Janeiro, Brazil
`werner@cos.ufrj.br`

Abstract. The investigation of contributions from Latin American researchers is highly relevant in the context of the Metaverse for education and immersive learning. In this way, the objective of this study is to characterize the state of the art of Metaverse for Education based on Latin American research. Based on our findings, papers are predominantly focused on empirical and development studies, suggesting an under-representation of theoretical and conceptual approaches which are crucial for deeper understanding. Additionally, there's a significant opportunity to expand the research to other Latin American countries, besides Brazil, which would encourage a broader diversity of approaches and perspectives.

Keywords: Metaverse For Education · Latin America · Systematic Mapping Study

1 Introduction

The Metaverse offers several advantages for education, making it a promising platform for transforming learning experiences [19]. One of the key advantages is its potential to enhance immersion and interaction, providing a more engaging and realistic learning environment. The immersive nature of the Metaverse, supported by advanced computing and socialization, allows for personalized and interactive learning experiences, which can significantly enhance student engagement and motivation [18]. Additionally, the Metaverse fosters innovation in educational modes and systems, offering a more attractive and effective approach compared to traditional courses. This innovation is further supported by the use of deep learning-based high-precision recognition models and natural generation models, which strengthen the Metaverse with various factors, such as mobile-based always-on access and connectivity with reality using virtual currency [18,19].

Moreover, the Metaverse has the potential to enrich and transform education, leading to increased learning outcomes and enhanced student engagement [17]. It also provides a safe environment for laboratory applications, procedural skills development, and Science, Technology, Engineering and Mathematics (STEM) education, offering opportunities for practical training and experimentation [17]. Furthermore, the Metaverse supports the creation of meaningful learning experiences through its key elements, including immersion, advanced computing, socialization, and decentralization, allowing instructional designers to develop innovative and effective learning experiences. The application of the Metaverse in teaching and learning has been found to enhance classroom teaching and learning, particularly for continuous assessment. Additionally, the Metaverse can facilitate speaking activities, role play, simulation, and small group learning activities with interaction, making it effective for language education [16].

In the context of Latin America, the relevance of investigating contributions from Latin American researchers is evident in the need to use of the current status of research collaboration in Latin America related to the Metaverse for education. This understanding allows researchers to detect main areas of opportunity, which in turn serves to improve future decision making in this area. Therefore, the objective of this study is to characterize the state of the art of Metaverse for Education based on Latin American research.

The work is organized as follows: Sect. 2 describes the research method adopted for the identification and inclusion of studies; Sect. 3 presents the answers to the defined research questions, which are discussed in Sect. 4. Finally, the conclusions of the studies are presented in Sect. 5.

2 Research Method

Research method of this work adheres to the three key stages of a systematic literature review [24]. Initially, the review is planned, involving the development and evaluation of a protocol. Following the validation of the protocol by the researchers, the execution phase of the review commences. This phase focuses on selecting studies, extracting data, and synthesizing this information. The final stage involves outlining how the results of the study will be disseminated. Details of the review process are provided in the subsequent sections.

2.1 Research Questions

In this work, the primary research question defined is: *what is the state-of-the-art of the Metaverse for Education across Latin America*. From this main research question, we established two secondary research questions (SRQ), as follows:

SQR1: What are the publication trends?
SQR2: How are research designed and validated?

In SRQ1, we intend to analyze the studies from a quantitative perspective, including cultural aspects. For example, observations on how the publication history is over time; the number of studies, authors, and affiliations by country; languages of the full text; and venues. Finally, SRQ2 was defined in order to analyze the studies from a point of view of the research methodology, such as research problem; contribution; and validation.

2.2 Search Process

PICO approach (Participants, Intervention, Comparison, and Outcome) was used to design and outline the objective of this secondary study [24]. However, the comparison variable was excluded due to it being a systematic mapping study, in addition to the focus of this work being on the observation of evidence without comparison criteria. The purpose of the study is defined as follows:

- Population: studies with educational purposes;
- Intervention: that reports the use of the Metaverse technologies to support the teaching and learning process;
- Outcome: whose at least one of the authors' affiliations is from a Latin American country.

Search process was designed to construct a search string that automatically retrieves studies from databases such as Scopus, Compendex, and Web of Science. To aid in formulating the search string, the purpose of the study defined based on PICO approach was used to design and outline the objective of this study. The "OR" boolean operator was employed to connect related terms, while "AND" was used to link the terms about population and intervention. In this way, the search string is defined as: *(metaverse) AND (learn* OR teach* OR train* OR edu*) AND ("Argentina" OR "Belize" OR "Bolivia" OR "Brazil" OR "Chile" OR "Colombia" OR "Costa Rica" OR "Cuba" OR "Dominican Republic" OR "Ecuador" OR "El Salvador" OR "Guatemala" OR "Honduras" OR "Mexico" OR "Nicaragua" OR "Panama" OR "Paraguay" OR "Peru" OR "Uruguay" OR "Venezuela")*.

2.3 Selection Criteria and Procedure

This section describes the conduction of the review phase. The systematic literature review process was performed in November 2023 based on 3 search engines: Scopus, Compendex, and Web of Science. For each search engine, the search string *(metaverse) AND (learn* OR teach* OR train* OR edu*)* was performed and returned 3631 documents in total – 1380 from Scopus, 1364 from Compendex and 887 from Web of Science. However, filters were applied considering affiliations' country and region of Latin America. After these filters, 3490 papers were excluded. For this reason, 141 papers (Scopus 61, Compendex 40, and Web of Science 40) followed the screening step. In this step, 64 duplicated papers were excluded, leaving a total of 77 papers. For each paper, inclusion and exclusion criteria (see Table 1) were applied in the title and abstract for each paper in order to select papers for the next step.

Table 1. Exclusion and inclusion criteria.

Exclusion Criteria	Inclusion Criteria
– Study is not a work that considers the Metaverse for education and none of the authors' affiliations are in Latin America	– Full-text study written in the Portuguese, Spanish, or English language
– Study is not a paper	
– It is not possible to access the full-text study	

Finally, 26 papers were rejected, remaining 51 papers, whose full texts were read. While reading the full text, exclusion criteria were applied again, being 23 papers rejected due to lack of access. Therefore, 28 papers have been considered in this review for data extraction (see Table 2). Figure 1 shows all the steps taken to find the final set of articles. The organization of the steps was inspired by the PRISMA method [26].

3 Results

In the preceding section, we outlined the selection process for the 28 studies, including the sources used, the definition of the search string, criteria for inclusion and exclusion, and other procedural details. In order to support analysis, Parsifal tool[1] and Microsoft Excel[2] were adopted. Parsifal is a tool designed to assist researchers in conducting systematic literature reviews. These studies are labor-intensive and require extensive effort from researchers. Parsifal aids in planning, conducting, and reporting these reviews. Data analysis and charts were created from Microsoft Excel. This section will address each research question, drawing on data extracted from these studies.

3.1 What are the Publication Trends (SQR1)?

As presented in Sect. 2.1, our objective is to examine the studies quantitatively, incorporating trends and cultural dimensions. This involves exploring trends over time in publication history, assessing the distribution of studies, authors, and institutional affiliations by country, evaluating the languages used in the full texts, and considering the various publication venues.

The selected papers in this study are presented in Table 2. Although the authors hail from Latin American countries, the majority of the works are written in English. This reflects the greater visibility of the papers, as the English language is widely adopted in international conferences and journals. Additionally, one can observe the nationality of the authors, as well as the collaboration

---

[1] https://parsif.al/.
[2] https://www.microsoft.com/pt-br/microsoft-365/excel.

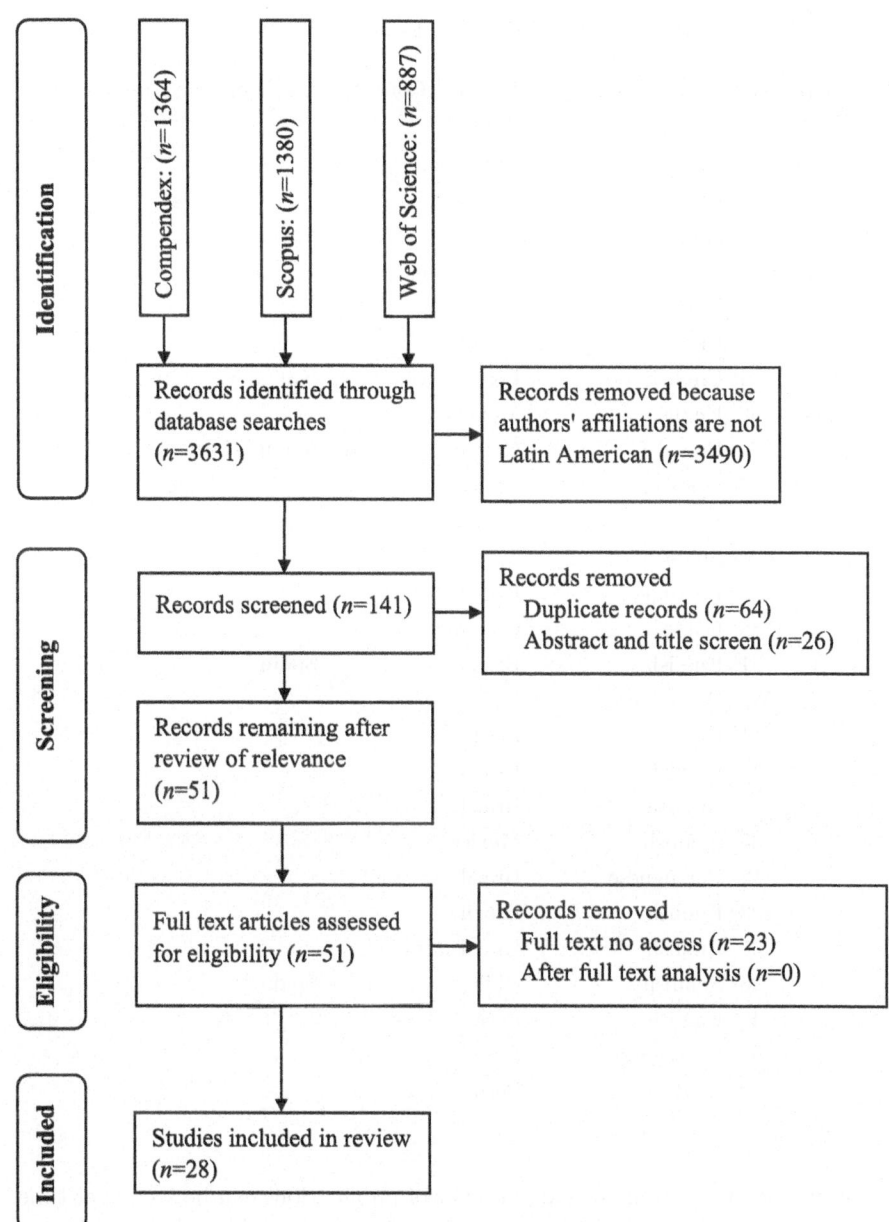

Fig. 1. Overview of the filtering process.

between countries within Latin America and other regions of the world. From the perspective of international collaboration, it is noted that there are few partnerships, regardless of the geographical region.

Table 2. Selected papers for data extraction.

Year	Ref.	Full-text Language	LATAM Country	Collaborating Country
2012	[33]	English	Panama	
2013	[32]	English	Colombia	
	[29]	Portuguese	Brazil	
	[21]	English	Colombia	Spain
2020	[14]	English	Colombia	
	[15]	English	Colombia	
2022	[17]	English	Brazil	
	[34]	English	Peru	Korea
	[6]	English	Mexico	
	[2]	English	Colombia, Ecuador	Spain, Morocco
2023	[27]	Spanish	Chile	
	[22]	Spanish	Ecuador	
	[20]	Spanish	Mexico	
	[13]	Portuguese	Brazil	
	[30]	English	Colombia, Mexico	
	[31]	English	Brazil	Spain
	[8]	Portuguese	Brazil	
	[11]	English	Peru	
	[1]	English	Brazil	
	[5]	English	Brazil	
	[25]	Spanish	Mexico	
	[12]	Portuguese	Brazil	
	[23]	English	Brazil	
	[35]	English	Brazil, Mexico	
	[28]	Spanish	Chile	Spain
	[4]	English	Peru	
	[9]	Portuguese	Brazil	
	[10]	English	Peru	

According to Fig. 2, an increasing number of publications can be seen over time. Especially, from the year 2022 onwards the number of publications is significant. This behavior may be related to the rebranding of the former company Facebook to Meta [17]. In October 2021, Facebook announced that it would change its corporate name to Meta. This change was more than a simple rebranding; it symbolized a strategic realignment of the company, which began to focus on the development of technologies related to the Metaverse. In addition, the period from 2014 to 2019 reveals an absence of works addressing the integration of the Metaverse within educational contexts. This lacuna suggests that, despite the concept of the Metaverse not being novel, its application and exploration in educational paradigms did not gain academic traction until more recently. This historical evidence void against the current proliferation of Metaverse-related research underscores the transformative impact of Meta's strategic realignment on academic and industry perspectives towards the potential of Metaverse technologies in education. Considering that the focus of this study is research carried out by Latin Americans, we analyzed which countries are involved in Metaverse for education research, based on the authors' affiliations.

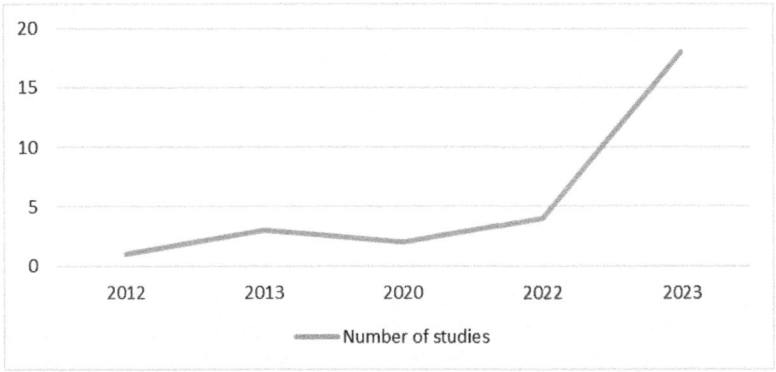

Fig. 2. Number of studies published per year.

According to Fig. 3, Brazil has a significant number of contributions. Some factors may contribute to this result, such as the size and diversity of the economy; population and human resources; and investments in research. Historically, Brazil has invested more in higher education and research than many of its Latin American neighbors. Although there have been fluctuations in funding, some Brazilian institutions, such as CAPES (from Portuguese, Federal Coordination Office for the Improvement of Higher Education Personnel) and CNPq (from Portuguese, National Council for Scientific and Technological Development), have played a crucial role in promoting research [3].

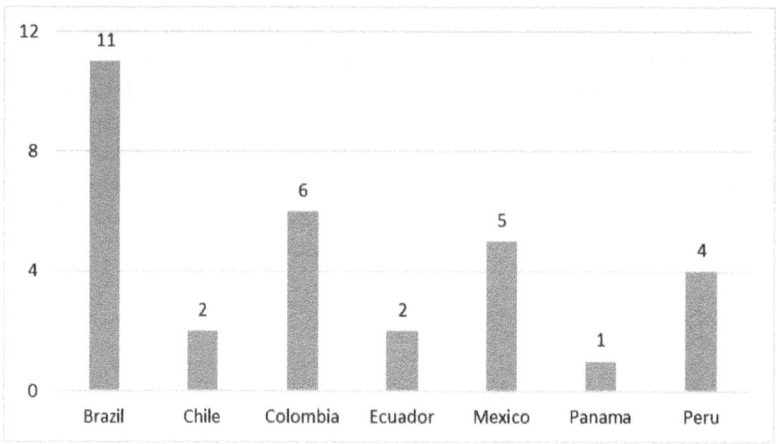

Fig. 3. Number of authors contributions per country.

On the other hand, it is evident that the challenges faced by countries with a reduced number of contributions are multifaceted, potentially involving issues related to infrastructure, funding, training, and international collaboration. To surmount these challenges and bolster research in the field, it would be advantageous for these countries to invest in technological infrastructure and actively seek international partnerships. Such measures could not only augment the volume of research conducted but also enhance the quality and impact of education through the integration of immersive technologies. This approach suggests a strategic pathway for leveraging immersive technologies to foster educational innovation and improve learning outcomes on a global scale.

In our next analysis, we seek to understand how the types of studies are distributed by venue. We consider primary studies to be research that involves the direct collection of information from primary sources, that is, from individuals or entities that are the objects of study themselves. On the other hand, secondary studies involve analyzing data that have been collected by other researchers or sources such as databases, existing literature, government reports, or previous studies. This may include reanalysis of existing data, systematic reviews, meta-analyses, or other forms of evidence synthesis. According to Fig. 4, the trend shows that publication preference is in journals. More specifically, secondary studies were published only in journals, while primary studies were published in both venues (conference proceedings and journals).

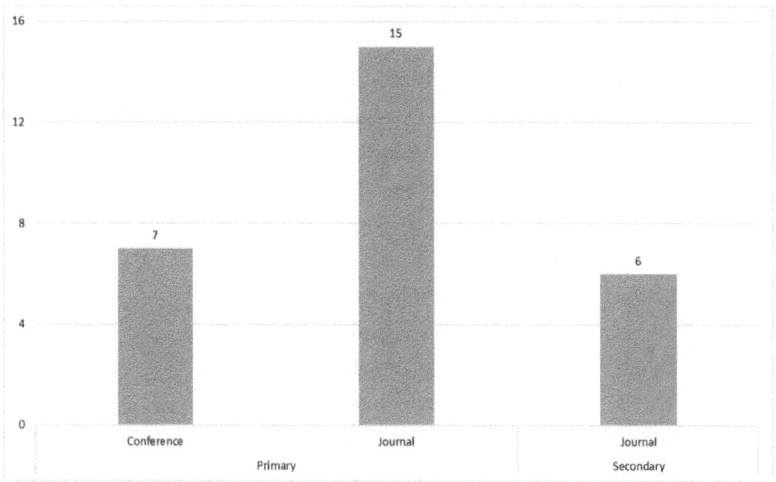

Fig. 4. Number of studies grouped by type of study versus venue.

3.2 How are Research Designed and Validated (SQR2)?

In this research question, we used three dimensions to support our data extraction inspired by [7]. The authors develop a categorization scheme by merging, extending, and revising previous studies, resulting in a four-dimensional framework encompassing problem, contribution, validation, and topic (see Table 3). We disregard the topic dimension. According to [7], each dimension has a specific purpose:

- Problem: what issue the paper would like to solve or the question the paper would like to answer;
- Contribution: what is the main result presented in the paper;
- Validation: what evidence the paper shows so that the contribution is valid.

In this way, each study was analyzed under the three dimensions and classified according to their respective sub-dimensions. Table 4, Table 5 and Table 6 present a description of each sub-dimension.

Table 3. Overview of the categorization scheme by [7].

Dimension	Sub-dimensions
Problem (see Table 4)	Development method
	Analysis method
	Specific instance
	Generalization or characterization
	Feasibility study or exploration
Contribution (see Table 5)	Theoretical
	Technological
	Empirical
	Perspectival
Validation (see Table 6)	Analysis
	Evaluation
	Experience
	Example
	No Validation

Table 4. Groups for problem adapted from [7].

Problem	Description
Development method	The paper investigates methods or tools for (better)doing/creating/modifying/evolving/automating/maintaining any educational process through the Metaverse
Analysis method	The paper investigates methods or tools for (better) analyzing/evaluating/measuring the quality/correctness of any educational process through the Metaverse.
Specific instance	The paper investigates how it can (better) design/implement/maintain/adapt/evaluate/analyze some particular system, specific practice, or other instance of any educational process through the Metaverse.
Generalization or characterization	The paper investigates how to generalize or provide important characteristics/varieties of the Metaverse for education process/technology/method/phenomenon
Feasibility study or exploration	The paper explores the Metaverse for education aspects in a completely new way or from a novel perspective

Table 5. Groups for contribution [7].

Contribution	Description
Empirical	The paper presents an empirical predictive study based on observed data
Perspectival	The paper presents a novel perspective on a specific research field or part of it
Technological	A paper in which the main contribution is of a technical nature
Theoretical	The paper relies on theoretical assumptions and presents an analytical model or methodology to solve a problem

Table 6. Groups for validation [7].

Validation	Description
Analysis	The paper presents a rigorous/convincing analysis of the contribution
Evaluation	The paper presents evaluation of the contribution in specific (replicable) situations
Example	The paper presents illustrations derived from practical situation
Experience	The paper presents evidences supporting the contribution by using third party & result collection
No Validation	The paper does not present any of the above mentioned validations

According to the Fig. 5, a large part of the studies is focused on *Development Method*, that is, studies that focus on useful features to improve the teaching process through the Metaverse.

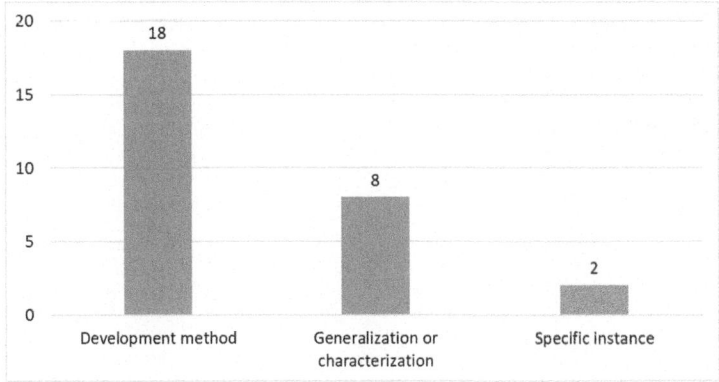

Fig. 5. Categorization of the problems addressed by the studies.

Furthermore, most studies made empirical contributions, that is, studies that carried out a controlled experiment, case study, field or observational study, survey of professionals and practitioners through questionnaires or interviews, and reports of lessons learned. Figure 6 presents the results.

Finally, we identified that a large part of Latin American research validated its studies through Evaluations, that is, studies that describe phenomena of interest involving the contribution of the article, the evaluation of the benefits or innovation of the contribution, the description of a feasibility study or pilot project involving the contribution of the article and the generation of results that fit the real data. Figure 7 presents the results.

4 Discussion

According to the findings, the trend shows a preference for publishing in journals. More specifically, secondary studies were published only in journals, while primary studies were published in both venues (conference proceedings and journals). This observation suggests a tendency in the research community to give preference to publications in journals, especially for studies that analyze and synthesize existing work, which may have implications for the way research is disseminated and discussed in the academic community. Considering the contributions of Latin American countries, Brazil stands out as a prominent example in terms of research and innovation. Brazil is described as having a rich pool of research talent, being home to several renowned universities and research institutions that attract and cultivate high-quality researchers. Historically, Brazil has invested more in higher education and research than many of its Latin American neighbors. Despite fluctuations in funding, some Brazilian institutions, such as CAPES and CNPq, have played a fundamental role in the country's scientific and technological advancement. These factors collectively contribute to

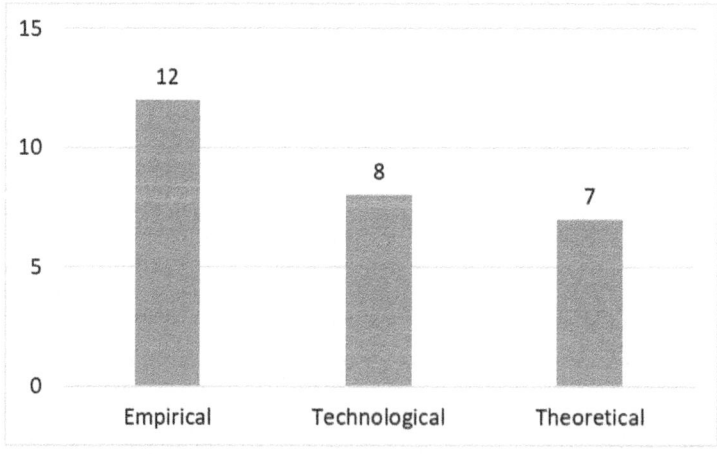

Fig. 6. Categorization of the problems addressed by the studies.

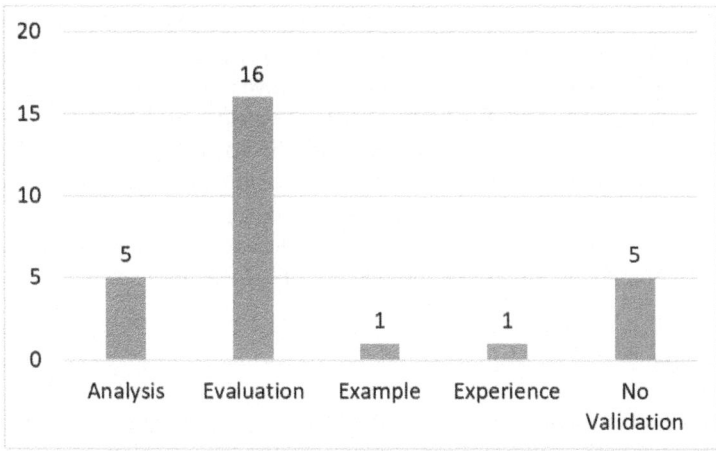

Fig. 7. Categorization of the problems addressed by the studies.

Brazil's ability to leverage its diverse talent and institutional resources for scientific advancement. From the point of view of the types of studies published, the preference for publishing in journals, especially secondary studies, reveals a tendency that may limit the dissemination of new practical and experimental research. This suggests an opportunity to increase focus on conferences and other forums that can facilitate the exchange of innovative ideas and practices.

Notably, only [30,35] have directly addressed the use of the Metaverse for disability education. This is a significant issue as Metaverse technologies have the potential to offer inclusive and accessible educational experiences for people with disabilities. The lack of focus in this area suggests a great research opportunity, where new studies can explore how the metaverse can be adapted or designed to meet the educational needs of people with different types of disabilities. This may include the development of accessible interfaces, adaptive content, and teaching methods that take advantage of the immersive and interactive capabilities of the metaverse to provide a more inclusive and equitable education.

5 Conclusion

This work aimed to characterize the state of the art of the Metaverse for education across Latin America. From the Scopus, Compendex and Web of Science databases, 141 studies of affiliations of Latin American authors were identified. After the inclusion and exclusion criteria, 28 studies were selected for data extraction.

Based on our findings, we highlight that the geographic concentration of research may indicate a lack of diversity in perspectives and approaches. Furthermore, the predominance of empirical and development studies suggests a possible under-representation of theoretical and conceptual approaches.

Furthermore, there is room to expand Metaverse research in education to other Latin American countries, encouraging a greater diversity of approaches and perspectives. As future work, we intend to investigate the processes through which learners build knowledge within virtual worlds, and to delve into sociocultural theories as a means to comprehend the social dynamics and cultural impacts that characterize educational experiences in the Metaverse. In addition, we also intend to broaden the discourse surrounding research themes and challenges associated with the integration of the Metaverse in educational settings, with a particular focus on trends prevalent in Latin America.

References

1. Almeida, L.G., Vasconcelos, N.V.D., Winkler, I., Catapan, M.F.: Innovating industrial training with immersive metaverses: a method for developing cross-platform virtual reality environments. Appl. Sci. **13**(15), 8915 (2023)
2. Alpala, L.O., Quiroga-Parra, D.J., Torres, J.C., Peluffo-Ordóñez, D.H.: Smart factory using virtual reality and online multi-user: towards a metaverse for experimental frameworks. Appl. Sci. **12**(12) (2022). https://doi.org/10.3390/app12126258
3. de Andrade, R.S., Martelli, D.R.B., Swerts, M.S.O., Oliveira, E.A., Martelli, H.: Scientific production of the Brazilian council for scientific and technological development (CNPQ) researchers in the field of oral medicine and oral pathology granted with a scientific productivity fellowship. Oral Surg. Oral Med. Oral Pathol. Oral Radiol. **126**(6), 553–554 (2018)
4. de la Asuncion, I.N.M., Vargas-Murillo, A.R., Palacios, R.J., de Jesús Guevara-Soto, F., Ypanaque-Pereira, I.L., et al.: Smart learning in virtual worlds: A systematic literature review on the usage and applications of metaverse in education. Int. J. Learn. Teach. Educ. Res. **22**(9), 85–101 (2023)
5. Baptista, R.M., et al.: Investigating engineering contributions in hackathons. Metaverse and blockchain as key components for e-commerce. In: 15th International Symposium on Project Approaches in Engineering Education and 20th International Conference on Active Learning in Engineering Education Workshop, PAEE/ALE 2023 (2023)
6. Bedolla, F.P.P.: Meeting my friends virtually. In: 2022 XII International Conference on Virtual Campus (JICV), pp. 1–3 (2022). https://doi.org/10.1109/JICV56113.2022.9934780
7. Bertolino, A., Calabró, A., Lonetti, F., Marchetti, E., Miranda, B.: A categorization scheme for software engineering conference papers and its application. J. Syst. Softw. **137**, 114–129 (2018). https://doi.org/10.1016/j.jss.2017.11.048
8. Borba, E.Z., Bassan, D., Oliveira, F.L.: Treinamento imersivo em realidade virtual: A percepção de experiência dos colaboradores numa indústria calçadista. Rev. Gestão e Desenvolvimento **20**(2), 250–272 (2023)
9. Câmara, J.A.: Ensino, realidade e metaverso no direito administrativo. Rev. Estudos Inst. (REI) **9**(3), 757–773 (2023)
10. Chamorro-Atalaya, O., et al.: The metaverse in university education during COVID-19: a systematic review of success factors. Int. J. Learn. Teach. Educ. Res. **22**(5), 206–226 (2023)
11. Chamorro-Atalaya, O., et al.: Inclusion of metaverses in the development of the flipped classroom in the university environment: bibliometric analysis of indexed

scientific production in scopus. Int. J. Learn. Teach. Educ. Res. **22**(10), 247–270 (2023)
12. Classe, T.M.d., Castro, R.M.d., de Oliveira, E.G.: Metaverso como um ambiente de aprendizado para o ensino híbrido. RIED. Rev. Iberoamericana Educ. Dist. **26**(2) (2023)
13. Classe, T.M.D., Castro, R.M.D., Sousa, H.P.D.S.: Evaluating students' technology acceptance of use of metaverse as an educational information system for hybrid education. In: Proceedings of the XIX Brazilian Symposium on Information Systems, SBSI 2023, pp. 197–205. Association for Computing Machinery, New York (2023). https://doi.org/10.1145/3592813.3592906
14. Díaz, J.: Virtual world as a complement to hybrid and mobile learning. Int. J. Emerg. Technol. Learn. (iJET) **15**(22), 267–274 (2020)
15. Díaz, J., Saldaña, C., Avila, C.: Virtual world as a resource for hybrid education. Int. J. Emerg. Technol. Learn. (iJET) **15**(15), 94–109 (2020)
16. Fernandes, F., Werner, C.: Towards immersive learning in object-oriented paradigm: a preliminary study. In: 2019 21st Symposium on Virtual and Augmented Reality (SVR), pp. 59–68 (2019). https://doi.org/10.1109/SVR.2019.00026
17. Fernandes, F.A., Werner, C.M.L.: A scoping review of the metaverse for software engineering education: overview, challenges, and opportunities. Presence Teleoper. Virtual Environ. **31**, 107–146 (2022). https://doi.org/10.1162/pres_a_00371
18. Fernandes, F.A.: MetaSEE: an approach to enable the metaverse-based software engineering education. Ph.D. thesis, Universidade Federal do Rio de Janeiro (2023)
19. Fernandes, F.A., Rodrigues, C.S.C., Teixeira, E.N., Werner, C.M.L.: Immersive learning frameworks: a systematic literature review. IEEE Trans. Learn. Technol. **16**(5), 736–747 (2023). https://doi.org/10.1109/TLT.2023.3242553
20. Godínes, J.C.V., Rueda, C.J.Á.: El trabajo colaborativo en los edit, explorando el aprendizaje inmersivo en el metaverso. Rev. Educ. Dist. (RED) **23**(73) (2023)
21. González Crespo, R., Escobar, R.F., Joyanes Aguilar, L., Velazco, S., Castillo Sanz, A.G.: Use of ARIMA mathematical analysis to model the implementation of expert system courses by means of free software OpenSim and Sloodle platforms in virtual university campuses. Expert Syst. Appl. **40**(18), 7381–7390 (2013). https://doi.org/10.1016/j.eswa.2013.06.054
22. Guun-Yoo, S., Ortega-Castro, J.C., Campaña-Ortega, E.M.: Arquitectura de un mecanismo de autenticación seguro para el metaverso en un ecosistema educativo. Rev. Conrado **19**(90), 320–325 (2023)
23. Júnior, D.P.A., Júnior, J.M., Campos, R.: Metaverse workspaces for active learning - Brazilian oil & gas company case. In: 15th International Symposium on Project Approaches in Engineering Education and 20th International Conference on Active Learning in Engineering Education Workshop, PAEE/ALE 2023 (2023)
24. Kitchenham, B., Charters, S.: Guidelines for performing systematic literature reviews in software engineering - version 2.3. Technical report. EBSE-2007-01, Keele University and University of Durham (2007)
25. Menéndez-Aponte, S.M., et al.: El metaverso y la educación en anestesiología. Rev. Chil. Anest **52**(3), 262–266 (2023)
26. Moher, D., Liberati, A., Tetzlaff, J., Altman, D.G., Group, P.: Preferred reporting items for systematic reviews and meta-analyses: the PRISMA statement. PLoS Med. **6**(7), e1000097 (2009)
27. Reyes Bravo, P., Contreras Aguilar, D., García Barrera, F.: Un metaverso para realizar actividades de gamificación en el área de gestión de personas. Ingeniare. Rev. chilena ingeniería **31** (2023)

28. Ruiz-Campo, S., Matías-Batalla, D., Boronat-Clavijo, B., Acevedo-Duque, Á.: Metaverses as teaching tool in higher education instructors training. Latin Am. J. Educ. Technol. **22**(1), 135–153 (2022)
29. Schlemmer, E., Marson, F.: Immersive learning: metaversos e jogos digitais na educação. In: 2013 8th Iberian Conference on Information Systems and Technologies (CISTI), pp. 1–7 (2013)
30. Segura, M., Osorio, R., Zavala, A.: Extended reality model for accessibility in learning for deaf and hearing students (programming logic case). Int. J. Mod. Educ. Comput. Sci. (IJMECS) **15**(4), 1–17 (2023). https://doi.org/10.5815/ijmecs.2023.04.01
31. Silva, I.N.d., García-Zubía, J., Hernández-Jayo, U., Alves, J.B.D.M.: Extended remote laboratories: a systematic review of the literature from 2000 to 2022. IEEE Access **11**, 94780–94804 (2023). https://doi.org/10.1109/ACCESS.2023.3271524
32. Torres-Arias, D.M., Trefftz, H.: Educational effectiveness of using a shared virtual immersive environment for teaching English as second language. In: Proceedings of the International Conference on Image Processing, Computer Vision, and Pattern Recognition (IPCV), p. 1 (2013)
33. Vernaza, A., Armuelles, V.I., Ruiz, I.: Towards to an open and interoperable virtual learning environment using metaverse at university of panama. In: 2012 Technologies Applied to Electronics Teaching (TAEE), pp. 320–325 (2012). https://doi.org/10.1109/TAEE.2012.6235458
34. Yong, Y.J., Lee, J.H., Kim, Y.S.: A study on the possibility of a change in culture and arts education curriculum by shooting "metaclassroom" in the covid-19 pandemic era. Cypriot. J. Educ. Sci. **17**(5), 1603–1621 (2022)
35. Zambiasi, L.P., Rabelo, R.J., Zambiasi, S.P., Romero, D.: Metaverse-based softbot tutors for inclusive industrial workplaces: supporting impaired operators 5.0. In: Alfnes, E., Romsdal, A., Strandhagen, J.O., von Cieminski, G., Romero, D. (eds) APMS 2023. IFIP Advances in Information and Communication Technology, vol. **689**, 662–677 Springer, Cham (2023). https://doi.org/10.1007/978-3-031-43662-8_47

Building Extended Reality Learning Communities in Universities: The CIRE-UNAH Case in Honduras

Marcos E. Zúniga-Solórzano[1](✉) and Ramon Fabregat[2]

[1] Research Institute of Applied Sciences and Technology (IICAT), Universidad Nacional Autónoma de Honduras, Tegucigalpa 11101, Honduras
marcos.zuniga@unah.edu.hn

[2] Broadband Communications and Distributed Systems Group (BCDS), Universitat de Girona, 17071 Girona, Spain
ramon.fabregat@udg.edu

Abstract. One of the most notable trends in Higher Education in recent decades is the implementation of various technologies focused on improving and innovating teaching and learning processes. Among these, technologies that offer immersive experiences stand out, such as Augmented Reality (AR), Virtual Reality (VR), and Mixed Reality (MR), which together with others have consolidated the concept of Extended Reality (XR). These technologies offer more meaningful experiences and enable the possibility of increasing student motivation for topics in different fields of knowledge. The National Autonomous University of Honduras (UNAH) has been making sustained efforts in recent years to incorporate and promote cutting-edge educational innovations. That is why, since 2021, UNAH has created the Extended Reality Innovation Center (CIRE-UNAH), a pioneering center in this field in Higher Education Institutions in the Central American region. The main goal of CIRE-UNAH is to enhance institutional capacities by bringing together teachers, researchers, and students who utilize XR technology to develop innovative products and services. Additionally, it aims to improve the digital and didactic skills of university professors to enhance the quality of teaching practices and student learning outcomes. This work highlights the theoretical principles that have led to the creation of CIRE-UNAH, the outcomes achieved so far, and the strengths, weaknesses, opportunities, and threats identified during the process.

Keywords: XR Learning Communities · Extended Reality · Educational Innovation · Higher Education · UNAH

1 Introduction

The National Autonomous University of Honduras (UNAH) is a public institution of higher education that is responsible by law for overseeing the level of higher education in Honduras. To fulfill its mission, the UNAH has proposed in its General Plan for the Comprehensive Reform of the UNAH [1] that it must diversify its educational programs while promoting the integration of science and technology innovations.

Both the General Plan for Comprehensive Reform [1] and the Academic Standards of the University [2] emphasize that the responsibility of UNAH is to encourage the creation and application of new knowledge. Furthermore, higher education at UNAH is characterized by constant innovation, and creativity linked with the development of science, art, and culture.

In this institutional context, UNAH recognizes the significance of enhancing its educational innovation capabilities to improve the quality of its teaching and learning processes. To achieve this goal, UNAH has initiated various activities to establish research and learning communities for immersive technologies. As a part of these efforts, UNAH has established the Extended Reality Innovation Center (CIRE-UNAH).

In recent years, Higher Education has witnessed a significant trend towards the adoption of various technologies that focus on enhancing and innovating teaching-learning processes. Among these technologies, immersive experiences stand out as they offer more meaningful experiences and can increase student motivation toward different fields of knowledge.

On the other hand, the market value of immersive technologies has been growing steadily and is expected to continue to do so in the future. This makes them one of the most important trends in global society. For a developing country like Honduras, this presents an interesting opportunity to participate in communities that develop science and technology based on Extended Reality (XR).

CIRE-UNAH has been established with three main objectives in mind. Firstly, to develop skills in the use of immersive technologies for creating products and services that can satisfy industry needs. Secondly, to create a technology-based entrepreneurship development center that promotes the establishment of companies based on these technologies. And finally, to enhance the digital and didactic skills of university professors to enhance the quality of teaching practices and improve student learning.

Section 2 provides an overview of the background and justification of CIRE-UNAH. In Sect. 3, the research methods for this work are described. In the Sect. 4 the theoretical framework that led to its development is explained. Following that, Sect. 5 details the organization's strategy. Section 6 discusses the outcomes achieved, as well as the strengths, weaknesses, opportunities, and threats identified during the process. Finally, Sect. 7 presents the conclusions of the process and outlines future work.

2 Background and Justification of the CIRE-UNAH

2.1 Background

A work plan has been developed to increase the international R&D&I indicators of the UNAH by integrating members of the university community who are related to the areas of engineering and applied science. This plan aims to stimulate research in these areas and generate interdisciplinary research programs that can lead to the development of new products, services, methods, and technological processes. The plan also aims to promote innovation and accelerate the development of technological applications within Honduras.

On the other hand, EON Reality Inc (EON) is a leading company in the world that specializes in transferring knowledge and skills using Augmented Reality (AR), Virtual

Reality (VR), and Mixed Reality (MR) for industries and education [3–8]. EON believes that knowledge is a basic human right and should be available to everyone on the planet. To make this possible, EON has developed software that supports AR, VR, MR, and XR knowledge and skills transfer on different types of devices, including mobile ones and immersive glasses [9].

To aid in economic recovery during the COVID-19 pandemic, EON introduced a Grant Guarantee Program designed to enhance immersive technology capabilities in educational institutions and UNAH decided to participate in the challenge to obtain these funds, technical support, and guidance from EON.

In February 2021, during a session, the UNAH University Council approved an agreement (No. CU-O-007-02-2021) regarding the "EON-XR Center Grant Guarantee Program by and between the National Autonomous University of Honduras (UNAH) and EON Reality Inc (EON)". This agreement now allows UNAH to develop educational and commercial solutions that make use of XR technologies. With this agreement, UNAH has partnered to promote immersive technology solutions, train high-level students, and establish learning communities around Extended Reality (XR).

2.2 Justification

A study presented by the Faculty of Economic, Administrative, and Accounting Sciences of the UNAH reveals that Honduras has a primarily primary, dependent, and peripheral economic structure. This configuration is a historical-rich-structural feature, according to the report [10]. The Observatory of Economic Complexity (OEC) of the Massachusetts Institute of Technology (MIT) indicates that the Honduran economy ranks 103rd worldwide and 94th in complexity. In 2019, the country had a trade balance of −4.2 billion dollars, of which 52.24% of exported goods were primary products, with animal or plant origin. The remaining 47.76% of these exports were light manufactures, which are classified in the textile industry [11].

The report discusses the state of the labor market, which plays a crucial role in analyzing the socioeconomic welfare of the country. Dissatisfaction with basic needs among large sections of the population remains unaddressed, hindering any significant improvement in the economic well-being of society's members [12].

The UNAH has expressed concern over the relatively low salary ranges that university graduates are receiving, as statistics show that only 12% of graduates can earn a monthly salary equivalent to 2 to 3 minimum wages. Furthermore, approximately 79% of the population with a university degree earn below 2 minimum wages as their monthly remuneration, which highlights a saturation in many knowledge areas within the labor market. As a result, it is necessary to explore new markets that have yet to be developed within the country.

XR technologies have had a significant impact on the industry and education sector. According to the Fortune Business Insights report [13], Table 1 shows the market values for these technologies in the year 2020 and forecasts for the year 2028. Based on these values, it is an interesting opportunity for Honduras to enter and secure its share of this market. This is especially true considering that it has a low investment cost for the development of innovative products and services. Honduras can leverage its pool of human resources to provide training and support for these technologies.

UNAH aims to support the social, business, and governmental development of Honduran society. To this end, CIRE-UNAH strives to facilitate the development, adaptation, implementation, and transfer of knowledge and disruptive technologies, as well as establish research and learning communities around XR technologies. The objective is to build capabilities that contribute to the transformation of Honduran society.

Table 1. Value and market trends of XR technologies to 2028.

Tecnology	Market value 2020 (billions)	Market value projected 2028 (billions)
XR	US$ 25.4	US$ 397.81

The Faculty of Engineering, through the Research Institute for Applied Sciences and Technology (IICAT), has initiated the development of the CIRE-UNAH intending to provide benefits to students and non-students of UNAH, people with limited resources, the industrial sector, and the government. The center will enhance the skills of professionals and stimulate a new market in the country based on research and development, using XR technologies.

The CIRE-UNAH in Honduras is the first of its kind in the Central American region as stated in [14]. Its primary objective is to impart knowledge to the industrial and educational sectors. By training and certifying 5,000 students and 700 business resource developers, the center aims to promote the use of XR technologies and create a public and private ecosystem to support it.

3 Research Methods

The research methodology used in this work is Design-Based Research (DBR), a process that helps create innovative educational experiences [15]. This methodology is focused on educational innovation and was developed by researchers who were creating technology-enriched learning environments [16]. It is a relatively new paradigm in educational research that typically employs mixed methods. Its main characteristic is that it is iterative, meaning it repeats the design, implementation, and analysis phases while also introducing new elements in each iteration that transform the process. DBR allows for a process of review and reformulation, making it easier to review and adapt the design to address any problems detected.

The implementation process of the XR learning community at UNAH through the creation of CIRE-UNAH is organized into 3 phases, which are:

1- Establishment and institutional positioning
2- Adequacy of infrastructure and initial academic offer
3- Evaluation and continuous improvement

Based on Fraefel's diagram [17], the Fig. 1 illustrates how these phases are founded on theories and requirements and involve actions of designing, implementing, and analyzing the project. The analysis of what has been achieved in turn informs the implications of the theory and begins a new phase.

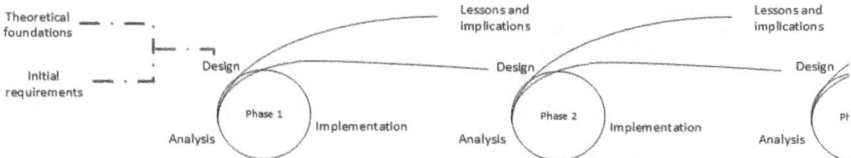

Fig. 1. Cycle of the Design-Based Research methodology.

The CIRE-UNAH's process and its objectives will be evaluated in each phase using various instruments, mainly the following:

- The Instructional Design Motivation Instrument (IMMS) to measure motivation levels [18].
- The acceptance of technology will be measured using the Technology Acceptance Model (TAM) or a modified version such as the Unified Theory of Acceptance and Use of Technology (UTAUT), which measures factors that influence users when faced with new technology.
- The impact evaluation will be visible on the contrast between the starting situation and what happens once the training has taken place. The objective is to try to determine if there were changes, the magnitude they had, which segments of the target population they affected, etc. [19].

4 Theoretical Foundations of CIRE-UNAH

4.1 Extended Reality

XR, which stands for "eXtended Reality," is a broad concept that unites different technologies such as Augmented Reality (AR), Virtual Reality (VR), and Mixed Reality (MR) into a single term [20]. It also includes related and complementary concepts such as Artificial Intelligence (AI) or 5G, as well as other innovations that arise from the advances in these technologies. The term XR has emerged due to the increasing convergence of these technologies, as they continue to advance and intermingle with each other. Additionally, XR also encompasses tools that exist between these realities, such as 360 video and holograms [21].

VR is a technology that enables users to fully immerse themselves in a virtual world using all their senses [6]. To achieve this, the user needs to wear a set of headphones and special glasses that isolate them from the outside world. There are two types of glasses available: those that come with an in-built screen and those that require a smartphone to be inserted into them. Both types of glasses are equipped with sensors that detect the user's head movements, allowing them to explore the virtual world. Some of these glasses also have controls that enable users to interact with objects within the virtual reality universe [22, 23] (Fig. 2).

AR is a technology that allows digital layers to be superimposed on a real-world environment. This is usually done using devices with a camera, such as a mobile phone or a tablet. Popular examples of AR include TikTok, Pokemon Go, and Snapchat, where users can see real-time images of the world around them with synthetic objects added to

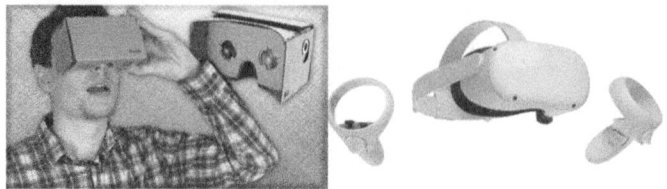

Fig. 2. Example of some XR glasses available in the market.

help them interact with reality. Additionally, users can record 3D images in these spaces [24].

Fig. 3. "Cuetaya: Land of Colors". A board videogame that uses AR [25].

MR is an advanced version of AR that combines real and virtual environments. This technology not only places virtual objects in the real environment but also enables these objects to interact with the environment in real time. In other words, MR makes virtual objects understand the environment in which they exist and react accordingly [26] (Fig. 3).

The concept of these realities can be visualized through the graph presented in Fig. 4 and proposed by [27]. As we move toward the left side of the graph, we approach the real world, while as we move toward the right side of the graph, we move closer to a completely virtual world.

To summarize, different types of technologies create immersive experiences:

- VR is a technology that allows users to experience and interact with a completely artificial digital environment.
- AR superimposes virtual objects onto the real-world environment.
- MR not only overlays virtual objects but also anchors them to the real-world environment.
- XR is an umbrella term that encompasses VR, AR, and MR, and the relationships between them.
- XR is the current and future of immersive technologies. As the market matures, accessing and transitioning between different XR technologies will become easier and they will eventually converge into a single one. In the long run, this unified XR experience will be accessed from the same device and it will be difficult to differentiate between the different technologies [28].

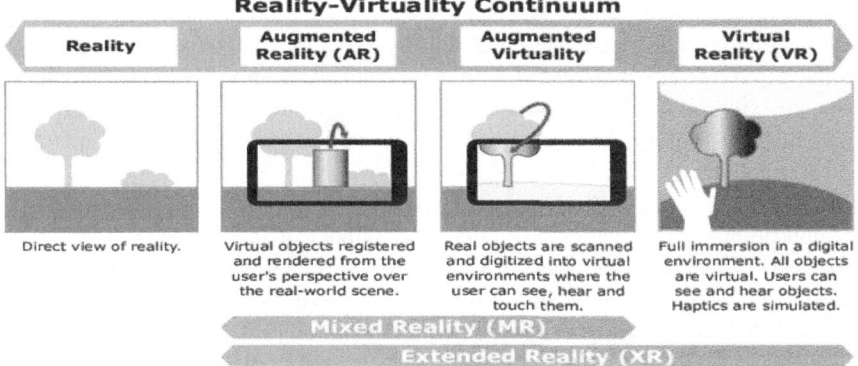

Fig. 4. Reality–virtuality continuum. Spectrum of physical and extended reality, with virtual reality at one end and the real world at the other [27].

4.2 Innovative Trends in Higher Education

Since 2017, the Higher Education Horizon Report has highlighted the positive impact of VR and AR implementation in classrooms. It has led to stronger learning processes, collaborative work, and peer learning. There are now a growing number of technology tools available on the market, such as ActionBound, Zapworks, Augmented Class, and EON-XR. These tools come packed with features to conduct remote learning and training in a hands-on, immersive environment [29].

The following technologies significantly impact the way we present content for learning and enable interaction with different pedagogical models. These models are described in the EduTrends Report, AR Edition [30]:

- Mobile Learning
- Gamification
- Digital Educational Materials and Open Educational Resources
- Hybrid Learning
- Learning Based on Experimentation

It is important to recognize the vast potential of VR and AR technologies and to explore their possibilities in the field of education. Experts predict that the medical industry will benefit the most from this technology, followed by the military, industrial, and tourism sectors. XR technologies also have the potential to revolutionize other industries such as fashion, entertainment, cultural heritage, and banking [13, 31].

4.3 Advantages of Using Extended Reality in Higher Education

There have been several studies that indicate the positive effects of using AR in education. These benefits include improved student motivation, engagement, performance, learning attitudes, interactions, and participation [32]. Current research in AR in education focuses on special educational needs, Industry 4.0, storytelling, 3D printing, mobile applications, and higher education [33].

In the field of health sciences education, in [34] suggest that using VR or AR can have many benefits, especially in ophthalmology training. These technologies can be integrated into conventional treatment processes and allow for safe repeated practice of low-complexity tasks without constant supervision by instructors or medical personnel. This could greatly reduce the costs associated with physical training facilities and trained medical personnel.

In the area of vocational education, a noteworthy example is the co-creation of an AR application for learning car painting. The authors of this application found that the students' time spent on the task had a moderate correlation with the dimensions of attention, relevance, and satisfaction. AR has the potential to increase the time dedicated to the task and, consequently, enhance student motivation [35].

5 Organizational Strategy of CIRE-UNAH

5.1 Mission, Vision, and Objectives of CIRE-UNAH

Mission Statement: Our goal is to provide top-notch training, research and development, and educational innovation services using extended reality applications. We strive to enhance the learning and training processes of our clients and stakeholders and become the most reliable Extended Reality Center in the region.

Vision Statement: By the year 2025, we envision becoming the leading Extended Reality Center in the Central American region. Our focus will be on teaching, developing, and innovating products and services using Extended Reality technologies. We aim to set the standard in our field and be recognized as the go-to reference for all Extended Reality needs in the region (Fig. 5).

Fig. 5. A banner on the web page of CIRE-UNAH

General Objective: To develop innovative solutions using AR, VR, and XR technologies, which can create new products and services in the national market and contribute to the productive transformation of Honduras.

5.2 Structure of CIRE-UNAH

The CIRE-UNAH is an institutional project comprising a coordinator, a teacher-researcher, and an assistant. Operational units have also been proposed to align with their objectives and areas of action. These units will be created based on budget availability and include the Educational Training and Innovation Unit, the Research and Development Unit, and the Technology-Based Entrepreneurship Promotion Unit.

To support the CIRE, various internal bodies of the UNAH assist. These bodies include the Directorate of Scientific and Technological Research, the Directorate of Educational Innovation, the Learning Resources Center / Executive Directorate of Technology Management, the Academic Vice-Rectory, and the Communications Direction. The core lab of the CIRE-UNAH is located in the Faculty of Engineering and provides the logistics, advice, and training capacity inside and outside the UNAH.

5.3 CIRE-UNAH Works Plan

The CIRE-UNAH has organized its work into three areas of action, which were addressed in 2023 using results-based planning. Below are the main points of these areas:

1. Training and Certification:
   - Spread awareness about the CIRE UNAH training program.
   - Provide certification for UNAH students in VR and AR.
   - Train and certify UNAH professors in VR/AR.
   - Certify the UNAH XR Mentor group in 3D modeling.
2. Research and Development
   - Establish the "Pumas in the Metaverse" community, which will provide a platform for teachers and students to research and develop immersive technologies.
   - Incorporate XR practices and experiences into technical and humanities training programs for young students.
   - Create fieldwork experiences that use immersive technologies.
3. Promotion of Entrepreneurship:
   - Enhance the entrepreneurial skills of UNAH students by providing training in technological entrepreneurship.

6 Discussion of the CIRE-UNAH Experience: Results and SWOT Analysis

CIRE-UNAH, despite being relatively new, has achieved significant results in terms of its management, which represents multiple benefits for the institution, including national leadership in the area of XR, increased scientific visibility through academic events, and increased expectations from students and teachers to incorporate these technologies in their teaching-learning processes. Some noteworthy achievements include:

- **Teaching.** Certification of 436 students and 72 teachers in the course "Adopting virtual reality and augmented reality solutions." The course, which is a 10-h training program on the EON Reality platform, allows participants to develop XR resources in 3D and 360 format.
- **Research.** Presentation of 6 papers on XR-based themes at international conferences held in Mexico, Guatemala, Nicaragua, and Honduras. These papers cover topics such as Cultural and Natural Heritage, Quantum Computing, Higher Education, and Industry 4.0.

- **Scientific Publications.** Publication of 1 article in an indexed magazine that discusses the use of XR to expedite the training process of optical technical staff (Fig. 6).
- **XR Communities.** Creation of the UNAH learning and research community on XR: "Pumas in the Metaverse" (named after the UNAH mascot) (Fig. 7).
- **Internationalization.** There have been two international academic exchange tours on the topic of XR, one with the Universitat of Girona in Spain, and another with the Ean University and the Konrad Lorenz in Colombia (Fig. 8).
- **Fundraising.** 3 proposals were presented in companion with local instances and Central American universities to obtain international funds.

Fig. 6. Scientific article published in an *academic* indexed in Scopus by a researcher associated with CIRE-UNAH.

Fig. 7. Poster inviting you to participate in the "PUMAS in the Metaverse" space.

Figure 9 outlines a SWOT analysis carried out with the experience that has been had in two years of management of the CIRE-UNAH.

Fig. 8. Dr. Esquivel, CIRE-UNAH Coordinator, during the visit to the VR Lab at Ean University in Colombia.

Strengths • Human teams from different internal units of the UNAH have shown commitment to the CIRE-UNAH establishment. • It has been possible to appoint 3 professors from the Faculty of Engineering to CIRE-UNAH with partial part-time assignments. • Support from EON Reality Inc., not only in the training processes but also in Fundraising for the CIRE-UNAH.	**Opportunities** • The "Pumas in the Metaverse" community has had significant acceptance among UNAH students. • Become the university that leads the topic of XR at the national and regional level. • There are approaches to have support between the CIRE-UNAH and the Honduran industry, both textile and in the coffee sectors. • Develop UNAH-CIRE's pedagogical strategies for education with immersive technologies and socialize them in academic events.
Weaknesses • The institutional bureaucracy has delayed some key processes for the advancement of CIRE-UNAH. • Lack of adequacy of a physical space adapted to the needs and conducive to the design and prototyping of the XR. • Lack of a Technology Transfer Office at UNAH to manage the technological transfer to the industry of the CIRE-UNAH future prototypes and products developed	**Threats** • That the XR issue stops being a priority for the authorities and they decide to stop promoting the CIRE-UNAH.

Fig. 9. SWOT analysis of CIRE-UNAH.

7 Conclusions

Thanks to the concrete decision and will of the UNAH community, the use of immersive VR/AR/XR technologies is being promoted and strengthened within the university. The establishment of CIRE-UNAH has helped create multidisciplinary teams, enabling a better understanding of immersive technologies. This has provided a platform for learning and reflection, which has resulted in the development of educational and research skills in this field.

The support provided by EON Reality Inc. as a strategic partner of UNAH has been instrumental in facilitating and validating the implementation of CIRE-UNAH. Through various shared experiences with international professionals from five different countries (United States, Spain, Turkey, Argentina, and Honduras), the UNAH team has been able to acquire good practices based on international standards.

Although the physical infrastructure planned for the CIRE-UNAH is not fully adapted yet, there is some technological equipment available such as Oculus Quest 2 and Magic Leap glasses, a 360 Camera, a 3D Scanner, and some webcams. Additionally, there are VR/AR adapters for mobile phones that allow immersive experiences. The Center also has a smart screen and software licensing on the EON Reality platform and using these resources from 2021 to 2023, the CIRE-UNAH has carried out training, transfer and dissemination, and research activities in the field of VR/AR/XR technologies. Some of the notable activities include:

- Socializing the CIRE-UNAH liaisons in Faculties and Regional Centers.
- Visiting consortia of companies and organizations to carry out training initiatives in immersive technologies with MSMEs and agricultural producers.
- Organizing an XR Fair as part of the UNAH Educational Innovation Day 2023.

In the future, we aim to foster and strengthen academic cooperation between universities and international organizations related to science and technology. A concrete action will be to encourage UNAH academics to join the Immersive Learning Research Network (iLRN) to establish an XR society in Honduras and propitiate an open space to share knowledge, lessons learned, and good practices. Additionally, we propose organizing VR-Day Honduras 2024 as a strategy to use this academic event that will involve more actors inside and outside UNAH to learn about the latest tools and developments in the Latin American region. Across time will be possible to incorporate some impact evaluations and conduct comparative studies between institutions.

During the initial phase of implementing the CIRE-UNAH, the validation process for the experience of teachers and students through the application of instruments has not yet been carried out. This process would enable us to determine the impact of XR knowledge on teaching practices. However non-formal consultations have been conducted with individuals who have completed the courses, and the feedback received has been significantly positive. There is also an expressed interest by them in continued training on the subject and also being part of the community "Pumas in the Metaverse".

Furthermore, we're considering adding video game development to CIRE-UNAH's thematic lines, as there are intrinsic relationships between both technologies. The synergy created with these technologies can lead to new developments in higher education.

References

1. Comisión de Transición: Plan General para la Reforma Integral de la Universidad (PGRI). UNAH, Tegucigalpa (2005)
2. UNAH: Normas Académicas de la UNAH. Publicaciones de la Reforma Universitaria 6. UNAH, Tegucigalpa (2015). https://vra.unah.edu.hn/gestion-academica/documentos-relacionados/fasciculos-de-la-reforma-universitaria. Last accessed 30 May 2023
3. Al-Allaq, A., Jaksic, N., Al-Amili, H. A., Mahmood, D. M.: The Application of Virtual Reality to (Mechatronics Engineering) by Creating an Articulated Robotic Work Cell Using EON Reality V9.22.24.24477. Alkej **17**(2), 18–30 (2021). https://doi.org/10.22153/kej.2021.04.001
4. Jaksic, N.: A virtual reality course using EON reality: students' experiences. In: 2018 ASEE Annual Conference & Exposition Proceedings, Salt Lake City, Utah (2018)
5. Massis, B.: Using virtual and augmented reality in the library. New Libr. World **116**(11/12), 796–799 (2015). https://doi.org/10.1108/NLW-08-2015-0054
6. Liu, Y., et al.: Virtual reality system for industrial training. In: 2020 International Conference on Virtual Reality and Visualization (ICVRV), pp. 338–339. Recife, Brazil (2020)
7. Subandi, J., Syahidi, A.A., Mohamed, A.: Mobile Augmented Reality Application with Multi-Interaction for Learning Solutions on the Topic of Computer Network Devices (Effectiveness, Interface, and Experience Design). In: 2020 Third International Conference on Vocational Education and Electrical Engineering (ICVEE), pp. 1–6. Surabaya, Indonesia (2020)
8. Gonzalez Almaguer, C.A., et al.: STEM competency-based learning for engineering and design students of the educational model TEC21. In: Proceedings of the 22nd International Conference on Engineering and Product Design Education (2020)
9. Jo, D.-S., Yang, U.-Y.Y., Son, W.-H.: Design evaluation system with visualization and interaction of mobile devices based on virtual reality prototypes. ETRI J. **30**(6), 757–764 (2008). https://doi.org/10.4218/etrij.08.0108.0209
10. OEC: Complejidad Económica de Honduras (2019). https://oec.world/es/profile/country/hnd. Last accessed 30 May 2023
11. OEC: ¿Qué exporta e importa Honduras (2019). https://oec.world/es/visualize/tree_map/hs92/export/hnd/all/show/2019/. Last accessed 30 May 2023
12. Rodríguez-Corea, H., et al.: Situación del Empleo en Honduras: Lineamientos para la formulación de una estrategia nacional de generación de empleo. UNAH, Tegucigalpa (2018). https://iies.unah.edu.hn/assets/Uploads/Situacion-del-Empleo-en-Honduras.pdf. Last accessed 30 May 2023
13. Fortune Business Insights: AR Market Size, Share & COVID-19 Impact Analysis (2022). https://www.fortunebusinessinsights.com/augmented-reality-ar-market-102553. Last accessed 30 May 2023
14. Zúniga Solórzano, M., Fabregat, R., Gross, E.: Realidad Aumentada y Tecnologías de Juegos para el Aprendizaje del Patrimonio Cultural y Natural en la UNAH. Managua (2021). https://www.researchgate.net/publication/356504294_Realidad_Aumentada_y_Tecnologias_de_Juegos_para_el_Aprendizaje_del_Patrimonio_Cultural_y_Natural_en_la_UNAH/citation/download. Last accessed 30 May 2023
15. Leinonen, T., Durall-Gazulla, E.: Design thinking and collaborative learning. Comunicar: Revista Científica de Comunicación y Educación **21**(42), 107–116 (2014). https://doi.org/10.3916/C42-2014-10
16. Salinas-Ibáñez, J., De-Benito, B.: Construction of personalized learning pathways through mixed methods. Comunicar: Revista Científica de Comunicación y Educación **28**(65), 31–42 (2020). https://doi.org/10.3916/C65-2020-03

17. Fraefel, U.: Professionalization of pre-service teachers through university-school partnerships Partner schools for Professional Development: development, implementation and evaluation of cooperative learning in schools and classes (2014)
18. Keller, J.M.: Motivational Design for Learning and Performance. Springer, Boston, MA (2010)
19. OIT: Guía para la Evaluación de Impacto de la Formación (2019). https://test-guia.oitcinter for.org/conceptualizacion/que-se-entiende-evaluacion-impacto. Last accessed 30 May 2023
20. Çöltekin, A., et al.: Extended reality in spatial sciences: a review of research challenges and future directions. IJGI **9**(7), 439 (2020). https://doi.org/10.3390/ijgi9070439
21. Xing, Y., et al.: Historical data trend analysis in extended reality education field. In: 2021 IEEE 7th International Conference on Virtual Reality (ICVR), pp. 434–440. Foshan, China (2021)
22. Draganov, I.R., Boumbarov, O.L.: Investigating oculus rift virtual reality display applicability to medical assistive system for motor disabled patients. In: 2015 IEEE 8th International Conference on Intelligent Data Acquisition and Advanced Computing Systems: Technology and Applications (IDAACS), pp. 751–754. Warsaw, Poland (2015)
23. Junfithrana, A.P., Suryana, A., Mahmud, M., Edwinanto, Asian, J.: Practical learning application program to enhance online course using oculus quest virtual reality. In: 2020 6th International Conference on Computing Engineering and Design (ICCED), pp. 1–4. Sukabumi, Indonesia (2020)
24. Javornik, A., et al.: What lies behind the filter? Uncovering the motivations for using augmented reality (AR) face filters on social media and their effect on well-being. Comput. Hum. Behav. **128**, 107126 (2022). https://doi.org/10.1016/j.chb.2021.107126
25. Tobar-Muñoz, H., Baldiris, S., Fabregat, R.: Co-design of augmented reality games for learning with teachers: a methodological approach. Tech Know Learn **28**(2), 901–923 (2023). https://doi.org/10.1007/s10758-023-09643-z
26. Bockholt, N.: Realidad virtual, realidad aumentada, realidad mixta. y ¿qué significa "inmersión" realmente? https://www.thinkwithgoogle.com/intl/es-es/futuro-del-marketing/tecnologia-emergente/realidad-virtual-aumentada-mixta-que-significa-inmersion-realmente/. Last accessed 30 May 2023
27. Iop, A., et al.: Extended reality in neurosurgical education: a systematic review. Sensors (Basel, Switzerland) **22**(16), 6067 (2022). https://doi.org/10.3390/s22166067
28. González-Vargas, J.C., Fabregat, R., Carrillo-Ramos, A., Jové, T.: Survey: using augmented reality to improve learning motivation in cultural heritage studies. Applied Sciences (Switzerland) **10**(3), 897 (2020). https://doi.org/10.3390/app10030897
29. Adams Becker, S., et al.: NMC Horizon report: 2017 Higher Education Edition. New Media Consortium, Austin, Texas (2017)
30. Observatorio de Innovación Educativa: EduTrends: Realidad Aumentada y Virtual. Tecnológico de Monterrey (2017). https://observatorio.tec.mx/wp-content/uploads/2023/03/13.EduTrendsRealidadVirtualyAumentada.pdf. Last accessed 30 May 2023
31. Fortune Business Insights: VR Market Size, Share & COVID-19 Analysis (2022). https://www.fortunebusinessinsights.com/industry-reports/virtual-reality-market-101378. Last accessed 30 May 2023
32. Bacca, J., Baldiris, S., Fabregat, R., Graf, S., Kinshuk: Augmented Reality Trends in Education: A Systematic Review of Research and Applications. J. Educ. Technol. Soc. **17**(4), 133–149 (2014). http://www.jstor.org/stable/jeductechsoci.17.4.133. Last accessed 30 May 2023
33. Avila-Garzon, C., Bacca-Acosta, J., Kinshuk, Duarte, J., Betancourt, J.: Augmented reality in education: an overview of twenty-five years of research. Contemporary Educ. Technol. **13**(3), ep302 (2021). https://doi.org/10.30935/cedtech/10865

34. Muñoz, E.G., Fabregat, R., Bacca-Acosta, J., Duque-Méndez, N., Avila-Garzon, C.: Augmented reality, virtual reality, and game technologies in ophthalmology training. Information **13**(5), 222 (2022). https://doi.org/10.3390/info13050222
35. Bacca, J., Baldiris, S., Fabregat, R.: Kinshuk: insights into the factors influencing student motivation in augmented reality learning experiences in vocational education and training. Front. Psychol. **9**, 1486 (2018). https://doi.org/10.3389/fpsyg.2018.01486

Special Track 2: Sustainable Development and Immerse Learning in the Climate Emergency

Amplifying Immersive Climate Learning

Maria Andrei(✉), Sharon Pisani, Alan Miller, Iain Oliver,
Catherine Anne Cassidy, Sonja Heinrich, and Richard Bates

University of St Andrews, St Andrews, UK
{ma306,sp259,alan.miller,iao,cc274,sh52,crb}@st-andrews.ac.uk

Abstract. Climate change poses an existential threat to our heritage and the way we live, yet its impacts are still often perceived as distant, which in turn acts as a barrier to achieving the behavioural and societal changes required to solve this emergency. This paper summarises impacts of climate change, psychological barriers to effective action, and how experiential climate learning can help overcome these challenges. Surveys of community perceptions of threats to cultural and natural heritage in Scotland's Western Isles, and the increasing engagement of heritage practitioners with this emergency point to the power of heritage as a positive actor in the climate crisis. A strategy for using virtual reality to extend experiential climate learning is proposed and evaluated through the creation and deployment of a climate heritage exhibit. The exhibit enables climate impacts and potential climate futures for the Western Isles to be experienced. The workflow used is then applied to global landscapes experiencing climate change. This demonstrates the way that virtual reality can represent the diversity of landscapes impacted by this crisis and enable immersive climate learning experiences.

Keywords: Climate Change · Virtual Reality · Heritage · Immersive Learning

1 Introduction

The impacts that climate change is predicted to have on the world's cultural and natural heritage are considered by the international scientific community as "one of the major challenges of the twenty-first century" [1]. Immersive climate education shows great potential in contributing to the resolution of the climate emergency. Yet, this is still an underdeveloped field that requires further technical, psychological and social evaluation [2,3]. This research aims to explore why Virtual Reality (VR) could be an effective climate communication tool for museums, analysing both external and internal projects. This serves as the foundation for the second research objective of this paper, which is the development of the first prototypes of immersive simulations of flooding caused by climate change in Scotland that enhance the user learning experience. This builds on insights we gathered through surveys where we investigated perceptions of climate change within vulnerable groups from Scotland's Outer Hebrides Isles.

2 Context of Research: Climate, Distance and Immersion

This work is based upon three fundamental concepts. Firstly, climate change is a global threat, but it manifests differently across different regions. For instance, in Scotland, coastal erosion and flooding are expected to intensify because of sea level rise and precipitation. Secondly, our collective response to climate change is limited by psychological distance from this phenomenon. Thirdly, that immersive technology has great potential as a communication tool within museums to transform climate change from an abstract concept to an experienced reality.

2.1 Climate Change in Scotland

In Scotland, scientists are urging the public to take urgent action into preserving the country's coastal environment [4]. Rising sea levels and extreme precipitation contribute to coastal erosion and flooding, impacting nearly a third of Scotland's coastal infrastructure [5]. Significant natural heritage sites for biodiversity and carbon sequestration are also endangered [4,6], with machair as a primary example. Machair is a rare soil that is particularly important to Scotland as approximately 67% of global machair resides in the country's Outer Hebrides islands [7]. Most cultivated machair can be found in the Isle of North Uist, playing a critical role in the economy of Hebridean people [8]. The isle also hosts UK's most complex saline lagoon system and kelp forests, some of the most productive ecosystems on Earth for marine biodiversity and for the global carbon sink. These offer coastal protection and act as soil fertilisers and animal feed in Scottish traditional agriculture [9,10]. Yet, these are at risk of extinction due to flooding since North Uist is mostly composed of low-lying land with shallow lakes and marshes [11,12]. Past flooding events already damaged roads and infrastructure [13], enhancing the isolation faced by islanders and reducing their access to vital health, educational and transportation facilities. The Scottish Environment Protection Agency (SEPA) predicts that 50 homes and businesses will be damaged by 2080 in the Isle of North Uist alone, with significant losses to arable land [12]. As it will be discussed in Sect. 3, the residents do not trust their government to take appropriate climate action because they believe that the public has yet to accept the reality of climate change.

2.2 Psychological Distance from Climate Change

The 2023 conference for the Network of European Museum Organisations (NEMO) remarked the public lack of acceptance of the reality of climate change as one of the biggest challenges in addressing the climate emergency. The conference further highlighted how the role of museums is shifting from powerful hubs of lifelong learning that safeguard heritage for future generations to a sector that is taking mass action against climate change [14]. Museum practitioners from across the globe emphasised their dedication to communicate the impacts of climate change effectively and drive ecological action. However, climate change information is often perceived as abstract by the public, which acts as a barrier to the actions needed from individuals, corporations and institutions to slow down and limit global warming [15]. Information perceived as concrete instead of abstract is demonstrated to have a much bigger influence on behaviour [16]. This phenomenon is called psychological distance and is described as "a subjective perception of distance between the self and some object, event, or person" [17]. This particularly develops with long-term complex processes such as climate change, as perceived distance is created amongst a multitude of dimensions: likelihood of occurrence, time, geographical space or social distance [18]. Most digital developments that illustrate the coastal impacts of climate change are in the form of web maps, such as the ones developed by SEPA [19] and Dynamic Coast [5]. The field of vulnerability mapping is becoming more pivotal in climate communication [20], but are these tools sufficient. Through a survey evaluated in [21], we discovered that digital maps might reinforce how abstract climate information is perceived.

While psychological distance creates passivity, personal experiences of climate change have been shown to drive concern and action [17,18]. For example, farmers who noticed changes in water availability and people who experienced floods or hurricanes are more inclined to support ecological initiatives. Perceived exposure to climate change has also been linked to pro-environmental behaviour [18]. Consequently, addressing psychological distance is crucial for effective climate communication, and investigating how museums can achieve this through their exhibitions is of great societal importance. Studies show that first-hand accounts of climate change are more powerful than second-hand information due to the Experience-Perception Link [22]. This suggests how psychological distance could be tackled by applying principles of experiential learning: the idea of observing, engaging with, and making sense of personal experiences as integral parts of the learning and understanding process [23,24]. For instance, extending experiential learning with Virtual Reality (VR) simulations of remote or future climate change has the potential to address multiple aspects of psychological distance by simplifying complex phenomena and by enhancing engagement with environmental issues [2,3,25,26]. What is more, 98% of the partakers in the aforementioned survey expressed that their preferred method of learning about climate change would be immersive Virtual Reality experiences when compared to digital maps and written articles [21].

2.3 Immersive Learning for Climate Education and Communication

Virtual Reality has shown many advantages in training and education, with participants studying for longer, making fewer errors and grasping abstract concepts more easily [27–29]. Museums have also leveraged immersive technology to engage people with the past through 3D reconstructions of historical sites, deriving great benefits in preserving and promoting heritage, and in building connections with local communities [30,31]. Since direct experiences of climate hazards are more powerful than second-hand information, and given VR's ability to simulate any location and time period, researchers have been prompted to explore how this technology can support understanding of long-term complex causal processes, such as ecosystem dynamics and climate change impacts. One study showed that fifth and sixth graders exhibited deeper understanding of causal relationships and change over time when they evaluated the reasons behind a fish die-off in a virtual pond [32]. These discoveries are of great value, as spatial and temporal space from the impacts of climate change adds to their perceived complexity and generate psychological distance, which in turn hinders ecological attitudes and behaviour [17,18]. People's remoteness from the ocean can lead to sea level rise being perceived as a distant phenomenon - "out of sight, out of mind" [25]. This is accentuated by the temporal distance between present and future states of the coast, as sea-level rise is "a slow and temporally distant process" [25]. 630 million people are living in areas that are expected to get flooded annually by 2100 [25]. This is addressed by a series of VR experiences titled *The Sea Level Rise Explorer* that simulate how three cities in the United States are projected to be flooded in 100 years. Nearly 1000 participants showed great interest in the simulations, agreeing that they are more impactful than 2D models or photographs because they turn "sea level rise into a reality" [25]. There has been consistent evidence showing that changes in attitudes and behaviour can occur when individuals feel the impact of an experience in a more concrete, immediate and approximate way [2]. Virtual reality has also been described as the "ultimate empathy machine" because it evokes an emotional response that brings participants closer to global issues such as climate change [2]. What is more, visualising climate change with Virtual Reality has the potential to immerse users in novel experiences which may otherwise be unattainable, impractical, resource-intensive, or perilous in the real world. For example, the practical impossibility of fast-forwarding time to witness the unfolding effects of climate change can be overcome through with VR. Varying formats of VR - immersive, desktop and mobile - have the capability to not only convey meaningful content, but to test human cognition, emotional responses, and reactions towards these global issues [2,3]. Despite these advantages, there is only a limited number of such projects, and most of them incorporate expensive hardware, while also not being available online. An additional gap within this research sphere is that some of the most challenging impacts of climate change are not yet represented, as is the case for Scotland.

3 Perceptions of Climate Change

This section analyses primary research accounts regarding perceptions of climate change that we collected from global heritage stakeholders, as well as from stakeholders and inhabitants living on the Isle of North Uist.

3.1 Heritage Stakeholder Perceptions of Climate Change

In September 2023, the Audiovisual, New Technologies & Social Media subcommittee of the International Council of Museums (AVICOM) hosted an online workshop titled *Museums, Virtual Reality and Sustainability in the Climate Emergency*. Attracting over 20 contributors[1] and 180 participants, this enabled us to survey heritage stakeholders who presented on their climate action initiatives.

Participants: Twelve stakeholders from the workshop responded to the Qualtrics survey which was distributed online during the event. They came from several European countries including Scotland, as well as Barbados, Egypt, Nigeria, the Philippines and the United Arab Emirates, and were predominantly between the ages of 25 and 44.

Materials: The survey had four sections: the first assessed perceptions regarding threats of climate change, such as coastal erosion and wildfires; the second section assessed opinions on the roles of heritage organisations, governments, digital tools and citizen science within monitoring climate change; the third question investigated how the stakeholders view the public and their individual understanding of climate change, and their opinions on museums and immersive technologies within climate communication; the final section of the survey evaluated perceptions of individual, community, and governmental climate actions. The questions were a mixture of Likert scale and qualitative questions. For Likert questions, the participants indicated their level of agreement with statements on a 5-point scale ranging from "Strongly agree" to "Strongly Disagree". An example is "The public underestimates the threats of climate change".

Results: Unsurprisingly, all the practitioners were worried about how their communities will be impacted by climate change. After highlighting how concerned they were about different effects of global warming, 11 stakeholders further noted that flooding events, exorbitant storms and heatwaves are the main threats to their home regions. When asked about any other concerns, their answers varied from glacial melts and coastal erosion, to resource scarcity and human perception i.e. humans not understanding "their impacts and responsibilities on climate change". All stakeholders strongly agreed that enhancing public understanding on the impacts of climate change is important, whilst stating that museums and galleries can support this mission and help public audiences become active. We carried out the same survey with seven stakeholders from the Isle of North Uist which was distributed as paper versions during a digital festival hosted as part of the *Aire air Sunnd* (Attention to Wellbeing) project in collaboration with the North Uist Historical society. All participants highlighted flooding, storm formations and coastal erosion as the primary climate hazards in their locality. When asked what they perceive to be the biggest challenges in resolving climate

---

[1] Contributers included practitioners from the Australian, Barbados and Timespan museums, alongside representatives from the University of Siena and the Red Cross.

change, some notable answers were "acceptance of its existence from major governments to individuals", "public and political will for change", "denia", and "assuming that it is likely to get the required behaviour changes needed when people assume their lifestyles can never be changed". All stakeholders believe that governments should take measures to respond to climate change, yet none trust their administration to do so effectively. Five practitioners highlighted the political system as one of the biggest challenges in resolving climate change, whilst others remarked the lack of a consensus on what actions can be taken by individuals, organisations and governments as a significant impediment. Most stakeholders strongly agreed that communicating the impacts of climate change is an integral part of our collective response to this complex issue, with four believing that museums should support this mission. What is more, all agreed that Virtual Reality is an effective communication tool. These results emphasise the high potential of applying immersive technology to successfully educate public audiences on climate change, which confirm the analysis in Sect. 2.3 (Fig. 1).

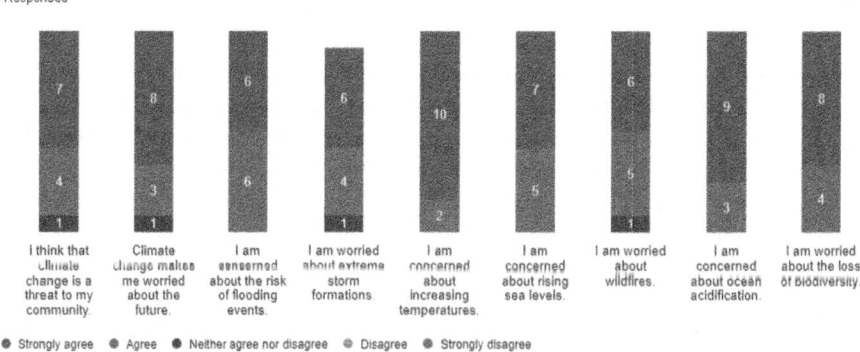

Fig. 1. Stakeholder responses about climate threats from the AVICOM workshop.

3.2 Community Perceptions of Climate Change

The previous insights further corroborate the results we have gathered through another community wellbeing survey distributed as part of the *Aire air Sunnd* project. This was first discussed in [33] and has now been completed. The wellbeing survey was developed by representatives of the North Uist Historical Society and researchers from the Universities of Aberdeen, St Andrews, and the Highlands and Islands. Key components of community and personal wellbeing were analysed, such as wellbeing connections to heritage, culture, Gaelic, natural heritage, and the use of digital tools.

Participants: The participants included 83 residents of North Uist and Benbecula. The study was advertised through the Historical Society's email and social media. Participants were self-selected. It was available online (via Qualtrics) and a paper version was made available in popular shops, cafes and restaurants and by request.

Materials: The survey had four sections: the first one gathered perceptions of residents regarding their heritage and wellbeing, including concerns about current issues such as the environment and Gaelic preservation; the second section gathered feedback and suggestion about the use of the Society's new premises; the third section was an Edinburgh-Warwick study assessing wellbeing, and the last section analysed technological connectivity and social media use amongst residents. The questions were a mixture of Likert scale and qualitative questions. For Likert questions, the participants indicated their level of agreement with statements on a 5-point scale ranging from "Unimportant" to "Very Important". An example item is "What is the importance of the North Uist land and sea environment in your life?".

Results: The combined results from all sections sum up the perceptions and wellbeing of the community. For instance, 92% of respondents said that the North Uist land and sea environment was important to very important in their life. Some of the environmental concerns highlighted by the respondents were coastal erosion, the loss of machair, climate change, and cases of flooding on the island. The community was also asked to voice its concerns in relation to decisions taken at a wider regional and national level. 69% felt that their concerns are not heard at a wider level, whilst 72% said they are not fully consulted on decisions that affect them. When asked to comment, community members said that there was a lack of meaningful engagement between government and community. This was exemplified in the recent opposition to the Scolpaig spaceport development and its environmental effects [34]. As per the stakeholders' perceptions, this creates a sense of distrust in the government and political systems to effectively deal with communities' concerns on areas that are of significant importance to the local community. In the same survey, the community members had an opportunity to add free-text comments on the importance of the natural environment to them. This allowed us to understand what the community values in its environment and why it is important for the effects of climate change to be better communicated.

The responses were coded into the following topics of importance: wellbeing, crofting, animals and biodiversity, exercise and water sports, and art and craft. These results show that the environment is central to the islanders, it is important "for health and wellbeing of body and mind". As with many of the Scottish isles, crofting has been integral to the culture of North Uist and is still being performed. One respondent commented on how they "live on a croft and grow trees to encourage bio-diversity". The community members are aware of the importance of traditional knowledge to maintain "environmentally friendly crofting traditions as implemented by our forebears", but they also see its importance for future generations: "The North Uist environment is important to me as it plays a huge part in my children's upbringing - from exploring the beaches, to taking a boat to uninhabited islands, crofting on the land...". They are also actively reporting on visible effects of climate change on their environment, with one respondent saying "I have realised how vulnerable our coastlines are, as e.g. how Busdara (East-) beach in Berneray has changed in a period of 12 years (Erosion on one side, filling up on the other)". When asked how they envisaged digital tools to be used in their community, workshops on developing digital skills were requested, as well as accessing heritage through websites or alternative media platforms. Almost 60% of the respondents said that digital exhibits that represent local place, stories, and objects will help communicate their heritage. This legitimises this research to similarly communicate climate change through holistic digital exhibits.

4 Developing Immersive Climate Learning Experiences

In previous projects[2] we leveraged game engines to allow people to visualise the past through VR reconstructions of cultural landscapes. Virtual reality represents an aspect of a holistic approach to heritage that explores cultural landscapes, investigating the relations between natural and cultural heritage. Since game engines allow dynamic adaptation, we propose utilising them to create immersive simulations of landscapes in their present and future states. Our research follows a practice based methodology which places creative and practical work at the centre of the inquiry process [35]. To achieve this, we offer a guide to the workflow and materials we have refined through our own developments of game enhanced climate simulations.

4.1 Workflow and Materials

After deciding on the climate effects to be represented, the first milestone is importing a 3D terrain model of the desired landscape into a game engine. If these 3D models are not readily available online, elevation data needs to be obtained and then developed into a 3D terrain model. To download terrain data, we have mainly been using the free academic platform Digimap, as it contains high quality data of most of the landscapes we have represented in 3D. The elevation data needs to be processed in a geographical information system (GIS) software. We have been utilising QGIS, which is a renowned cross-platform software that is also open-source and regularly gets updated. The next step is inputting the updated elevation map into a 3D terrain generator software. World Machine is our program of choice as the software is very intuitive to use and we have a professional license readily available within our team. However, the free version of World Machine also offers high quality outputs that are compatible with game engines that allow for VR development. The 3D terrain model gets imported into a game engine, which generates a virtual landscape that has the exact heights of the real one. We have done most of our VR modelling in Unreal Engine (UE), as this has been shown to render more realistic virtual environments, which

---

[2] Previous projects from our research group can be accessed at https://www.openvirtualworlds.org/reconstructions/.

can be more useful in training and education [36]. UE has been developed by Epic Games, and is written in C++. It provides its own complete programming language for game scripting called Blueprint, which allows for any 3D modelling of climate scenarios. This is how we developed climate simulations of flooding in Scotland. Using Blueprint, we programmed that a second body of virtual water starts rising over 10 s when the user presses a specific button on the keyboard or joystick. The interaction also triggers rain to start, which was build using the Niagara particle system available in Unreal Engine. Unreal also offers its own design and environment tool-kits such as Brushify that enable users to freely model the textures and composition of the virtual landscape so that it resembles the physical one. To assess our simulations and gather insights from relevant stakeholders and communities, we have been collecting primary data through surveys built in Qualtrics, a free and accessible tool that comes with its own data analysis features. To divide answers into clear categories, we have predominantly been applying Likert scale questions alongside open-ended questions.

4.2 Simulating Climate Change in Scotland

One key objective has been to develop VR projects of climate change in Scotland, building on simulations of how the Tentsmuir nature, is expected to inundate in 100 years [21]. We then developed a VR experience that visualises a 10-meter future flood in Glasgow (Fig. 2). This is based on the height of sea levels when CO_2 concentrations were as high in the past as they are now [37]. We further applied our holistic approach through an exhibition about the St Kilda volcanic archipelago, the UK's only Marine and Dual UNESCO World Heritage Site that is part of Scotland's Outer Hebrides isles [38]. This was installed in Taigh Cearsabagh museum in North Uist. The objective of this exhibition was to highlight the natural and cultural heritage of this once inhabited islands. The exhibit comprised of a virtual tour of St Kilda as it looked like in 1810. This is both engaging and exploratory, enabling visitors to interact with the subject in an immersive way. However, this is complemented with an archive of local stories and songs, local biodiversity, and current views of St Kilda. These seamlessly connect to other elements of the exhibit that address the biggest climate threats to the archipelago: a VR simulation of an extreme storm in St Kilda, and an interactive digital poster that educates on these threats and promotes climate actions that visitors can take. In this context, the information about climate threats is not presented as a pessimistic account of adversity, but rather as motivation for the safeguarding of precious and unique biodiversity.

We also developed a simulation of flooding in the Isle of North Uist (Fig. 3). This experience was not showcased as a stand-alone exhibition, but as an activity at the aforementioned digital festival we hosted on the island. In order to better represent the issues and threats, the flooding simulation was shown alongside virtual walk experiences exploring the archaeology and history of the island. The virtual walks are further discussed in [33]. The addition of the flooding simulation enabled visitors to appreciate the context of the climate change discussion that was present in the exhibit. Through the combination of these exhibits, visitors

Fig. 2. Simulation of Future Flooding in Glasgow.

Fig. 3. Simulation of future flooding in the Isle of North Uist.

could visualise the effects of climate change within the context of their own community and heritage, which in turn could reduce the psychological distance driven by both the temporal and identity separation between the perceived 'self' of the individual and the effects of climate change. A place name activity was also carried out. This was based on a desire by the community to record local place names, as communicated through the survey discussed in Sect. 3.2. Through an online digital map, visitors contributed the Gaelic names of places that are at the risk of being lost. Again, whilst the discussion on climate change in this activity was not a direct one (visitors were not asked to write places that have been affected by climate change alone), participants still engaged with the climate change discussion, and were naturally putting in names that they believed will be lost soon, either due to erosion or abandonment as a consequence of harsher conditions. This simulation was evaluated by 19 participants, nine who joined the festival and ten who assessed the simulation at a subsequent workshop at our institution. This was achieved through the same feedback survey used with the other climate simulations which was available on paper and online, and shared with the users during the events. Six participants responded that the immersion was their favourite element of the simulation, with some mentioning that it allowed them to relate more strongly with the topic of the exhibits. Others stated that "VR is a great way to visualise the effects of climate change", "it helps to make the impacts of climate change hit home", and that "it really shed light into how impactful climate change is beyond abstract data". All participants agreed that VR will help climate communication. Perhaps the most interesting part of the feedback was that over half of the users said that they wanted to learn more about the topic, and that they were likely to research it after interacting with the simulation. This indicates how immersive climate education experiences are likely to drive action beyond the user's interaction with the exhibit.

4.3 Applying Methods to Global Landscapes

To explore the use of VR in climate communication, we developed a series of immersive climate educational experiences. The simulations address various effects of climate change, such as rising temperatures alongside China's Silk Road, Icelandic melting glaciers, and the bleaching of the Great Barrier Reef. Users can explore the virtual environments and visualise them through throughout different time periods, from how these landscapes looked like in the past to how they are expected to change in the future because of climate change. The VR experience regarding Icelandic glaciers leveraged the concept of virtual museums, which redefines engaging with heritage - the user is able to virtually explore a gallery of 3D exhibits and displays on glacial melt in Iceland. For each case study, an accompanying web gallery was built for accessibility that incorporated panoramic photos and videos of the VR experiences amongst other digital artefacts, such as photography, videos and infographics [39]. These were evaluated by an average of ten participants per project through individual workshops to test if the immersive technology enhanced the learning experience through usability and user satisfaction. The online questionnaire was built in Qualtrics and shared with the participants after the interaction with the exhibit. It contained a mix of open-ended ended questions and Likert statements on a 5-point scale ranging from "Strongly agree" to "Strongly disagree", addressing both the simulations and web gallery. Some of the statements were "I thought the system was easy to use" and "I enjoyed this way of learning". The feedback was predominantly positive, with users stating that the VR simulations fostered a more engaging and interactive learning experience, whilst simplifying a complex phenomenon like climate change. Most participants answered that they were more likely to engage with ecological action after visualising climate change in VR, indicating that immersive technology has the potential of being an effective communication tool. However, a small number of participants stated that the simulation was not an interesting learning experience, with some mentioning that they would have preferred more gaming elements. This holistic approach is one key element that can help museums talk about climate change in their exhibits whilst addressing the challenge of climate fatigue. This refers to a phenomenon that is yet to be widely researched in museums, where people disassociate with the climate change discussion due to its negative or depressing effects [40]. This is reflective of the museum fatigue phenomenon which demonstrates that users often lose interest after engaging with an exhibit for a while [41]. However, it has been shown that using more positive narratives can promote action and engagement in visitors [41]. Thus, this is what aims to be addressed through climate learning exhibits.

5 Challenges

Although VR has great potential as an effective climate communication tool implemented by the heritage sector, it also poses several limitations. Building climate simulations is resource and skills intensive, and some groups of people might not want to engage with it, or might physically be unable to do so. Furthermore, it is an ongoing challenge within research to measure behaviour change effectively, especially over longer periods. If this is not addressed, we might not be able to attest the effect of immersive technology on psychological distance and human action. To address these limitations and support the heritage sector in halting climate change, we are proposing a holistic approach to heritage that integrates digital engagement, including VR. This includes exploring cultural landscapes and the relations between cultural and natural heritage, both tangible and intangible.

6 Future Work

This holistic approach will be further developed through a global strategy, as we aim to showcase climate effects in various landscapes, ranging from polar environments to islands (Fig. 4).

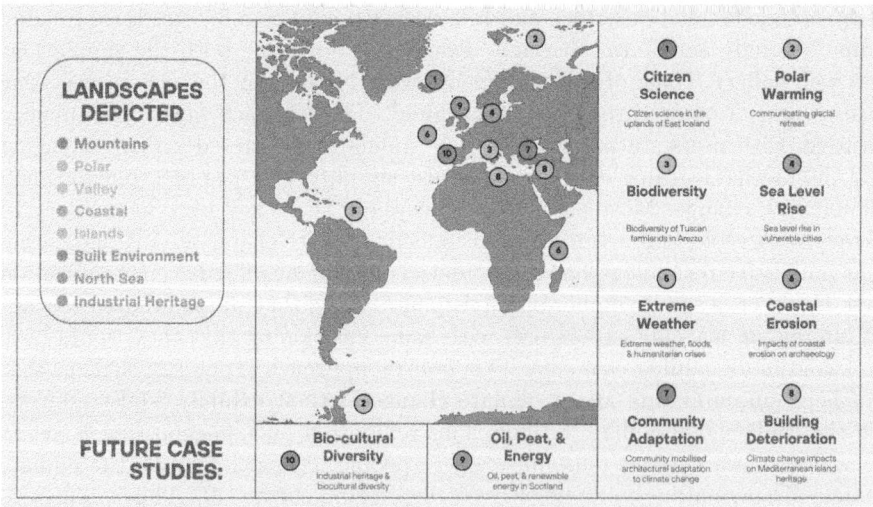

Fig. 4. Planned case studies for climate projects.

This will include building, to our knowledge, the first immersive climate simulations of the Western Antarctic Peninsula in collaboration with the Discovery Point in Scotland, which will be integrated with the climate simulations of Scotland during the development of the museum's upcoming Antarctic climate gallery. This will allow us to expand our evaluation methods and investigate more in depth how perceptions of climate change are impacted through VR experiences that display both global and local impacts. We are further collaborating with Heritage Malta to develop a hub for multi-sensory experiences about the local heritage and the effects of climate change to help visitors engage with Maltese history and identity through Virtual and Augmented Reality.

References

1. UNESCO: Case studies on Climate Change and World Heritage. UNESCO Digital Library (2007)
2. Markowitz, D., Bailenson, J.: Virtual reality and the psychology of climate change. Curr. Opin. Psychol. **42**, 60–65 (2021)
3. Queiroz, A.C.M., Kamarainen, A.M., Preston, N.D., da Silva Leme, M. I.: Immersive virtual environments and climate change engagement. In: Proceedings of the Immersive Learning Research Network, pp. 153–164. ILRN, USA (2018)
4. GOV.UK Committee on Climate Change: UK Climate Change Risk Assessment 2017 Evidence Report - Summary for Scotland. UK Climate Change Risk Assessment (2017)
5. Hansom, J.D., Fitton, J.M, Rennie, A.F: Dynamic coast - national coastal change assessment: summary. The National Coastal Change Assessment Reports (2017)
6. Fitton, J., Hansom, J.: A national coastal erosion susceptibility model for Scotland. Ocean Coast. Manage. **132**, 60 (2016)
7. Beaumont, N.J., Jones, L., Garbutt, A., Hansom, J.D., Toberman, M.: The value of carbon sequestration and storage in coastal habitats. Estuar. Coast. Shelf Sci. **137**, 32–40 (2014)
8. Owen, N.W., Kent, M., Dale, P.: Ecological effects of cultivation on the machair sand dune systems of the Outer Hebrides, Scotland. J. Coast. Conserv. **6**, 155–170 (2000)
9. Angus, S.: Scottish saline lagoons: impacts and challenges of climate change. Estuar. Coast. Shelf Sci. **198**, 626–635 (2017)
10. Greenhill, L., Sundnes, F., Karlsson, M.: Towards sustainable management of kelp forests: an analysis of adaptive governance in developing regimes for wild kelp harvesting in Scotland and Norway. Ocean Coast. Manage. **212**, 105816 (2021)
11. Angus, S.: The implications of climate change for coastal habitats in the Uists, Outer Hebrides. Ocean Coast. Manage. **94**, 38–43 (2014)
12. Scottish Environment Protection Agency: Flood Risk Management Plan Outer Hebrides Local Plan District (2021)
13. AmPaipear: Uist battles rising floods (2022)
14. Gibbs, K., Sani, M., Thompson, J.: Lifelong learning in museums - a European handbook. The Network of European Museum Organisations, Italy (2006)
15. van Lange, P.A.M., Bastian, B.: Reducing climate change by making it less abstract. Sci. Am. **320**(4) (2019)
16. Borgida, E., Nisbett, R.: The differential impact of abstract vs. concrete information on decisions. J. Appl. Soc. Psychol. **7**, 258–271 (1977)

17. Wang, S., Hurlstone, M., Leviston, Z., Walker, I., Lawrence, C.: Climate change from a distance: an analysis of construal level and psychological distance from climate change. Front. Psychol. **10**, 230 (2019)
18. McDonald, R., Chai, H., Newell, B.: Personal experience and the 'psychological distance' of climate change: an integrative review. J. Environ. Psychol. **44**, 109–118 (2015)
19. SEPA Flood Risk Management Maps. https://map.sepa.org.uk/floodmap/map.htm. Accessed 1 Mar 2024
20. De Sherbinin, A., et al.: Climate vulnerability mapping: a systematic review and future prospects. Wiley Interdisc. Rev.: Clim. Change **10**(5), 600 (2019)
21. Andrei, M., Miller, A., Oliver, I.: Work-in-progress-visualising the impacts of climate change with immersive technology. Immersive Learn. Res. - Acad. **1**(2), 100–104 (2023)
22. Lang, C., Ryder, J.D.: The effect of tropical cyclones on climate change engagement. Clim. Change **135**, 625–638 (2016)
23. Fromm, J., Radianti, J., Wehking, C., Stieglitz, S., Majchrzak, T., vom Brocke, J.: More than experience?-on the unique opportunities of virtual reality to afford a holistic experiential learning cycle. Internet High. Educ. **50** (2021)
24. Mughal, F., Zafar, A.: Experiential learning from a constructivist perspective: reconceptualizing the Kolbian cycle. Int. J. Learn. Dev. **1**(2), 27–37 (2011)
25. Calil, J., et al.: Using virtual reality in sea level rise planning and community engagement an overview. Water **13**, 1142 (2021)
26. Scurati, G., Bertoni, M., Graziosi, S., Ferrise, F.: Exploring the use of virtual reality to support environmentally sustainable behavior: a framework to design experiences. Sustainability **13**(2), 943 (2021)
27. Buttussi, F., Chittaro, L.: Effects of different types of virtual reality display on presence and learning in a safety training scenario. IEEE Trans. Vis. Comput. Graph. **24**(2), 1063–1076 (2018)
28. Makransky, G., Petersen, G.B.: The cognitive affective model of immersive learning (CAMIL): a theoretical research-based model of learning in immersive virtual reality. Educ. Psychol. Rev. **33**(3), 937–958 (2021). https://doi.org/10.1007/s10648-020-09586-2
29. Němec, M., Fasuga, R., Trubač, J., Kratochvíl, J..: Using virtual reality in education. In: 15th International Conference on Emerging eLearning Technologies and Applications (ICETA), pp. 1–6. IEEE, Slovakia (2017)
30. Cassidy, C.A., et al.: Digital pathways in community museums. Museum Int. **70**, 126–139 (2018)
31. Kennedy, S., et al.: Exploring canons and cathedrals with open virtual worlds: the recreation of St Andrews Cathedral, St Andrews day, 1318. In: 2013 Digital Heritage International Congress (DigitalHeritage), pp. 273–280. IEEE, France (2013)
32. Grotzer, T., et al.: Turning transfer inside out: the affordances of virtual worlds and mobile devices in real world contexts for teaching about causality across time and distance in ecosystems. Technol. Knowl. Learn. **20**, 43–69 (2015)
33. Pisani, S., Miller, A. H. D., Morrison, M.: Digitising the cultural landscape of north Uist. In: Proceedings of the 9th International Conference iLRN 2023, pp. 397–407. ILRN, USA (2023)
34. Severin, C.: Scottish spaceport near protected areas approved despite local opposition. The Guardian (2023)
35. Candy, L.: Practice based research: a guide. Creat. Cogn. Stud. Rep. **1** (2006)
36. Checa, D., Bustillo, A.: A review of immersive virtual reality serious games to enhance learning and training. Multimed. Tools Appl. **79**, 5501–5527 (2020)

37. National Geographic. https://education.nationalgeographic.org/resource/climate-milestone-earths-co2-level-passes-400-ppm/. Accessed 1 Mar 2024
38. Northern Heritage. https://northernheritage.org/st_kilda/. Accessed 1 Mar 2024
39. Open Virtual Worlds. https://www.openvirtualworlds.org/reconstructions/. Accessed 1 Mar 2024
40. Kerr, R.: Amid worrisome signs of warming, "climate fatigue" sets in. Science **326**(5955), 926–928 (2009)
41. Ferreira, M., Nisi, V., Nunes, N.: Interactions with climate change: a data humanism design approach. In: Proceedings of the 2023 ACM Designing Interactive Systems Conference, pp. 1325–1338. Association for Computing Machinery, USA (2023)

Creating Authentic Historical Costumes to Augment Virtual Humans for Cultural Heritage

Junyu Zhang[✉][iD], Alan Miller[iD], and Perin Westerhof Nyman[iD]

School of Computer Science, University of St Andrews, St Andrews, UK
{jz87,alan.miller,pwn2}@st-andrews.ac.uk

Abstract. Benefiting from the simulation of 3D technologies, the evolution of virtual humans allows them to have a realistic human-like appearance and behaviour, interacting with users and the environment. Today, the application of digital avatars has expanded to computer visualization exhibitions, movies, animations, game engines, etc. This paper investigates a methodology for applying virtual humans to support the digital reconstruction of cultural heritage in virtual reality applications, focusing on converting 2D design sketches of historical costumes into a tangible reality within an immersive VR environment. Through the creation and application of authentic historical outfits, this approach enriched the authenticity of digital avatars, and further expanded the interpretation and representation of cultural heritage for educational and cultural institutions. In addition, this paper evaluated the impacts of avatars on enhancing learning and visiting experiences on the promotion of cultural history diversity. This research is beneficial for exploring how immersive VR technologies bring about equitable quality education and promote learning opportunities in the context of cultural heritage. At the time of writing, the results of this research are adopted in immersive exhibits in the Timespan Museum, West Highland Museum, Finlaggan Museum and Taigh Chearsabhagh, aimed at providing an immersive virtual time travel experience to strengthen lifelong cultural education values and further support the sustainable development goals.

Keywords: Virtual Humans · Cultural Heritage · Virtual Reality

1 Introduction

Virtual Humans (VHs) are widely used in various fields, including computer visualization exhibitions, movies, animations, game engines, non-player characters (NPCs) contribute to a better sense of immersive storytelling. Moreover, the increasingly developed technologies such as Virtual Reality (VR), Augmented Reality (AR), or Mixed Reality (MR) provide realistic 3D simulations for potential users. Through affordable devices, it is more accessible for people to use VR headsets or mobile devices to explore high-fidelity virtual representations to acquire equitable quality education and lifelong learning opportunities.

In cultural heritage digitization, 3D technologies, particularly VR, offer immersive and interactive experiences [9]. This facilitates advanced archiving, management, and digital storytelling, engaging audiences with historical collections [27]. VR is crucial in contemporary museums for mass communication and culture popularization [5]. The instantiation of "virtual museums" exemplifies the symbiotic integration of technology with cultural heritage, contributing significantly to research investigations and cultural preservation. VR has been adopted as an efficient method for cultural organizations to attract visitors. It allows the immersive exploratory experience with augmented environments. In Helmsdale, Scotland, the Timespan Museum provides virtual reality representations of the 1800s Caen township [20]. The Castle of Corsano implements VR application, providing immersive experiences [10]. The virtual reconstruction of St Andrews Cathedral enables the public to immerse themselves in the past history through Virtual Characters in VR. [17]. Researchers have highlighted [34] interactive and personalized cultural experiences led by virtual technologies in virtual museums.

With technical advances, virtual agents can simulate realistic human appearances and even interact and communicate with users [15,29]. Benefiting from the growth of real-time performance and improved fidelity quality, the use of virtual characters has been expanded from screening displays to immersive environments [35]. Today, VR benefits from the existence of virtual avatars. For instance, VHs expand the personalized and interactive user experience. The interaction effect of VR was discussed by Mori and Hoshino (2005), who built a storytelling interactive system that allows users to talk with the character and change the discourse of the story and indicated it is important for entertainment and education [22]. They can even perform more active roles or play various purposes in the diverse virtual worlds. However, it is difficult to find enough work on how virtual characters strengthen the virtual exhibition of cultural heritage. To better promote and preserve the cultural heritage via high-fidelity technology, the presence of VHs wearing authentic costumes plays an important role in augmenting the historic scene as well as providing deeper engagement.

This study introduces the process of creating realistic virtual characters in authentic historical outfits and presenting them in the VR environment, with a focus on their rigging body mesh, historical outfits, and animation across four case scenarios (West Highland Museum - Jacobite 1646, Finlaggan Trust in Lords of the isles 1540, Timespan Museum - Iron Age, Highland Clearances 1813 and Herring Boom, Taigh Chearsabhagh Museum - St Kilda 1890). By leveraging digital exhibits to enhance visitor experiences, we aim to enrich the cultural learning among the public through exploring the potentials of authentic VHs in immersive 3D environments. This methodology can contribute to the development of authentic digital humans in a 3D environment, supporting the preservation of cultural heritage digitally and promotion of inclusive cultural learning opportunities emphasised by sustainable goals of United Nations.

2 Related Work

Reconstructing VHs for exhibition is a challenging interdisciplinary task that requires collaboration among graphic designers, computer scientists, historians, and archaeologists. The recreation of VHs typically involves manual modeling [19], supported by various 3D software. However, interaction necessitates additional steps for animating virtual characters [12]. Real-time and realistic cultural heritage representations necessitate specific physical device requirements, such as memory, graphic cards, and processing speed, impacting the fidelity and quality of VHs.

The study of reconstructing VHs in cultural heritage necessitates consideration of the trade-off between responsiveness and detail, as it involves a common challenge known as the Uncanny Valley effect. This concept, proposed by a roboticist in the 1970s, signifies that the pursuit of highly realistic VHs may elicit negative effects in user interaction [23] and disrupt the level of immersion that visitors experience in the digital environment [28]. This concern is pervasive in the realm of 3D computer technologies. Despite concerted efforts to create highly realistic virtual characters, computer representation has fallen short of providing flawless depictions due to humans acute sensitivity to identifying imperfections [7]. The Uncanny Valley effect may render reconstructions less realistic and divert users attention from the landscape, architecture, and artifacts rather than enhancing their experience.

The application of VHs in virtual environments has been widely discussed. In the computer visualization-based environment, the existence of avatars allows new interactions and expressions [24]. Additionally, virtual characters in immersive virtual environments can significantly influence users experiences, potentially imparting a positive impact on the learning process [14]. For example, Wagner et al. (2006) employed VHs with augmented reality technology in art history education, noting increased user engagement and performance [33]. In the realm of educational entertainment, a study proposed by Agung et al. (2022) supported the idea that VHs can enhance the overall experience and generate interest. In their game designed for collecting artwork descriptions, the addition of virtual characters was found to promote enjoyment and engagement among players [1]. Further supporting this notion, research on serious games posited that the presence of VHs can be considered an efficient method for assisted learning, consequently improving engagement and knowledge absorption [13]. Evidently, the incorporation of digital avatars in virtual environments contributes positively to the user experience.

Furthermore, VHs play an essential role in shaping peoples perceptions of both present and past environments [7]. The presence of VHs has been considered in various contexts to aid in digital reconstruction. For example, a straightforward approach involves populating scenes with characters in static poses, enriching the digital environment and creating a profound sense of immersiveness. When virtual characters are strategically placed as background decorations, their presence can enhance the impression of artefacts, thereby offering a more informative and immersive environment [3]. Moreover, VHs can engage in dynamic communications coupled with interactive measures. In the visualization of the ancient agora of classical Athens, users can navigate around historic scenes, exploring the daily activities of VHs and fostering greater engagement by posing questions related to their professional topics, thereby enhancing the interactive experience [32].

Another common application of virtual characters in the cultural heritage domain is virtual guides. Bogdanovych et al. (2009) emphasized the significance of VHs as carriers of knowledge. Their resulting model demonstrates the utility of enhancing the educational process for history students by immersing them deeply in the daily life of the ancient city of Uruk in 3000 B.C [4]. In an effort to enhance the visitor experience at the third-largest living history museum in the United States, Decker et al. (2021) employed rendered characters as virtual guides to convey information [11]. Within virtual environments, digital agents can introduce tourist attractions, showcase ancient artefacts, or narrate the historical stories behind the heritage for potential participants [19]. From these perspectives, the utilization of digital characters in cultural heritage digitalization spans from their role as decorative elements in the virtual world to assuming practical roles as knowledge carriers or guides. They prove to be valuable not only for educational purposes but also for providing interactive guidance to those seeking information transfer.

As time progresses, the utilization of virtual reality in the cultural heritage sector has gained popularity, bringing a special opportunity for potential users, who can visit the past landscapes, buildings, and artefacts, and even explore the mysterious stories behind the heritage that have faded into history. However, the exploration of static objects and scenes can only provide a limited user experience. To stimulate the audience, adopting more attractive measures should be considered. Populating VHs in historic scenes can enhance the overall environments presence and improve the interaction between the audience and their surroundings [3,19]. The existence of VHs can increase the realism of the simulation and render the user experience more authentic, which is strengthened by the above analysis of the effects that virtual human interactions have on user engagement, sense of immersion, and learning effectiveness. Additionally, inconsistencies in realism may lead to the uncanny valley effect [18]. Therefore, the creation of VHs should prioritize achieving a high degree of realism [16]. Overall, it is found that placing VHs in the context of cultural heritage can strengthen its exhibition. However, attention should be given to maintaining consistent realism in VHs to mitigate any uneasiness felt by users.

3 Methodology

The method we applied to this research is the following steps, which can be utilized in any relevant research regarding the reconstruction of VHs in the context of cultural heritage:

1) Conduct historical research and form the design sketch of characters.
2) Create 3D models of historic clothing and accessories.

3) Binding skeleton, body, and outfit.
4) Collect historic archives and recreate virtual faces.
5) Import virtual models and add 3D textures to refine the details of outfit.
6) Equip digital avatars with animations.

We aim to create authentic historical outfits to augment the performance of VHs in digital exhibitions of cultural heritage, which requires technical processions in three different software: Unreal Engine 5, Marvelous Designer, and Blender. Unreal Engine 5 is a sophisticated 3D game engine that supports high-quality simulations and asset creation. Our research utilizes it to import VHs and historical clothing, thereby creating immersive and interactive historical experiences for VR users. Blender, a free and versatile 3D modelling program, plays a pivotal role in our VR projects for system binding, body and head creation, and data modification. It enables the reconfiguration and animation of avatars imported from Unreal Engine. Complementing Blender, Marvelous Designer specializes in creating 3D digital clothing for game engines and VFX. It combines 2D and 3D environments to design realistic clothing with dynamic textures and movement. Together, these tools provide a comprehensive solution for developing and animating virtual avatars and clothing in virtual reality environments. In the following section, we introduce the importance of historic research in the 3D reconstruction of VHs and certain techniques used and challenges faced during the practical work.

4 Historic Research

Before implementation, we conducted an extensive archival survey to gather sketches, paintings, historical photographs, and literature. The collection of relevant materials related to clothing enabled the creation of 2D annotated sketches. The historical research and analysis of existing information contribute significantly to ensuring the reliability of the simulated designs.

Historic clothing stands as an integral component of historical characters. To correspond to the correct historic or cultural atmosphere, virtual characters are typically adorned in relevant costumes. Historic fashion, based on its exceptional value, has garnered attention from academia. Museums recognize fashion, including clothing and dress, as a serious subject of study [31]. Collaborating with costume collections allows us to open the door to knowledge and understanding of the way of life among forebears [2]. Historical clothing, being a part of peoples lives, often contains valuable information. The recreation of historic outfits for the realistic virtual agents in Pre-Clearance Caen area is meticulously prepared and modelled. We propose that each character exhibited in the historic scene will wear clothing authentic to the time, place, occupation, and activity. This work has primarily relied on the support from Dr. Perin Westerhof Nyman, an expert on historical clothing at the University of St Andrews. Dr. Nyman conducted searches of written and visual records, designing the main clothing style as the authentic reference for digital modelling. A context document was produced to provide sufficient references to relevant images of clothing and sketches for each character.

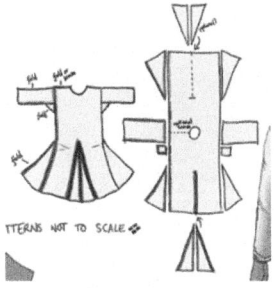  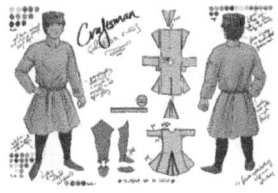

Fig. 1. Iron Age Clothing Design.

Fig. 2. Outfit in Finlaggan Lord of the Isles.

Fig. 3. Craftsman Outfit in Whitehorn.

Scenario 1 - Iron Age Kildonan: Throughout the Iron Age, individuals consistently donned a simple style of shirt. This shirt, akin to the basic outer tunic or gown, is crafted with geometric cuts but is slightly shorter than the outer garments (see Fig. 1). For women, it extends to calf length, while for men, it reaches thigh length. Typically, glimpses of the shirt can be seen at the wrists and/or neckline. The woman's dress could add some volume to the waist crafted with a slightly wider design, later cinched by a belt. Those of middling or higher social status would wear shirts made of bleached linen, whereas individuals of lower status would opt for coarser bleached or unbleached linen, often in a light grey-brown shade.

Scenario 2 - Finlaggan Trust: Figure 2 represents the historical design for the attire of an average female of middle status in the Lord of the Isles. Based on historical research, a woman of middle-class standing at the time was not notably impoverished or engaged in strenuous labour in kitchens or fields. However, she likely did not belong to the noble or aristocratic class either. Possible roles could include being a higher-status household servant, a lady-in-waiting to noblewomen, or a prosperous craftswoman. Underneath this garment, she would wear a standard shift and hose. One intricate aspect of this dress pattern involves the sleeves, which are tailored in the 'grande assiette' style. In this style, the back of the sleeve extends over the shoulder blade on the back of the dress. The front of the gown skirt is intended to be flatter and less voluminous than the back. The neckline is designed to ascend onto the shoulders, and the 'skirt' of the hood should reach just below the point where the neck meets the shoulders. Additionally, it is noteworthy that most aprons during this period would be tied around the natural waist, the narrowest point of the torso. The apron 'string' would typically be about 1/4" (less than 1 cm) wide in real life.

Scenario 3 - Whitehorn: The character and clothing design for scenario three is grounded in the historical context of the early medieval. In Fig. 3, we observe the fundamental geometrically cut gown that was prevalent during this era. Notably, gowns featuring gores in the front, back, and sides were most commonly worn by individuals of middling and higher social status. During this

Fig. 4. Characters in Highland Clearance.

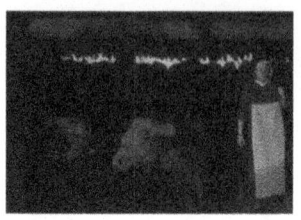

Fig. 5. An Animated Character in Cultural Heritage 3D Environment.

Fig. 6. Historic Short Gown Archives.

period, working women typically wore ankle-length gowns, while those of higher status donned floor-length or longer garments, especially for special occasions or 'best dress' events. Wool was the primary fabric for clothing in earlier periods, with the possibility of nobility and royalty incorporating silk garments into their wardrobes from the late 11th century onward (approximately 1070s and later). The gentry also began adopting silk from the early 14th century onward. For the general populace and nobility and royalty during outdoor activities or travel, wool garments were the norm. This practice persisted even for the aristocracy when not attending formal events.

Scenario 4 - St Madoes Pictish Costume: The clothing design for St Madoes draws primarily from the Whithorn 1023 assets created in Marvellous Designer. Given that the historical period in St Madoes slightly deviates in its timeline, a few minor adjustments were made to align with the specific historical context. There are deviations from the Whitehorn outfit design. The 'pillbox' cap, as seen in the Whitehorn design for some men, is not utilized in St Madoes (compared with Fig. 3). Additionally, monks' leather and metal belts have been replaced with cloth or rope belts. There is a distinction in the use of cloaks between individuals of higher and lower status. Lower-status individuals may wear a cloak, but in a more natural colour and fastened with a simple cloak pin or an annular or penannular brooch, as opposed to the more ornate disk brooch. Regarding the colour palette, medieval dye colours on wool, such as purple, highly saturated red, and deep blue, were associated with higher status. In contrast, yellows, and various browns, which were easier to achieve, were more common. Green, a colour obtained by overdyeing woad with a yellow dye, typically through welding, was somewhat less prevalent but still feasible in this historical setting.

Scenario 5 - Highland Clearance: The historical costumes in the Pre-Clearance comprise a blend of Highland and Lowland styles (see Fig. 4). Two of the characters represent average Highland labourers from the 1810s, resembling workers in common clothing elsewhere. The foundational elements for male characters include a blue hat, a linen-textured blue or white checked shirt, a kerchief tied around the neck, a waistcoat, a short jacket, dark trousers, and leather shoes.

Additionally, the costumes incorporate various tartans or checked elements. For female characters, the style lines are akin to those of working women or fishwives anywhere, spanning the 18th, 19th, and early 20th centuries. Although there have been certain changes in skirt fullness and length, as well as the shift from a bedgown to a blouse waist at the end of the 19th century. Generally, the female workers wear bedgowns over skirts but sometimes under, with aprons tied around their high waist, and have shawls or kerchiefs or both to cover their hair and necklines and linen caps (locally called mutches). The major different aspects, however, are influenced by the Regency fashions, both clothing styles of the male and female have a little higher waistline than usual. Figure 5 shows an example of a reconstructed, realistically animated virtual character from the 2D sketch to the 3D simulation in this research.

More information about clothing patterns design can be referenced from, respectively, Dorothy K. Burnhams book Cut my Cote (the early nineteenth-century shirt from the ROMs collection) and Linda Baumgartens book Costume Close-Up: Clothing Construction and Pattern 1750–1790 (the late eighteenth-century shirt from Colonial Williamsburgs collection), along with online sources like National Galleries Scotland, SCRAN, British Library, and others. Figure 6 illustrates the drawings and collections of the short gown recorded in one of the listed books. From these archives, we have acquired patterns for mens shirts and waistcoats, mens trousers, mens short jackets, and womens short jackets and petticoats, aligning with our objectives for 3D reconstructions. These series provide us with an overview of how Scottish citizens living in the Highlands might have appeared during the 1800s. Additionally, we explored other valuable historical sources related to the age, the area, and the narrative behind ancient Highlands. For instance, The Scottish Clearance written by T. M. Devine provides an illustrative account of peoples lives in the Highlands throughout history, complementing the array of data sources for our historical research.

Summary: In essence, our aim is to present VHs adorned in authentic costumes to simulate a historical impression through the support of advanced 3D technologies. These collections of historic costumes offer rare insights into the history of human populations [8]. We thus believe that the historic outfits worn by realistic digital characters in the VR environment can provide a greater understanding of past living conditions and the information behind the heritage.

5 Implementation

Enhancing the immersive visiting experience of VHs in heritage exhibitions can be achieved through animation support. Rendering animated virtual characters contributes to augmenting the real-time cultural heritage environment [26]. Specifically, mixed-reality simulations of virtual humans can execute various human-like activities, allowing the representation of diverse ceremonies and events in the cultural heritage site [25]. Utilizing animation packs or creating new animations can optimize VHs performance in the environment. Unreal Engine features a user-friendly function supporting external animation resources, known as Retargeted Resources. Modify the base skeleton of virtual humans to match the imported one by selecting Compatible Skeletons in asset details. Through the Rigging add-on, new animations generated by Blender can import into Unreal Engine. After adding a new bone to a digital asset, reveal the bone hierarchy in Edit Mode stemming from the root bone. Extend additional bones along the Y-axis by selecting the head of the root bone. In Object Mode, select everything (model and armature), then use Ctrl P to parent with Automatic Weights, rigging the bone and the 3D object. Before importing into Unreal, ensure correct location, rotation, and scale in Blender by setting everything in the Scene Collection to 0 and scale to 1 for both mesh and armature. Finally, export the FBX document, including both the Armature and Mesh. Timeline functionality can attach the object with animation. In Pose Mode, use the shortcut 'I' to insert pose or motion changes between different points in time. When exporting the animation from Blender, select 'Armature only' as the object type. Unreal Engine excels at reproducing textures on assets' surfaces in relation to light, providing authentic reactions for a lifelike virtual human representation. Strengthening the visual effect and immersion involves enhancing the texture of clothing fabric to be more realistic. Commonly used properties include Base Colour, Roughness, Normal, Secularity, or Ambient Occlusion. For instance, Ambient Occlusion can simulate self-shadowing within the crevices of a surface, while Normal maps add significant physical detail by modifying the 'normal' or facing direction of each pixel. These visualization techniques contribute to creating a plausible virtual world. Avatars should be reconstructed to approach humanoid characteristics, comprising photo-realistic textures, high-quality meshes, and rigging to achieve increased plausibility in the virtual environment [21].

Fig. 7. An Avatar in Highland Clearance.

Fig. 8. Avatars in Iron Age.

6 Evaluation

Heritage landscapes separately represent their unique time and cultural background. Exploring authentic VHs creations in diverse cultural scenarios broadens the methodology. Figure 7 and 8 present screenshots in Unreal Engine created by the Open Virtual World at the University of St Andrews, featuring digitized medieval characters adorned in historically accurate attire in Highland Clearance and Iron Age, as described in the preceding scenarios. Historical clothing is integral to advancing the application of VHs in the domain of cultural heritage. Users can gain insights into the cultural nuances and social shifts that have shaped human history by visualizing the changes in historical outfits over time. Figure 9 showcases an integrated summary of the changes of clothing from Pre-Roman Britain to 1550s. It serves as a valuable foundation for creating realistic and culturally authentic VHs in diverse cultural landscape contexts. Understanding the intricacies of historical fashion enables a more authentic and immersive experience, fostering a deeper connection between users and cultural heritage being preserved through virtual simulations. In essence, the study of historical clothing acts as a crucial bridge, connecting the past with cutting-edge technology, and enriching the application of VHs in cultural heritage contexts.

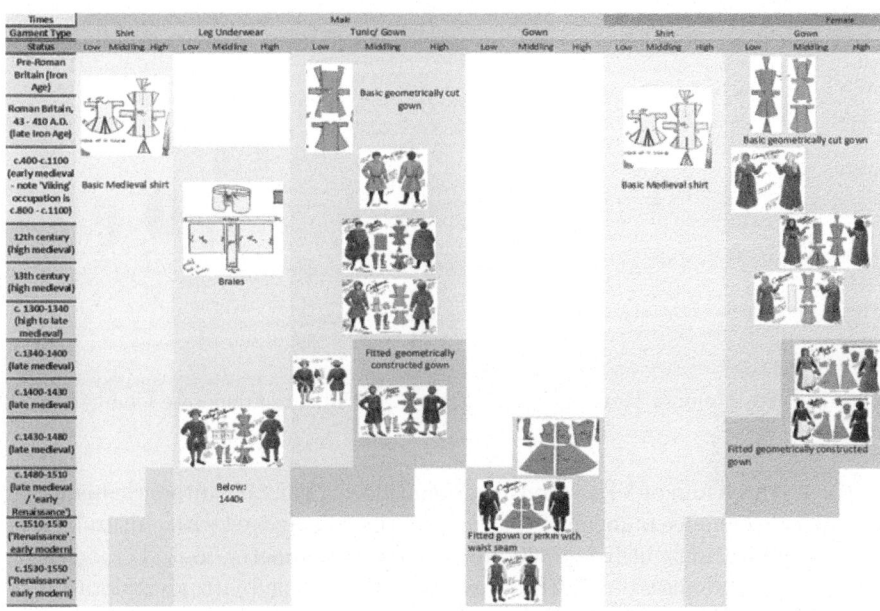

Fig. 9. Integrated Changes of Clothing from Iron Age to 1550s.

Considering the implementation of VHs in cultural heritage scenarios requires support from physical devices, this research adopted a system performance test to measure resource usage. The charts below indicate a series of data collected under the scene of Highland Clearance, evaluating the performance of animated characters using the following computer resources under both screen and VR headset conditions. Scenario one and two represent the performance of 1 and 4 avatars in an empty environment, while scenarios three to seven depict 0, 2, 4, 8, and 16 avatars in the same cultural landscape. The framerate measurement is calculated using the Xbox Game Bar tool. Data, such as FPS, CPU, GPU, and RAM usage, are visible on the screen. For the Number of Triangles and Resolution, those details can be found in the statistics of Unreal Engine. The results are generated on a PC with a 12th Gen Intel(R) Core(TM) i5-12600K CPU and NVIDIA Geforce RTX 3080 Ti GPU with 64 GB RAM. The scene of the heritage landscape contains 129,009,600 triangles. The box and whisker chart can visualize the lower quartile, upper quartile, maximum, minimum, and mean value of the data. Figures 10 and 11 respectively showcase the memory usage and framerate changes in different scenarios. Overall, the addition of avatars increases the pressure on framerate speed and systematic memory usage. From scenario four to seven, the simulation's consistency and system responsiveness are lower in VR headset compared to screen, particularly with more animated avatars, resulting in lower data values. However, under the scenario with only two animated avatars in the heritage landscape, the framerate remains steady at approximately 46–47 KHz in both modes.

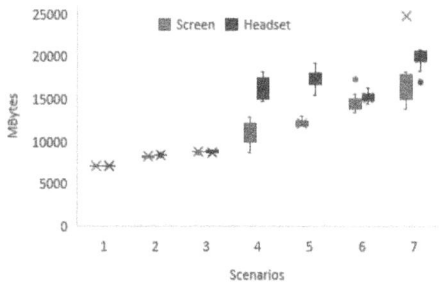

Fig. 10. Memory Usage.   **Fig. 11.** Framerate Changes.

The research aim of VHs reconstruction concentrating on authentic historical clothing is to enhance immersive visiting experiences engaged with cultural learning. VR applications, utilizing 360 images, photogrammetry, and 3D modelling, have transformed access to cultural resources and enabled virtual exploration of ancient buildings and historical collections, providing immersive learning experiences [6]. Recognized as an efficient tool, especially for children and diverse learning environments, researchers actively explore VR applications in education [30]. 3D reconstruction of virtual inhabitants wearing authentic outfits reflects the traits of the historical period, helping the audience learn about the culture. In addition, realistic humans can perform the role of increased in-presence feeling of the scene. Dynamic virtual environments and characters surpass traditional learning approaches, serving as engaging educational methods for history, heritage, and culture.

This research adopted on-campus recruitment and in-person exhibits at the museum and a Heritage Day, advertising study details to reach potential participants. This survey reached out to museums and heritage organisations including visitors to the West Highland Museum and museum practitioners in the Highland Scotland, and students from University of St Andrews. The VR environment is based on VR headsets connected to the PC, and the physical details of the device remain the same as in the above systematic measurement. The scenario of cultural heritage is set in the 1800s Highland Clearance. At the time of writing, 37 participants were invited to participate in experiencing the virtual journey depicting the ancient Scottish scene. All responses are anonymized, and an ethical agreement description is provided before collecting the data. User feedback was collected through a questionnaire, and the data were evaluated through chart visualization. Questions relevant to digital learning experiences and the performance of VHs in the historical scene were prepared. In the analysis, a bar chart was used to compare option preferences among "Strongly Agree", "Agree", "Neutral", "Disagree", and "Strongly Disagree". The age groups of the 37 participants ranged from below 16 (5.4%), 16–19 (8.1%), 20–24 (43.2%), 25–29 (24.3%), and over 30 (18.9%), with up to 56.8% of them having previous VR experience. The main result obtained from Fig. 12 indicates that 94.6% of respondents strongly believed the use of VHs in a heritage context strengthens exhibitions and enhances their imagination of history and culture, with 91.9% in agreement. It was identified that 94.6% of them firmly enjoyed this learning method, and digital exhibits can complement physical counterparts like museums, as indicated by 33 out of 37 participants. However, 8.1% of them disagreed with the notion that the exhibit was engaging. Participants commented that it is an enjoyable way of exploring the lost world, seeing virtual humans, animals, and entering the building was a plus. However, the rendering performance of dynamic movement sometimes glitches, affecting the experience and leading to a decrease in engagement. They suggested that such a topic requires further investment to provide people with a better experience. Based on the data, it can be concluded that VHs strengthen cultural heritage exhibitions. Young people show an inclination to support the use of such exhibits for learning, and cultural institutions may consider incorporating digital technology to enhance their physical exhibitions to bring about interesting cultural learning opportunities.

The following section discusses future improvements. Firstly, to deepen engagement, enhance interactions between avatars and the environment with vivid animations for a more compelling experience is considered. Secondly, technical limitations in this research include navigation issues, particularly the first-person perspective camera not fully following the avatar, which will be addressed by adjusting its position. Additionally, the simulated performance of dynamic scenes in the VR preview significantly impacted user engagement. Thirdly, to augment the cultural learning experience, additional information within scenes can be provided through storytelling measures like storyboards. Positive feedback was received for virtual exhibits with VHs in cultural heritage, enhancing exploration of past landscapes and providing an enjoyable learning opportunity. Authentic characters have the potential for active roles in digital learning objectives, but technology limitations require more resources for simulation consistency. In the future, we aim to integrate VHs with language models to enhance interactive communication among users and scenarios, offering quality learn-

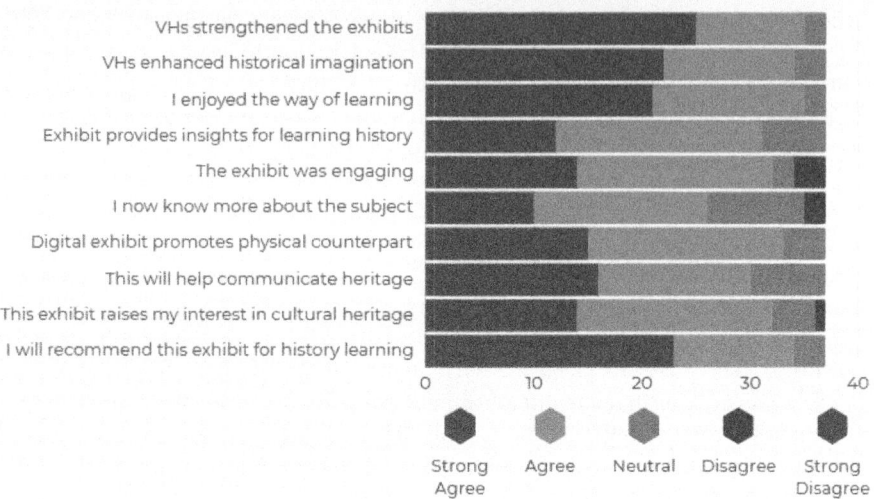

Fig. 12. User Data Visualization.

ing opportunities aligned with sustainable development goals, such as chatbots. This advanced approach can allow users to experience historical environments and expand cultural knowledge, fostering awareness of climate change's impact on communities and heritage legacy over time.

7 Conclusion

In this paper, we introduce a methodology for creating authentic VHs focusing on authentic historical outfit applications to augment cultural heritage in a 3D environment. The proposed methodology involves creating VHs by converting 2D design sketches into reality within the immersive VR environment. The evaluation section describes the computer resource usage of VHs in a cultural heritage context and presents user feedback between different educational stakeholders on the digital learning experience and avatar performance. Through this research, it is possible to look back to the lost world of heritage legacy and further people's understanding and knowledge about culture and history with a fun learning experience. Students, visitors, and museum professionals actively engaged in and enjoyed this creative learning method, highlighting the practicality of this research in promoting inclusive learning opportunities. This research offers new insight into applying realistic digital humans in a 3D reconstruction environment for cultural heritage, promoting lifelong cultural educational values emphasized by the sustainable goals of the United Nations through VR headset techniques. Contributing to digital heritage protection also benefits sustainable and inclusive development in local communities. In future work, we expect to enrich user engagement by focusing on animation and storytelling measures and to expand the potential of VHs in the 3D cultural heritage environment through language models to promote cultural sustainable awareness.

References

1. Agung, A., Savchyn, R., Paliyawan, P., Thawonmas, R.: Cute helper: a study on the effect of virtual character expressions on players' engagement in a game for collecting artwork descriptions. In: 2022 IEEE Conference on Games (CoG), pp. 588–589 (2022). https://doi.org/10.1109/CoG51982.2022.9893683
2. Alvarado, I.: Costume preservation: where science and art meet. Mus. Int. **XLV**(3), 28–32 (1993)
3. Antunes, R.F., Correia, L.: Virtual simulations of ancient sites inhabited by autonomous characters: lessons from the development of easy-population. Digit. Appl. Archaeol. Cult. Heritage **26**, e00237 (2022)
4. Bogdanovych, A., Rodriguez, J.A., Simoff, S., Cohen, A.: Virtual agents and 3D virtual worlds for preserving and simulating cultures. In: Ruttkay, Z., Kipp, M., Nijholt, A., Vilhjálmsson, H.H. (eds.) Intelligent Virtual Agents, pp. 257–271. Springer, Heidelberg (2009)
5. Carrozzino, M., Bergamasco, M.: Beyond virtual museums: experiencing immersive virtual reality in real museums. J. Cult. Heritage **11**(4), 452–458 (2010). https://www.sciencedirect.com/science/article/pii/S1296207410000543
6. Cecotti, H.: Cultural heritage in fully immersive virtual reality. Virtual Worlds **1**(1), 82–102 (2022). http://dx.doi.org/10.3390/virtualworlds1010006
7. Chalmers, A., Parkins, J., Webb, M., Debattista, K.: Realistic humans in virtual cultural heritage. In: Shehade, M., Stylianou-Lambert, T. (eds.) Emerging Technologies and the Digital Transformation of Museums and Heritage Sites, pp. 156–165. Springer, Cham (2021)
8. Coleman, E.A.: Preserving human packaging. Mus. Int. **XLV**(3), 4–7 (1993). https://unesdoc.unesco.org/ark:/48223/pf0000095234
9. Cruz-Neira, C., Sandin, D.J., DeFanti, T.A.: Surround-screen projection-based virtual reality: the design and implementation of the cave. In: Proceedings of the 20th Annual Conference on Computer Graphics and Interactive Techniques, SIGGRAPH 1993, pp. 135–142. Association for Computing Machinery, New York (1993). https://doi.org/10.1145/166117.166134
10. De Paolis, L.T., Chiarello, S., Gatto, C., Liaci, S., De Luca, V.: Virtual reality for the enhancement of cultural tangible and intangible heritage: the case study of the castle of Corsano. Digit. Appl. Archaeol. Cult. Heritage **27**, e00238 (2022)
11. Decker, J., Doherty, A., Geigel, J., Jacobs, G.D.: Bridging past and present: Creating and deploying a historical character to engage audiences through AR and VR. In: Shehade, M., Stylianou-Lambert, T. (eds.) Emerging Technologies and the Digital Transformation of Museums and Heritage Sites, pp. 139–155. Springer, Cham (2021)
12. Feng, A., Casas, D., Shapiro, A.: Avatar reshaping and automatic rigging using a deformable model. In: Proceedings of the 8th ACM SIGGRAPH Conference on Motion in Games, MIG 2015, pp. 57–64. Association for Computing Machinery, New York (2015), https://doi.org/10.1145/2822013.2822017

13. Gamage, V., Ennis, C.: Examining the effects of a virtual character on learning and engagement in serious games. In: Proceedings of the 11th ACM SIGGRAPH Conference on Motion, Interaction and Games, MIG 2018. Association for Computing Machinery, New York (2018). https://doi.org/10.1145/3274247.3274499
14. Garcia, B., Chun, S., Kicklighter, C., Mai, B., Palma, M., Seo, J.H.: Studying design attributes of virtual characters to support students' perceived experiences in virtual reality lectures. In: 18th International Conference on Cognition and Exploratory Learning in Digital Age (CELDA 2021) (2021). https://files.eric.ed.gov/fulltext/ED621382.pdf
15. Gratch, J., Rickel, J., Andre, E., Cassell, J., Petajan, E., Badler, N.: Creating interactive virtual humans: some assembly required. IEEE Intell. Syst. **17**(4), 54–63 (2002). https://doi.org/10.1109/MIS.2002.1024753
16. Karuzaki, E., et al.: Realistic virtual humans for cultural heritage applications. Heritage **4**(4), 4148–4171 (2021)
17. Kennedy, S., et al.: Exploring canons & cathedrals with open virtual worlds: the recreation of St Andrews Cathedral, St Andrews day, 1318. In: 2013 Digital Heritage International Congress (DigitalHeritage), vol. 2, pp. 273–280 (2013)
18. MacDorman, K.F., Chattopadhyay, D.: Reducing consistency in human realism increases the uncanny valley effect; increasing category uncertainty does not. Cognition **146**, 190–205 (2016)
19. Machidon, O.M., Duguleana, M., Carrozzino, M.: Virtual humans in cultural heritage ICT applications: a review. J. Cult. Herit. **33**, 249–260 (2018)
20. McCaffery, J., Miller, A., Vermehren, A., Fabola, A.: The virtual museums of Caen: a case study on modes of representation of digital historical content. In: 2015 Digital Heritage, vol. 2, pp. 541–548 (2015)
21. Molina, E., Jerez, A.R., Gómez, N.P.: Avatars rendering and its effect on perceived realism in virtual reality. In: 2020 IEEE International Conference on Artificial Intelligence and Virtual Reality (AIVR), pp. 222–225 (2020)
22. Mori, H., Hoshino, J.: Key action technique for digital storytelling. In: Kishino, F., Kitamura, Y., Kato, H., Nagata, N. (eds.) Entertainment Computing - ICEC 2005, pp. 36–47. Springer, Heidelberg (2005)
23. Mori, M., MacDorman, K.F., Kageki, N.: The uncanny valley [from the field]. IEEE Robot. Autom. Mag. **19**(2), 98–100 (2012)
24. Oliver, I.A., Miller, A.H., Allison, C.: Virtual worlds, real traffic: interaction and adaptation. In: Proceedings of the First Annual ACM SIGMM Conference on Multimedia Systems, MMSys 2010, pp. 305–316. Association for Computing Machinery, New York (2010). https://doi.org/10.1145/1730836.1730873
25. Papaefthymiou, M., et al.: Gamified AR/VR character rendering and animation-enabling technologies, pp. 333–357. Springer, Cham (2017)
26. Papagiannakis, G., Schertenleib, S., Ponder, M., Arevalo, M., Magnenat-Thalmann, N., Thalmann, D.: Real-time virtual humans in AR sites. In: 1st European Conference on Visual Media Production (CVMP) 2004, pp. 273–276 (2004)
27. Psomadaki, O.I., Dimoulas, C.A., Kalliris, G.M., Paschalidis, G.: Digital storytelling and audience engagement in cultural heritage management: a collaborative model based on the digital city of Thessaloniki. J. Cult. Heritage **36**, 12–22 (2019)
28. Schwind, V., Wolf, K., Henze, N.: Avoiding the uncanny valley in virtual character design. Interactions **25**(5), 45–49 (2018). https://doi.org/10.1145/3236673
29. Sylaiou, S., Fidas, C.: Virtual humans in museums and cultural heritage sites. Appl. Sci. **12**(19), 9913 (2022)

30. Tost, L.P., Economou, M.: Worth a thousand words? The usefulness of immersive virtual reality for learning in cultural heritage settings. Int. J. Archit. Comput. **7**(1), 157–176 (2009)
31. UNESCO: Concept of digital heritage. https://en.unesco.org/themes/information-preservation/digital-heritage/concept-digital-heritage
32. Vosinakis, S., Avradinis, N.: Virtual agora: representation of an ancient Greek agora in virtual worlds using biologically-inspired motivational agents (2016)
33. Wagner, D., Billinghurst, M., Schmalstieg, D.: How real should virtual characters be? In: Proceedings of the 2006 ACM SIGCHI International Conference on Advances in Computer Entertainment Technology, ACE 2006, pp. 57-es. Association for Computing Machinery, New York (2006)
34. Warwick, T.: Conference report: digital heritage: digital communities in action, centre for digital heritage, university of York, 12th July 2014. J. Cult. Herit. **15**(5), 580–581 (2014). https://doi.org/10.1016/j.culher.2014.09.005
35. Zell, E., Zibrek, K., McDonnell, R.: Perception of virtual characters. In: ACM SIGGRAPH 2019 Courses, SIGGRAPH 2019. Association for Computing Machinery, New York (2019). https://doi.org/10.1145/3305366.3328101

What the Amazon Can't Deliver: Lessons Learned from Virtual Reality-Based Sustainability Education

Kristian H. Träg(✉) [iD] and Miriam Mulders [iD]

University of Duisburg-Essen, Universitätsstr. 2, 45141 Essen, Germany
kristian.traeg@uni-due.de

Abstract. With Virtual Reality technology becoming an increasingly popular method to convey knowledge, sound pedagogical principles are needed to implement Virtual Reality effectively in classrooms. This paper proposes a pedagogical model that provides guidelines for educational practitioners before, during, and after Virtual Reality instruction. For elucidation, concrete examples as well as generative learning tasks are provided. These are based on a Virtual Reality learning experience developed by *greenpeace* and its evaluation studies. Finally, some general strengths and weaknesses of the proposed model are discussed.

Keywords: Virtual Reality · Pedagogy · Instructional Guidelines

1 Introduction

Recently, a lot of effort is being put into empirical research on finding the most efficient way to integrate Virtual Reality (VR) technologies into the classroom. Such technologies appear promising for learning, especially in constructivist and interactive approaches [1–3]. However, meaningful instructional guidelines on how to integrate VR learning applications into the everyday classroom are missing. This article provides initial recommendations on how to effectively implement VR learning experiences into classrooms. Examples of learning activities, based on Wittrock's Theory of Generative Learning [4–6], and a comprehensive model for briefing and debriefing activities that accompany the virtual experience are provided. In general, the article tries to point out that a VR based learning experience alone is not sufficient to create a meaningful learning environment. It requires pedagogically valuable accompanying briefing and debriefing actions which subsequently need to be empirically validated.

2 Theoretical Background

2.1 Learning in VR

There are multiple theories that include a framework for learning with technologies that provide a high degree of vividness and sense of presence, called immersive technologies, like VR [7]. A major framework for learning with VR technology is the Cognitive

Affective Model of Immersive Learning (CAMIL), wherein affective and cognitive factors like interest, motivation, or cognitive load mediate the effect of agency and presence on learning outcomes [8]. Agency is to be understood as a sense of control over one's own actions [8, 9], while presence refers to the feeling of actually "being there" in regards to a virtual environment [8]. Within this framework, presence, flow, and prior knowledge are relevant factors for gathering knowledge and perspective taking [10].

Similarly, Dengel and Mägdefrau [11] relate learning effects in virtual learning environments to the motivational, emotional, and cognitive potential of the learning situation, as well as to activities during learning. Their educational framework for immersive learning (EFiL) again cites the perception of presence as a relevant factor, but also considers instructional affordances, like the quality of the materials [11].

The meaningful immersive VR learning framework (MiVRL) stresses that providing meaningful learning opportunities is more important than creating high degrees of immersion [12]. Meaningful learning here refers to the generative process of using cognitive and motivational resources to actively connect prior knowledge with the to-be-learned material [5, 6]. Immersive learning environments should include segmented tasks that build on prior knowledge and practice constructive activities that are relevant to the targeted skill to foster knowledge transfer [12].

Common ground among the above models is found in the focus on cognitive factors. Indeed, immersive virtual environments seem to be related to higher cognitive load [13–15]. All models also stress the importance of presence and agency. This means that these factors should be considered when planning lessons around a VR application. Another relevant factor might be the experience of flow or perceiving an activity as satisfying and feeling as one with the activity [16]. Flow has a positive effect on learning and correlates with presence [17, 18].

With prior knowledge and agency as key factors, classes that rely on learning with immersive VR might have to find ways to relate that knowledge to the new information provided through interactive means. According to the Generative Model of Learning, perceptions and meanings are usually generated to be consistent with prior experiences [6]. This means that new information can be more easily related to prior knowledge and prior practical experience. The kind of task chosen should fit the to-be-learned material [5]. Fiorella and Mayer add that meaningful learning outcomes are enhanced with higher cognitive engagement, supporting higher degrees of constructive (inter-)activity over passive modes of learning [5]. They point out eight ways of designing generative tasks: summarizing (stating the main point of the learned material in own words), mapping (visualizing or organizing material in a map), drawing (depicting the contents of a lesson in a drawing), imagining (creating mental images of the learned material), self-testing (answering questions about the material), self-explaining (explaining the contents to oneself), teaching (explaining the contents to someone else), and enacting (engaging in task-related movements or object manipulation) [5].

2.2 Previous Findings

A multitude of studies have shown benefits of VR use in classrooms. The experience of flow and presence in VR might be beneficial for attitudes towards VR learning [19] and learner satisfaction [10]. Setyowati et al. [20] were able to increase participation via VR instructional media. Another study found positive effects of VR for learning car detailing, a procedural learning task [21]. Hence, presence and flow seem to be the main factors that influence learning outcomes in VR [10, 19].

However, Hamilton et al. [22] note that while many studies find immersive VR advantageous, oftentimes only short interventions with inadequate methods of measuring learning outcomes are implemented. Only rarely are long-term effects of VR-based interventions investigated [23]. This is tied to another flaw within many research designs: the lack of consideration for greater curricula. Mulders et al. [12] argue that VR-based interventions can only be effective if they are part of a lesson plan, not just novelty gadgets. Indeed, designing virtual learning environments to fit cognitive, affective, and motivational needs is only one aspect of suitable VR-learning. In the formal classroom setting, pedagogical and instructional implications should be considered for effective implementation [24].

First, students' prior knowledge should be addressed before its usage, as this is required to gauge the level of content detail and scaffolding that should be provided. Additionally, constructive learning activities before as well as after the virtual experience should be included to fully exhaust the interactive, high-agency nature of VR technology [4, 12]. Generative learnings tasks seem to positively affect transfer, retention, and motivational factors [4, 25, 26]. Moreover, immersive VR works in part through the mechanism of presence [8], which is also linked to better generative task performance [25].

2.3 Briefing and Debriefing a VR Learning Experience

The synthesis of the models for immersive VR [8, 11, 12] as well as generative learning strategies [4–6] can result in practical recommendations for teachers and schools on how VR technologies can be used to enhance learning in classrooms. It is advisable to differentiate between before, during, and after the virtual learning experience. On a theoretical level, we introduce a model here (see Fig. 1), which will be filled with exemplary content in the next step using a specific virtual learning application by *greenpeace*.

For the briefing of students, the above frameworks suggest that prior knowledge should be activated [8, 11, 12]. This includes ensuring that all students have a somewhat similar basis of knowledge before going into the VR intervention. Therefore, background information about the topic at hand should be provided in a short opening prompt that is engaging enough to also capture the students' interest [27]. A more basic prerequisite for working with VR applications is a sufficient number of devices as well as students' technical knowledge on how to operate those. Teachers should ensure that students understand how their devices work, so that the learning experience is not impaired by technical difficulties [28], which in turn might be detrimental for cognitive load [29]. Before the virtual learning experience starts, students should also be reminded that the virtual world they are about to encounter is different from the real world [30].

During the virtual experience, teachers should be ready to assist students if they have any questions, be it technical or content-related. Additionally, background noise or other distractions or interferences with the virtual experience should be avoided. Also, providing helpful information just in time in VR or breaking down a complex VR into smaller segments can prevent overload.

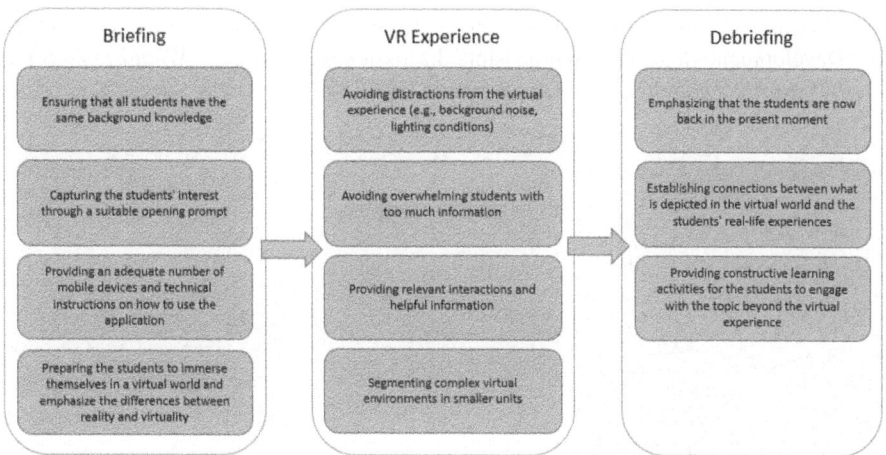

Fig. 1. Pedagogical model for working with VR. The model lays out tasks for teachers before, during, and after use of a VR application.

To start the debriefing phase, teachers may emphasize that students have left the virtual world and are now back in the present moment [30, 31]. Next, a link between the information gathered in the virtual experience, students' prior knowledge, and their real-life experiences should be established. This can be enhanced by providing constructive learning activities that encourage students to engage with the topic beyond the virtual experience [4].

Using an app from *greenpeace*, the model will be filled in the following with specific recommendations that accompany the use of the app before, during, and after. For this purpose, a short overview of the findings of its evaluation project will be given next.

3 The *Greenpeace* Project

In one recent study, we [32] have investigated the aforementioned application. It allows students to virtually visit four locations that would be difficult to experience first-hand in a regular classroom setting. This includes specific landmarks like the Amazon rainforest and the Great Barrier Reef (see Fig. 2), as well as more general settings, like a German forest before and after soil sealing. Here, they can explore their surroundings, interact with avatars resembling residents, and gather information on the environmental impact that human actions have had there. The Amazon rainforest setting deals with deforestation for meat production and its impact on the Brazilian indigenous population and local wildlife. The Great Barrier Reef setting focusses on the rise in water temperature and its effect on the flora and fauna underwater. The German forest setting deals with soil sealing and the dispersal of local birds through unsustainable agricultural use, while the supermarket setting illuminates global supply chains in food production.

This application in particular is interesting because *greenpeace* provided an elaborate manual specifying the prerequisites and thematical framework for a lesson in which their app could be introduced [33]. This includes pedagogical impulses on the 17 Sustainable Development Goals [34] and possible discussion threads (i.e., *"What are possible solutions for the challenges you encountered?"*; [33], p. 11).

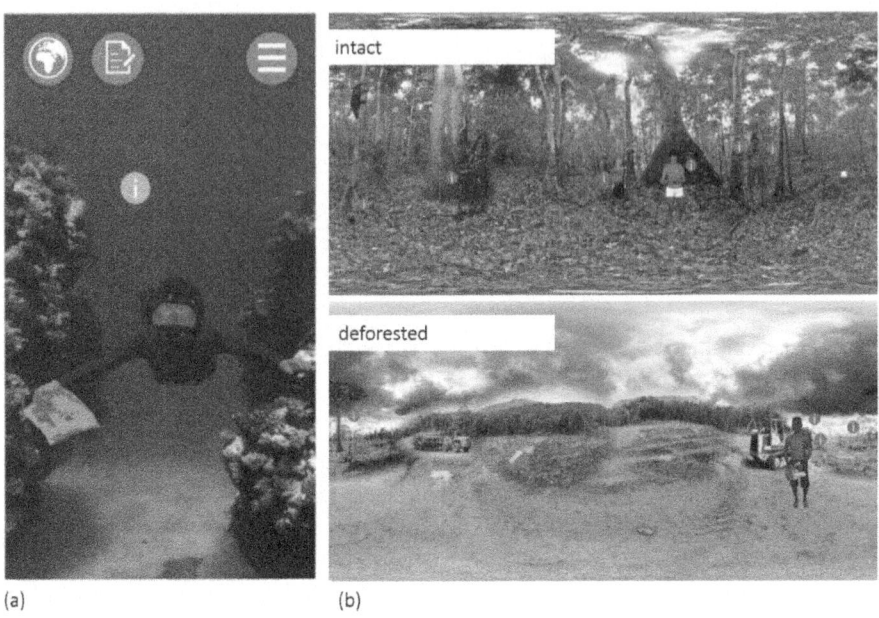

Fig. 2. Screenshots of the *greenpeace* application. (a) shows an underwater scape at the Great Barrier Reef. (b) shows intact and deforested versions of the Amazon rainforest.

Detailed evaluation results can be found in [32, 35, 36]. The first of those papers focuses more heavily on the quantitative portions of the utilized mixed-methods approach, where 172 students from eight German secondary schools filled in questionnaires on self-assessed knowledge, interest and attitudes after either a lesson with the *greenpeace* application or a traditional lesson. In short, change in self-assessed knowledge and attitude was achieved when using the app, yielding small effects (Cohen's d between 0.34 and 0.42). However, this was highly dependent on school form, with academic track students seemingly having an easier time learning with the app whereas students in vocationally oriented schools performed better in the control condition [32]. The second paper looked more thoroughly at possible moderators within the experimental condition. For self-assessed knowledge, the analysis indicated that flow and presence were moderators of the difference between pre- and posttest scores [35]. Especially students with little prior knowledge benefited from experiencing flow and presence. The analysis also revealed a high correlation between flow and presence ($r = .58$), as well as significant correlations between flow and self-assessed knowledge, interest, and two out of three attitude measures [35]. The third paper presents results of eight focus group interviews that 84 of the experimental group students (between 2 and 25 per school) volunteered for, and is more focused on the qualitative portions [36]. A content analysis [37] of those follow-up focus group interviews showed that students mentioning a change in attitude or behavior was often related to them talking about their feeling of presence during the lesson [36]. This corroborates the quantitative findings and supports the role of presence for learning in virtual environments, as hypothesized by the theoretical frameworks [8, 11, 12].

Curiously, there has been a discrepancy in statements by teachers and students. While teachers seemed critical of the high information density provided by the application and pointed out that some students had difficulties with selecting relevant information, many students stated that they found the amount of information beneficial for their learning experience. In total, students rated the app-based lesson on average a 7.5 out of 10 ($N = 62$), indicating a favorable rating [36].

Teachers and students agreed that they would like to see more and similar applications for other school subjects. According to one teacher, a virtual environment might lend itself to visualizing abstract scientific concepts that would otherwise be difficult to grasp, like electricity or molecular forces. Students seemed more interested in the world travelling aspects, which could support more immersive language learning. Students and teachers also agreed in their wish for a higher degree of interactivity. They proposed a more gamified version, where the application gives learners additional tasks to complete [36].

Generally, while students seemed very enthusiastic about VR use in the classroom, teachers were more skeptical. Especially for attitudinal and behavioral change, teachers remarked that the application might not give students enough time to reflect on the new information and could be more relatable, e.g., by addressing products students more commonly use, instead of tropical wood or nuts. Teachers did, however, seem content with using apps like the present one again in their classes. One teacher expressed that their students enjoyed the lesson a lot, even seemed surprised by the technical capabilities of their phones, and that making learning fun carries inherent value.

Based on our findings of the *greenpeace* project, the following section aims to explore requirements and ramifications for curriculum-oriented VR use in classrooms, what these kinds of applications can and cannot achieve, all while considering both teachers' and learners' perspectives.

4 Pedagogical Implications

4.1 What the App Can Do

Working with the *greenpeace* application offered an opportunity to apply concrete pedagogical procedures to the previously laid out model (see Fig. 1). In the recent study of Mulders et al. [32], the application was designed in a way that does not require preparatory steps, like downloading any data or sharing private information, but only a stable internet connection. The briefing section implemented in the study by Mulders et al. [32], started with a prompt on the 17 Sustainable Development Goals [34]. This could, for example, come in the form of a short explanatory video, as they are often found on video platforms like YouTube. A hypothetical question like *"In which ways would you like to design the 21st century?"* [33] could allow teachers to segue to SDGs, if students bring up tasks that are adjacent to those. Another possible learning activity might be a multiple-choice test with subsequent resolution as an option to bring students onto a similar level of background knowledge [8, 11, 12]. A key or legend explaining symbols that will be encountered in the intervention should also be provided, if necessary, to avoid confusion [9, 26, 27]. For example, the i-symbol is frequently used to indicate that more information is available. Tapping an icon with an i on it might lead to students finding additional information on whichever item they are currently examining within the VR application.

During the intervention in the study of Mulders et al. [32], teachers were mainly concerned with answering arising questions, helping with technical difficulties, and making sure that distractions were kept to a minimum, for example by asking students who had already finished the virtual exploration to remain quiet while others were still working. The *greenpeace* app, in its current version, is already designed to avoid overloading students and is divided into four different segments (here: habitats), allowing for various interactions. Only the simultaneous presentation of spoken and written text should be avoided in future versions in line with the modality effect [38].

In the study of Mulders et al. [32], the debriefing opened with welcoming students back to reality and continued with a quiz. This was followed by a reflective discussion in class, where thoughts, emotions, or specific parts of the exploration that made an impression on the students could be addressed. While the quiz is a self-testing generative task and mainly based on retrieval-based learning, the discussion incorporates parts of the summarizing and self-explaining techniques, in that the ideas conveyed through the application need to be stated in one's own words and made sense of to be able to discuss them with others [5]. Teaching, or explaining to other students what they have just learned, was not investigated within the study of Mulders et al. [32] but would also be a suitable generative learning task. For example, instead of having all students select the same learning habitat in the presently used application, teachers could split the class into groups. Those could in turn explain the different learning experiences in the different habitats to each other [5].

Following up on the lesson, additional learning experiences could be mapped out as mentioned in the focus groups. Examples include a homework assignment or class field trip to find out about products in local supermarkets that use components produced in the Amazon rainforest. For example, students could be split into groups to find a specific number of products from different aisles and check them for ingredients that might originate from the Amazon, or compare their prices with products that are more sustainably produced. This might make the experience more relatable to the real-life environment of students, as suggested by some teachers in the focus group. These practical examples for the model are summarized in Fig. 3.

Overall, pedagogical conclusions can be drawn. VR applications can positively affect knowledge in students [10]. While the quantitative knowledge measures of the *greenpeace* project can be criticized, students in the delayed focus groups were still able to recall large parts of the information they received during the VR class, meaning some degree of retention took place [35]. Still, this means that VR applications for classroom use should come with a plan on how to thematically lead up to the VR intervention to activate prior knowledge, and how to debrief the students afterwards. The *greenpeace* manual offered guiding questions for group discussions [33], however other kinds of

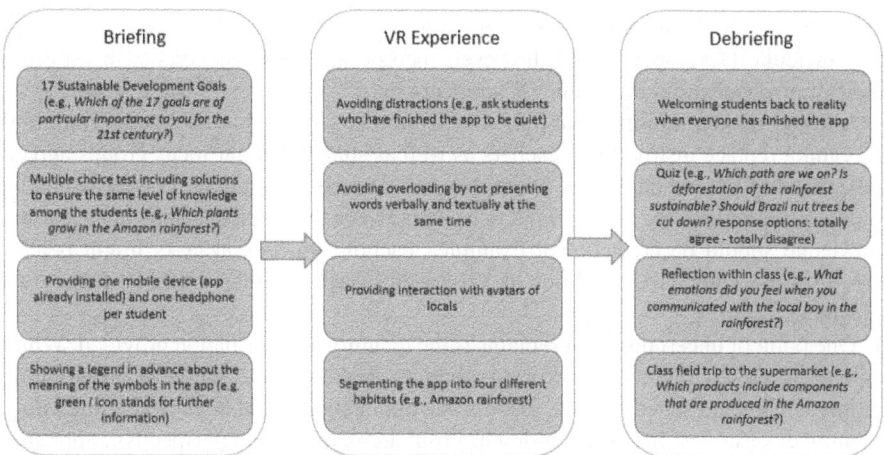

Fig. 3. Example tasks for the pedagogical model for working with VR. The examples are specific for sustainability education via the *greenpeace* application.

activities are desirable, like generative learning tasks to foster meaningful learning and higher engagement [5].

Students reported they had discussed general issues in the Amazon rainforest with peers and parents [36]. On one hand, this implies that learning in VR could be a useful starting point for teaching topics that lend themselves to open discussions, like social sciences. On the other hand, this also shows that VR-based lessons need to be planned with enough time for students to reflect on their experiences, as noted by some of the teachers.

For behavioral consequences from those attitudinal changes [39], statements from the focus groups were mixed. Students seemed at least somewhat eager to change their behavior, e.g., by buying fewer products that require palm oil. However, whether those ideas develop into long term behavior or even inspire more environmentally friendly actions remains unclear. As expressed above, teachers were critical as to whether this sort of intervention would at all be able to induce long term changes in behavior.

The overall benefits of this sort of intervention seem to lie partly in its novelty for students, but also in the ability of VR to make distant, abstract, or otherwise difficult to grasp topics palpable through perceived presence [8, 10, 11, 17–19]. In contrast, limitations and implications of what this setup cannot do will be discussed in the following chapter.

4.2 What the App Can't Do

No single method, application, or technology can be a miracle cure for all pedagogical ailments. Within the *greenpeace* project, teachers reported that they found their students to be more fatigued after the VR lesson than they were after conventional lessons, implying VR interventions should be kept short and only make up a part of a class, not its entire runtime. Naturally, because VR applications often require learners to move around, they put a higher physical strain on students than common sedentary classes. This kind of strain should generally be kept in mind when integrating VR-based technology into curricula. Developers could, however, incorporate a mix of tasks with differing levels of physical strain into their VR applications.

It has to be kept in mind that VR in education is supposed to be a supporting tool and cannot replace instruction. Teachers as well as students in our focus groups agreed that a blend of VR-enhanced and (what they considered) conventional classes would be optimal. It should also be kept in mind that a fit between the method and the to be learned knowledge should be created. For example, teaching procedural tasks might benefit more from the interactive qualities of VR-based instruction than teaching declarative knowledge [21].

One point of uncertainty that remains is the quantity of information provided. While students asked for a more open world to explore, teachers were skeptical of the information density and stated that the *greenpeace* application could be narrower regarding the number of topics, but more in-depth. From a cognitive load perspective, apps that provide more concise information would likely be beneficial [14, 27], however, from a developer standpoint, creating a singular, more encompassing application might seem more economically viable. A solution could be to give teachers the opportunity to lock and unlock specific parts of content. This could also play into a more gamified approach [3, 19, 40].

With *artificial intelligence* (*AI*) showing the potential to be an increasingly viable tool in application and game development [41, 42], future VR applications for classroom use might be able to utilize procedurally generated surroundings that are adapting to the learner. A higher degree of interactivity as requested by some students [36] could possibly be achieved with the help of large language models [43–45], for example by pairing the representation of a resident or expert avatar with a chatbot who can answer questions or accompany the learning experience [46, 47]. This would also lead to a more unique learning environment for each student, which could in turn encourage a more extensive exchange between students, since every one of them would have had a slightly different experience with the application.

Finally, some prerequisites should be addressed. Students with little prior experience in VR might struggle with VR-based instruction [32, 48], although research results are mixed [49]. This implies that efforts of VR-based instruction might be futile without at least a certain degree of media literacy or technological savviness [50]. Applications like the *greenpeace* VR experience might also not be able to uphold the air of novelty the more popular VR becomes. There is possibly a conflict between the benefits of prior experience with VR technology and the engagement provided by the novelty effect [51], as well as a possible link between lack of prior experience with VR and change of real-life behavior, making attitudinal and behavioral change less likely the more experienced the user becomes [52].

5 Conclusion

In the present paper, we provided a model for VR-based teaching that is sub-sectioned into three parts: before, during, and after the VR experience. For each section, pedagogically sensible generative activities as well as general recommended actions for instructors are included. This model was developed with the *greenpeace* application in mind. However, teachers as well as researchers should easily be able to adapt, adjust, and expand this by no means complete model for their own needs and applications. We hope that this model will be able to help popularize the integration of VR technology in classrooms, not for its own sake, but for the sake of pedagogically sound instruction that fits the learning task.

References

1. Bailenson, J.: Experience on demand: What virtual reality is, how it works, and what it can do. W. W. Norton & Company, New York, NY, US (2018)
2. Elmqaddem, N.: Augmented reality and virtual reality in education. myth or reality? Int. J. Emerg. Technol. Learn. (iJET). **14**, 234–242 (2019). https://doi.org/10.3991/ijet.v14i03.9289
3. Kavanagh, S., Luxton-Reilly, A., Wuensche, B., Plimmer, B.: A systematic review of virtual reality in education. Themes in Sci. Technol. Edu. **10**, 85–119 (2017)
4. Buchner, J.: Generative learning strategies do not diminish primary students' attitudes towards augmented reality. Educ. Inf. Technol. **27**, 701–717 (2022). https://doi.org/10.1007/s10639-021-10445-y
5. Fiorella, L., Mayer, R.E.: Eight ways to promote generative learning. Educ. Psychol. Rev. **28**, 717–741 (2016). https://doi.org/10.1007/s10648-015-9348-9
6. Wittrock, M.C.: Learning as a generative process. Educational Psychologist. **45**, 40–45 (2010). https://doi.org/10.1080/00461520903433554
7. Cummings, J.J., Bailenson, J.N.: How immersive is enough? a meta-analysis of the effect of immersive technology on user presence. Media Psychol. **19**, 272–309 (2016). https://doi.org/10.1080/15213269.2015.1015740
8. Makransky, G., Petersen, G.B.: The cognitive affective model of immersive learning (CAMIL): a theoretical research-based model of learning in immersive virtual reality. Educ. Psychol. Rev. **33**, 937–958 (2021). https://doi.org/10.1007/s10648-020-09586-2
9. Johnson-Glenberg, M.C.: The necessary nine: design principles for embodied VR and active stem education. In: Díaz, P., Ioannou, A., Bhagat, K.K., Spector, J.M. (eds.) Learning in a Digital World: Perspective on Interactive Technologies for Formal and Informal Education, pp. 83–112. Springer, Singapore (2019). https://doi.org/10.1007/978-981-13-8265-9_5
10. Mulders, M.: Learning about victims of holocaust in virtual reality: the main, mediating and moderating effects of technology, instructional method, flow, presence, and prior knowledge. Multimodal Technol. Interact. **7**, 28 (2023). https://doi.org/10.3390/mti7030028
11. Dengel, A., Mägdefrau, J.: Immersive learning explored: subjective and objective factors influencing learning outcomes in immersive educational virtual environments. In: 2018 IEEE International Conference on Teaching, Assessment, and Learning for Engineering (TALE), pp. 608–615. Wollongong, Australia (2018). https://doi.org/10.1109/TALE.2018.8615281
12. Mulders, M., Buchner, J., Kerres, M.: A framework for the use of immersive virtual reality in learning environments. Int. J. Emerg. Technol. Learn. (iJET). **15**, 208–224 (2020). https://doi.org/10.3991/ijet.v15i24.16615
13. Breves, P., Stein, J.-P.: Cognitive load in immersive media settings: the role of spatial presence and cybersickness. Virtual Reality (2022). https://doi.org/10.1007/s10055-022-00697-5
14. Makransky, G., Terkildsen, T.S., Mayer, R.E.: Adding immersive virtual reality to a science lab simulation causes more presence but less learning. Learn. Instr. **60**, 225–236 (2019). https://doi.org/10.1016/j.learninstruc.2017.12.007
15. Han, J., Zheng, Q., Ding, Y.: Lost in virtual reality? cognitive load in high immersive VR environments. JAIT **12**, 302–310 (2021). https://doi.org/10.12720/jait.12.4.302-310

16. Csikszentmihalyi, M.: Flow and education. NAMTA. Journal **22**, 2–35 (1997)
17. Kye, B., Kim, Y.: Investigation of the relationships between media characteristics, presence, flow, and learning effects in augmented reality based learning. Int. J. Educ. Media and Technol. **2** (2008)
18. Janssen, D., Tummel, C., Richert, A., Isenhardt, I.: Virtual environments in higher education – immersion as a key construct for learning 4.0. Int. J. Adv. Corp. Learn. **9**, 20 (2016). https://doi.org/10.3991/ijac.v9i2.6000
19. Bodzin, A., Araujo-Junior, R., Hammond, T., Anastasio, D.: Investigating engagement and flow with a placed-based immersive virtual reality game. J. Sci. Educ. Technol. **30**, 347–360 (2021). https://doi.org/10.1007/s10956-020-09870-4
20. Setyowati, R.R., Rochmat, S., Aman, Nugroho, A.N.P.: Virtual reality on contextual learning during Covid-19 to improve students' learning outcomes and participation. Int. J. Instruct. **16**, 173–190 (2023). https://doi.org/10.29333/iji.2023.16110a
21. Tai, K.H., Hong, J.C., Tsai, C.R., Lin, C.Z., Hung, Y.H.: Virtual reality for car-detailing skill development: Learning outcomes of procedural accuracy and performance quality predicted by VR self-efficacy, VR using anxiety, VR learning interest and flow experience. Comput. Educ. **182**, 104458 (2022). https://doi.org/10.1016/j.compedu.2022.104458
22. Hamilton, D., McKechnie, J., Edgerton, E., Wilson, C.: Immersive virtual reality as a pedagogical tool in education: a systematic literature review of quantitative learning outcomes and experimental design. J. Comput. Educ. **8**, 1–32 (2021). https://doi.org/10.1007/s40692-020-00169-2
23. Hill, T., du Preez, H.: A longitudinal study of students' perceptions of immersive virtual reality teaching interventions. In: 2021 7th International Conference of the Immersive Learning Research Network (iLRN), pp. 1–7 (2021). https://doi.org/10.23919/iLRN52045.2021.9459334
24. Fischer, H., Arnold, M., Philippe, S., Dyrna, J., Jung, S.: VR-based learning and teaching. a framework for implementation of virtual reality in formal education. In: INTED2021 Proceedings, pp. 3304–3314. IATED, Online Conference (2021). https://doi.org/10.21125/inted.2021.0694
25. Klingenberg, S., Jørgensen, M.L.M., Dandanell, G., Skrivor, K., Mottelson, A., Makransky, G.: Investigating the effect of teaching as a generative learning strategy when learning through desktop and immersive VR: A media and methods experiment. Br. J. Edu. Technol. **51**, 2115–2138 (2020). https://doi.org/10.1111/bjet.13029
26. Klingenberg, S., Fischer, R., Zettler, I., Makransky, G.: Facilitating learning in immersive virtual reality: Segmentation, summarizing, both or none? J. Comput. Assist. Learn. **39**, 218–230 (2022). https://doi.org/10.1111/jcal.12741
27. Pellas, N., Kazanidis, I., Palaigeorgiou, G.: A systematic literature review of mixed reality environments in K-12 education. Educ. Inf. Technol. **25**, 2481–2520 (2020). https://doi.org/10.1007/s10639-019-10076-4
28. Okimoto, M.L.L.R., Okimoto, P.C., Goldbach, C.E.: User experience in augmented reality applied to the welding education. Procedia Manufacturing. **3**, 6223–6227 (2015). https://doi.org/10.1016/j.promfg.2015.07.739
29. Skulmowski, A., Xu, K.M.: Understanding cognitive load in digital and online learning: a new perspective on extraneous cognitive load. Educ. Psychol. Rev. **34**, 171–196 (2022). https://doi.org/10.1007/s10648-021-09624-7
30. Lewers, E.: Durch raum und zeit?: medienkritische auseinandersetzung mit virtual reality im geschichtsunterricht. Medienimpulse **60** (2022). https://doi.org/10.21243/mi-02-22-20
31. Bunnenberg, C.: Mittendrin im historischen geschehen? geschichte für heute **13**, 45–59 (2020)
32. Mulders, M., Träg, K.H., Kirner, L.: Go green: evaluating an XR application on biodiversity in German secondary school classrooms Instr. Sci. (2025). https://doi.org/10.1007/s11251-024-09697-1

33. greenpeace: Augmented Reality-Anwendung: Der Artenvielfalt auf der Spur | Greenpeace, https://www.greenpeace.de/ueber-uns/umweltbildung/augmented-reality-anwendung-artenvielfalt-spur. Last accessed 05 June 2023
34. United Nations: Transforming our World: The 2030 Agenda for Sustainable Development (2015). https://sdgs.un.org/publications/transforming-our-world-2030-agenda-sustainable-development-17981
35. Mulders, M., Träg, K.H.: Presence and Flow as Moderators in XR-Based Sustainability Education. Sustainability **15**, 16496 (2023). https://doi.org/10.3390/su152316496
36. Mulders, M., Träg, K., Kirner, L.: Artenvielfalt im unterricht - ergebnisse qualitativer befragungen von schüler:innen zum einsatz von XR. In: Workshops der 21. Fachtagung Bildungstechnologien (DELFI) in Aachen, pp. 89–98. Gesellschaft für Informatik e.V., Bonn (2023). https://doi.org/10.18420/wsdelfi2023-24
37. Kuckartz, U., Rädiker, S.: Fokussierte Interviewanalyse mit MAXQDA: Schritt für Schritt. Springer Fachmedien, Wiesbaden (2020). https://doi.org/10.1007/978-3-658-31468-2
38. Leahy, W., Sweller, J.: Cognitive load theory, modality of presentation and the transient information effect. Appl. Cogn. Psychol. **25**, 943–951 (2011). https://doi.org/10.1002/acp.1787
39. Ajzen, I., Fishbein, M.: Attitudes and the attitude-behavior relation: reasoned and automatic processes. Eur. Rev. Soc. Psychol. **11**, 1–33 (2000). https://doi.org/10.1080/14792779943000116
40. Araujo-Junior, R., et al.: Flood Adventures: Evaluation Study of Final Prototype. In: Bourguet, M.-L., Krüger, J.M., Pedrosa, D., Dengel, A., Peña-Rios, A., Richter, J. (eds.) Immersive Learning Research Network, pp. 426–435. Springer Nature Switzerland, Cham (2024). https://doi.org/10.1007/978-3-031-47328-9_31
41. Kavouras, I., Rallis, I., Doulamis, A., Doulamis, N.: Evaluating the feasibility of fast game development using open source tools and AI algorithms. In: Krouska, A., Troussas, C., Caro, J. (eds.) Novel & Intelligent Digital Systems: Proceedings of the 2nd International Conference (NiDS 2022), pp. 124–133. Springer International Publishing, Cham (2023). https://doi.org/10.1007/978-3-031-17601-2_13
42. French, F., Levi, D., Maczo, C., Simonaityte, A., Triantafyllidis, S., Varda, G.: Creative use of OpenAI in education: case studies from game development. Multimodal Technol. Interact. **7**, 81 (2023). https://doi.org/10.3390/mti7080081
43. Su, J., Yang, W.: Unlocking the power of ChatGPT: a framework for applying generative AI in education. ECNU Rev. Educ. **6**, 355–366 (2023). https://doi.org/10.1177/20965311231168423
44. Guo, K., Zhong, Y., Li, D., Chu, S.K.W.: Effects of chatbot-assisted in-class debates on students' argumentation skills and task motivation. Comput. Educ. **203**, 104862 (2023). https://doi.org/10.1016/j.compedu.2023.104862
45. Ifelebuegu, A.O., Kulume, P., Cherukut, P.: Chatbots and AI in Education (AIEd) tools: The good, the bad, and the ugly. J. Appl. Learn. Teach. **6**, 332–345 (2023). https://doi.org/10.37074/jalt.2023.6.2.29
46. Khosrawi-Rad, B., Schlimbach, R., Strohmann, T., Robra-Bissantz, S.: Desgin knowledge for virtual learning companions. In: Proceedings of the 2022 AIS SIGED International Conference on Information Systems Education and Research, p. 6 (2022)
47. Khosrawi-Rad, B., et al.: Conversational agents in education – a systematic literature review. In: ECIS 2022 Research Papers, p. 18. Timisoara, Romania (2022)
48. Sagnier, C., Loup-Escande, E., Valléry, G.: Effects of gender and prior experience in immersive user experience with virtual reality. In: Ahram, T., Falcão, C. (eds.) Advances in Usability and User Experience, pp. 305–314. Springer International Publishing, Cham (2020). https://doi.org/10.1007/978-3-030-19135-1_30

49. Calvert, J., Hume, M.: Improving student learning outcomes using narrative virtual reality as pre-training. Virtual Reality **27**, 2633–2648 (2023). https://doi.org/10.1007/s10055-023-00830-y
50. Zender, R., Weise, M., von der Heyde, M., Söbke, H.: Lehren und Lernen mit VR und AR-Was wird erwartet? Was funktioniert? In: Proceedings der Pre-Conference-Workshops der 16. E-Learning Fachtagung Informatik (DeLFI 2018). Frankfurt a. M. (2018)
51. Wu, B., Yu, X., Gu, X.: Effectiveness of immersive virtual reality using head-mounted displays on learning performance: a meta-analysis. Brit. J. Educ. Tech. **51**, 1991–2005 (2020). https://doi.org/10.1111/bjet.13023
52. Jun, Y.: The Differential Effects of Virtual Reality (VR) on the Novice and Experienced VR Users. Asia Marketing Journal **25**, 61–70 (2023). https://doi.org/10.53728/2765-6500.1610

Immersive Learning of Cerebral Visual Impairment: Understanding Vision Through Dynamic Immersive Simulations

Catherine Anne Cassidy[(✉)], Iain Oliver, Kamila Oles, Helen St Clair Tracy, Andrew Blaikie, and Alan Miller[(✉)]

University of St Andrews, St Andrews, UK
{cc274,iao,kgo1,hsct1,ab312,ahr1}@st-andrews.ac.uk

Abstract. Many different brain-based impairments of vision can affect how someone experiences the world. Those conditions, called Cerebral Visual Impairments (CVI) are often difficult to explain and understand as each individual has their own unique experience of how they see and how their conditions affect them. However, people with CVI benefit substantially if those close to them understand their condition well enough to know which simple steps will make their world easier to navigate, interpret and understand. This paper summarises efforts to create immersive virtual reality visualisations which help those without CVI to better understand various CVI conditions. Two environments types are explored; classrooms and a climate change museum. A visual interface has been created which simulates various effects of CVI. Through this mechanism the user tailors their experience by selecting different impairments and their level of severity which then reacts dynamically to the environment chosen. Through experiential learning from a perspective of the world differing from their own, users gain exposure to CVI and potentially understand changes they can make to better support those affected. Evaluation and feedback demonstrates the simulation's effectiveness as a research platform in its ability to help refine understanding of the dynamic nature of the impairments. The simulation is also effecting in establishing change in understanding, potentially leading to broader accessibility standards in schools, public spaces and beyond.

Keywords: Cerebral Visual Impairment · Virtual Reality · Immersive Learning · Wellbeing · Sustainable Development

1 Introduction

Experiential learning offers the opportunity for an active learning process, where learners engage with the subject and construct their understanding, adding to previous knowledge. Though valuable experiential learning is, its applicability is often confined, due to our limited ability to experience phenomena, whether it is barriers of space, time, cost or perception. If one is not able to experience something then it is difficult for experiential learning to be applied.

Cerebral Visual Impairment (CVI) is a condition where these barriers are exemplified. The way a person's brain functions can impair their visual perception of the world. It is difficult to explain the impairment as it is usually unconscious to the affected person, is complex to describe and manifests in varied ways. Some visual impairments, especially due to eye disease, are straight forward to illustrate for another to experience. The dynamic qualities of how cerebral visual impairments manifest is much more difficult to visualise. By understanding CVI better, those looking after a person affected by CVI can be empowered to change the environment to make the physical world more accessible and therefore improving the visual experience for those affected by CVI.

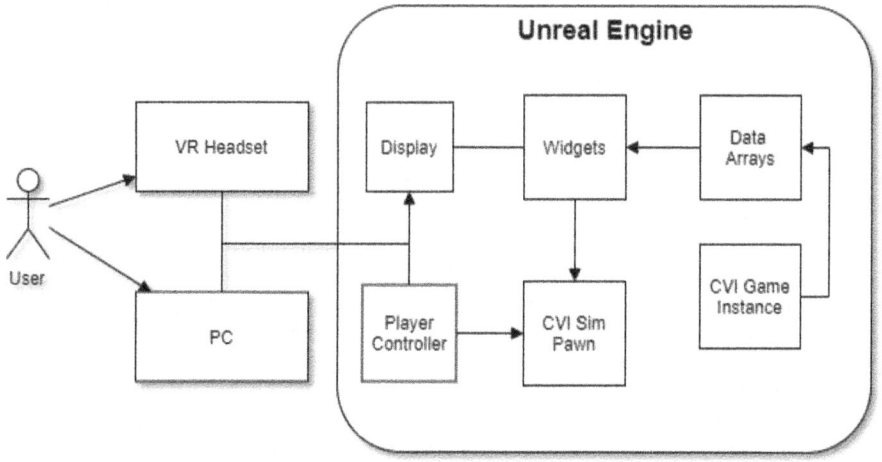

Fig. 1. CVI SIM Architecture.

Computer simulations and game technologies offer the possibility of extending experiential learning. Through immersive virtual reality (VR) we can experience what it might have been like to visit a Medieval cathedral, walk on the surface of Mars or scale the edge of a volcano. This paper reports and explores efforts to visually represent CVI through an immersive simulation experience, called CVI-SIM, illustrated in Fig. 1, so that carers, teachers and the public sector can better understand the effects of the condition, and be better equipped to improve environments such as homes, schools and museums to help rather than hinder people with CVI. The discussion is organised into the following sections:

1. What is CVI, who it affects and its manifestations,
2. Previous work and relativity to the topic,
3. VR's role to visualise and experience CVI,
4. The CVI Campus virtual environments,
5. Workflows and infrastructures for the CVI simulation,
6. Methodology for evaluation, and
7. Reflections and future work.

2 Cerebral Visual Impairment

It has been estimated that 40% of the brain is dedicated to processing vision [18]. Many different processes from different part of the brain are synchronised to enable a person to see clearly, recognise things and people, and safely navigate the world around them [6]. If any of the visual processes are not working typically, they can give rise to a condition called CVI, which is an umbrella term for one or many of the visual impairments from the brain [15,20]. How CVI manifests varies considerably from person to person, depending on which areas of the brain are affected and how severely. A common cause is brain damage before, during or just after birth causing a lack of oxygen to the brain [19]. Another cause is premature birth [9,10]. CVI can also be acquired at any time in life due to brain injury or disease. In stroke survivors, representing around 2% of the UK population, as many as three quarters may be affected by CVI [8] and arguably, all affected by dementia will at some point be affected by CVI. With 40% of the brain dedicated to processing vision, almost anything that can affect the brain at any time in life can affect a vision processing area causing CVI, including multiple sclerosis, traumatic brain injury, brain tumours and infections.

Table 1. Common Cerebral Visual Impairments featured in CVI-SIM.

Cerebral Visual Impairment	Description
Reduced Visual Acuity	Reduces the sharpness of vision, resulting in blurred or softer view
Reduced Contrast Sensitivity	Where the subtle differences between shades and tones of colours can't be seen clearly, or at all
Simultanagnosia	Difficulty of processing multiple visual stimuli simultaneously, particularly in complex or noisy environments, leading to an inability to perceive and interpret their visual surroundings
Lower Visual Field Impairment	Aspects of the field of vision appear blurred frequently in the lower part of the visual field
Dyskinetopsia	Things that move fast are not seen clearly due to motion blur

CVI has been found in 3–4% of primary school children in a large NHS funded study [22]. Of those children, 80% had difficulties in school [22]. That percentage in children across the UK suggests around half a million children may be affected by CVI, and the vast majority struggling in school as a result. In children who attend special schools, the numbers are much higher, two small studies have found 23.5% [3] and 58% [22]. There are two things all most everyone in the population affected by CVI have in common, firstly, as it is missed in standard sight tests, in almost everyone so it is unknown, undiagnosed and unsupported.

Secondly, the majority have difficulties as a result. Most are affected by a type of CVI that affects visual perception, it is difficult to describe or show what it looks like compared to typical vision. The condition is called simultanagnosia [7]. A list of common CVI conditions and their descriptions are listed in Fig. 2[1].

More research is needed to establish the percentage of the population likely affected by CVI, but the numbers are vast. Common difficulties include not being able to find things, especially in cluttered and crowded places. An inability to stay focused on one thing, difficulty reaching for things accurately, making the person appear clumsy and affecting handwriting. Reading, recognising faces, recognising facial expressions, remembering routes and going down stairs are further common difficulties [6]. A person with CVI can become completely overwhelmed and incapacitated, leaving them vulnerable [17].

CVI affects unconscious parts of the brain, meaning the person is not aware they have a visual impairment, only that things are difficult. They can't tell another person what they need because they don't know, because their vision is 'normal' to them.

3 Related Work and Context

The Cerebral Visual Impairment Society of Scotland (CVI Scotland) is a charity which is dedicated to sharing and developing understanding of CVI, through their global leading website resources (www.cviscotland.org), and is used in almost every country in the world [20]. Some of these resources embody previous and complementary efforts in visualising CVI which informed the trajectory of our VR simulation project, which included:

- Photographs with curated filters imitating the effects of different CVIs created from direct engagement with the CVI community.
- Videos in common environments, for example a beach and shop, were shown to adults with CVI, who described what they could see. By covering what they could not see, in consultation with medical CVI experts, a filter was created to make the worlds first simulation of visual perception difficulties associated with CVI.

This led to early iterations of CVI-SIM, which included:

- Using a game environment to simulate CVI effects, whilst viewing and interacting with a screen, keyboard and mouse or game controller. This enabled live interaction filtered by CVI effects.
- Videos created from game scenarios. This offered flexibility in creating scenarios and applying a range of CVI effects but without live interaction.

The work reported in this paper adds a third phase where the user is immersed in the experience. Through engagement with adults affected by CVI, CVI-SIM was created to 'behave' like different cerebral visual impairments, but

---

[1] Summary of discussion available in extended form in [23].

interacting with a virtual world. With different levels of severity, the programme is tailored to an individual's CVI and through a virtual reality head-mounted display (VR HMD), the simulation experience is more authentic and closer to an actual CVI experience.

Previous efforts to demonstrate visual impairments for understanding have laid a foundation for CVI-SIM and the research. Non-VR goggles simulate eye impairments which are considered static and duplicated using filters, such as glaucoma, cataracts and macular degeneration, and help associate real world difficulties for those unaffected [1,25]. However non-VR goggles limit an unaffected person's understanding to the world immediately around them, which spurred exploration using gaming technologies. Lewis et al. developed a simulation for the same impairments and asked users to navigate a virtual indoor environment in a task-driven evaluation [12] which has been further explored by Väyrynen, Colley and Häkkilä in a virtual city environment while wayfinding and with target location tasks [21]. A study focused on empathy was conducted by Krosl et al. using XREye, an immersive simulation using gaming technologies and a VR HMD [11]. Visual impairments tested included myopia, hyperopia, presbyopia, corneal disease, and age-related macular degeneration using various immersive methods including a virtual VR environment, augmented reality (AR), and 360° images in VR HMD. Greater feelings of empathy were felt by users using XREye and those passively watching, while those who had an immersive experience rated higher levels of empathy than those watching the 2D simulation.

Prior VR experience projects of the CVI-SIM team lay the foundations for this experimental and collaborative work. A long standing relationship between the research team and Timespan Museum and Art Gallery has developed a digital representation of Caen, a pre-clearances Highland village in the Strath of Kildonan, now since updated with three new virtual reconstructions and experiences [16]. The Picts & Pixels exhibition at the Perth Museum and Art Gallery adopted a mixed reality approach incorporating physical objects, 3D models, virtual reconstructions and virtual reality in parallel to one another in an gallery experience [5]. A virtual exhibit template (VRET) formulated virtual historical experiences for the Tomintoul & Glenlivet Discovery Centre, Skriuklaustur in the East of Iceland, and the Finlaggan Trust in Islay [4].

This work also fits within and can be considered part of efforts to realise the United Nations Agenda 2030. The United Nations Agenda 2030 was adopted by all United Nations Member States in 2015, and provides a shared blueprint for peace and prosperity for people and the planet. At the heart of the agenda are 17 Sustainable Development Goals (SDG) and an associated 169 targets. This work contributes to the realisation of Agenda 2030 as it contributes to SDG 3 'Ensure healthy lives and promote well-being for all at all ages', by contributing to the health and well being of people with CVI, Target 3.4. It also contributes to SDG 4 'Ensure inclusive and equitable quality education and promote life long learning opportunities for all' and applies to Targets 4.4 'Relevant skills' and 4.7 'Education for sustainable lifestyles for all'. The CVI-SIM includes a virtual museum environment with curated galleries focused on climate change and its effects on cultural and natural heritage, which addresses SDG 13 'Take urgent action to combat climate change and its impacts'.

4 Representing CVI Through Virtual Reality

Virtual Reality with a HMD as a primary engagement method is a highly immersive approach to visualising visual impairments from the brain. It places the user in the first person perspective as they themselves have to navigate common environments with the given simulated impairment. A robust VR HMD in parallel with a gaming computer would seamlessly operate more dynamic impairments of CVI to be simulated at varying intensities, something that would not be possible with simpler setups. The user is then placed into any simulated environment, therefore requiring a VR system which would interact seamlessly with a game engine.

Fixed and dynamic impairments were chosen to be simulated in CVI-SIM, an example of which are demonstrated in Table 1[2]. As a person with CVI may have one or a combination of a few conditions, it was imperative to simulate impairments distinctly but with clear integration with one another.

Unreal Engine 5 (UE5) handles the rendering and physics simulation of the virtual environment. It also provides an interface to the user input which allows the navigation and menus to be implemented simply in a platform independent manner. It also provides APIs to interact with the environment and to alter the rendering of the environment, which allows the CVI-SIM system to be implemented.

A menu system allows users to select VR HMD or screen and mouse combination for their preferred interaction method. From there, a video highlighting the various impairments included in CVI-SIM, preset 'demo' impairment combinations, or the fully customisable settings are available to select. The demos are a preselected combination of impairments at mild, significant, or profound severities. The customisable CVI setting menu simulates any single impairment or combination of simulated impairments to the user's chosen severity. After either experience is chosen, the user selects what virtual environment to simulate the chosen impairments in, which includes classrooms, a museum, or a room devoid of any detail to view impairments without stimuli.

The settings menu allows the user to change the CVI severity settings whilst using the system. UE5 contains a system call UMG for creating a menu that create buttons which are triggered with a mouse or VR pointer, and then change stored settings, open and close menus and trigger code to move the user to different parts of the simulated environment. Once the menu is closed these settings are applied, changing the CVI filters which is handled by the Pawn component of the system.

The player character component receives information from the game engine and the menu system component. It receives the processed user inputs from the

---

[2] Discussion of classrooms and images in extended form in [2].

game engine which trigger events in the blueprints. These determine the players movement, direction the player is facing, and whether to open the menus. The player movement and direction is then passed back to the game engine which calculates the world position, relevant physics, and what to render. This component receives the updated filter settings from the menus and applies them by modifying the filter parameters. The logic driving the dynamic filters is also within this component. This uses information about the visual scene from the game engine as well as the current state of the filters to determine the filters' behaviour. This is communicated to the filter component in the form of frequently updated filter parameters.

The Pawn component of the system takes in input events and translates them into movement requests to the UE5 system which then applies the physics of the environment. It initialises the visual filters open the menu it receives the settings changes to apply to the filters. The dynamic filter logic is located in this part and is updated every tick, which happens every time a frame is rendered. It also opens and closes the menus.

The visual effects of CVI are applied to the visual that the user sees using post-processing effects using two methods. The first and simpler method is the existing Post Processing effect in UE5. The settings are adjusted to provide the correct effect, adjusting settings based on the value set by the user. The second method of producing these effects is by creating a dynamic material and adding it to the post-processing system. These are implemented as a Material in UE5. The dynamic material takes the existing render, changes it to achieve the effect and then outputs it again. This process can also read parameters that have been set by the Pawn. Multiple such materials are used, with the next one taking the output from the previous one.

Reduced Visual Acuity is simulated using a Gaussian disk blur effect with the acuity values passed through a formula and used as the radius for the blur effect. The formula was adjusted to be consistent with LogMAR visual acuity scoring. The formula is $r = 10^b * 3$ where r is the radius and b is the set blur value. The Reduced Contrast Sensitivity impairment uses UE5's default contrast adjustment system but using a formula for the correct relationship between the input value and the contrast. The formula is $C = 1 - \cos(c * \pi * 0.5)$ where c is the input contrast value and C is the result. The Reduced Visual Field impairments are created by a post-processing effect which masks part of the image with a soft edge. This is created by placing predefined images of the data and adjusting their size to the supplied values.

Simultanagnosia is a more complex effect as it reacts to stimuli in an environment. To simulate it in CVI-SIM, it uses a post-processing effect to visualise supplied values from a secondary source, from inside the Pawn. This reads the environment being rendered to the user and determines the number size and complexity of the object in the user's field of vision. This is then combined with the impairment severity settings to determine the strength of the effect to be applied. It also determines which object the system should focus on as Simultanagnosia presents similar to tunnel vision, however the focus moves around

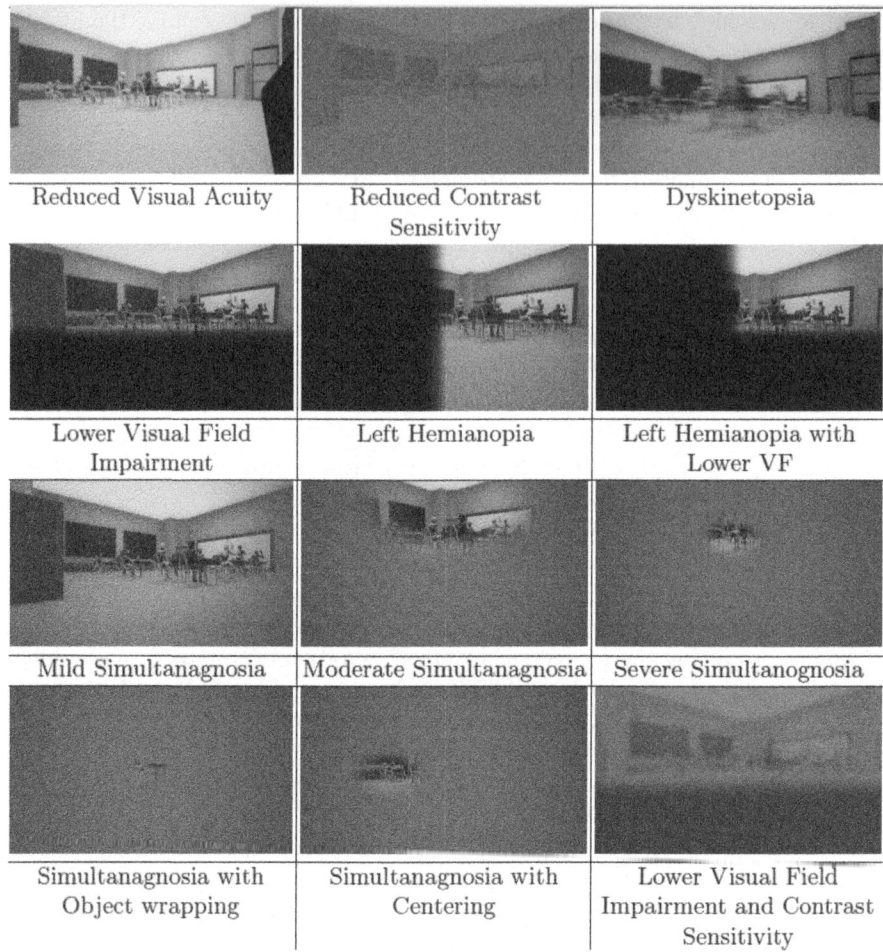

Fig. 2. Cerebral Visual Impairment visualisation of conditions.

the field of view and 'sticks'. It can also involve seeing only one object at a time on top of the tunnel vision. Two modes of this effect are present to select which are informed by the CVI community; one where the entire object stays visible through the tunnel vision and the other where the object begins to fade from view.

The visual field blur effect is visualised as a mask applied to part of the screen which is blurred while the other part is not. The last effect is a motion blur which simulates Dyskinetopsia. This effect is applied by using the UE5 post-processing system where the target frames per second of the motions blur effect is changed to alter the strength of the effect.

CVI-SIM is offered as a VR HMD experience or onscreen on a laptop or monitor, depending on the user's preference. The Meta Quest ecosystem was chosen

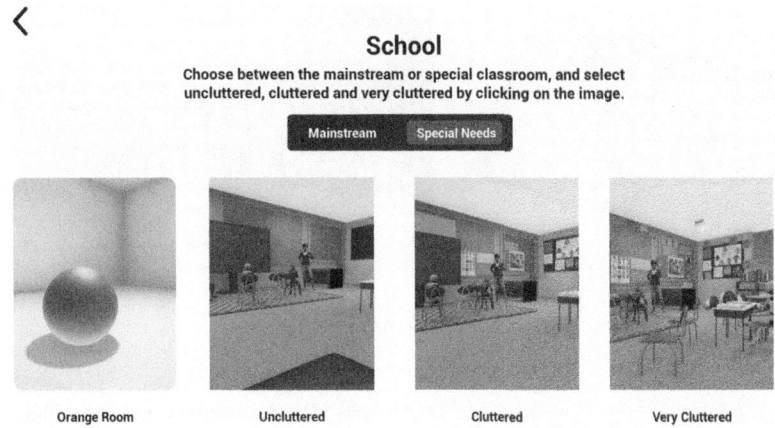

Fig. 3. Selection of classroom types.

as a powerful and customisable VR HMD option which has been tested and used extensively with previous immersive projects [4,5]. The VR HMD paired with a gaming laptop through a tethered connection. In the VR HMD option, users navigate an environment with a combination of head tracking and forward and back motions on the controller's thumbstick. A less controller-dependent navigation option was chosen to not break a user's first person experience and encourage head and body motion, more closely replicating a real experience.

5 The CVI Campus

The CVI Campus is an expansive and extendable virtual environment developed in UE5. Early iterations of the CVI-SIM included various classroom settings, but have been expanded to include a museum. There are future plans to expand the environments to include homes, a beach, neighbourhood and shopping complex. The environments reflect real settings, including commonly found complexity, clutter, movement and noise.

Classrooms. Two types of school classrooms are available to the user; a mainstream or a special needs classroom, which has been design on real classroom configuration and details. Figure 3 shows the top level menu for selecting between the two types. The user then selects the levels of 'clutter' in the classroom, which provides more visual stimulus. Those classrooms are then duplicated multiple times to allow switching between different levels of clutter, noise and amount of children and movement. The classrooms are all physically joined together in the virtual environment by two long corridors, however the menu selection is a faster method of navigation between all the classroom options.

Fig. 4. Climate Change Museum.

The Orange Room, inspired by work with children with complex CVI using orange therapy tents only has a large ball of strong contrasting colour to show the effect of having no distractions [13].

Climate Change Museum. After discussions for expansion of testing and feedback in the public sector, a museum was constructed to demonstrate an unfamiliar space which can have varying levels of complexity. The museum houses curated exhibits on the effects of climate change, and includes video and 3D objects displayed at different heights, moving projected shapes, and interpretation text in varying sizes and colour combinations. The layout of the museum is shown in Fig. 4 as well as examples of exhibitions. Users are expected to walk through the entrance and reception, through the galleries, out through a garden space and exit through the gift shop. This environment is similar to a real world museum, but not overly complicated of a floor plan. However, the stimulating details in combination with narrow passageways and windows can create a confusing layout for someone with CVI to navigate. Development of the climate change virtual museum is reported in [14,24].

6 Outreach and Stakeholders

The simulation of CVI is relevant to a number of stakeholders connected to people with CVI through work, leisure and family. These include:

- Parents, as accommodations in the home can be transformative for an affected person including learning, confidence and independence skills.
- Teachers, all of whom likely have children with CVI across their classes.
- Medical professionals and therapists, especially those in the vision sector.
- Museums and public sectors, as accessibility is considered in design and hosted activities in these spaces.

Central to the efforts of CVI Scotland is reaching out to stakeholders, making it easy for them to better understand the condition and how people with CVI can best be supported. There is a website, social media, conference proceedings,

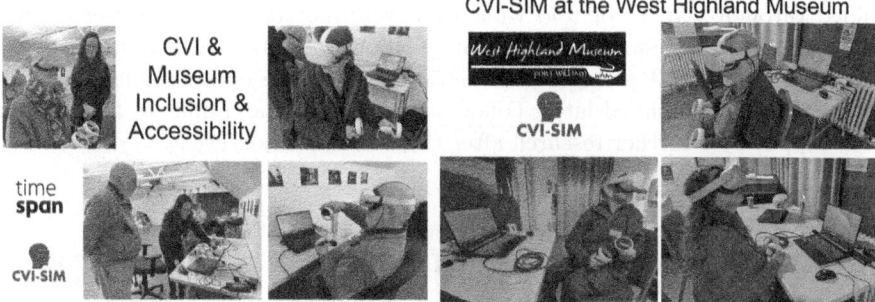

Fig. 5. CVI training in the museum sector.

workshops, research and expert advice to projects and partners. The CVI-SIM fits into a spectrum of resources which include textual descriptions, images, videos, simulations and now VR simulations. Demonstrations of the CVI-SIM have occurred with stakeholders who may be experts in CVI, work with people with CVI but not experts in the field, as well as those unaware of the complexities of CVI.

7 Testing and Evaluation

Adoption of practice-based research methods support interdisciplinary work with stakeholders. Initial formal evaluations occurred leading to early data which inform on further iterations of design. Collaboration with CVI experts led to the development of tailored investigations applicable to stakeholders and potential end users. Evaluations were carried out alongside the CVI-SIM's first public immersive outreach events, such as in museums, shown in Fig. 5.

Demonstrations of CVI-SIM occurred at common spaces for the stakeholders, including museums (public sector), a special school (teachers and parents), and universities (medical professionals). CVI-SIM was set up on its mobile setup with a laptop and VR HMD, and connected to a projector if available for greater group engagement for larger audiences. Participants sat through a brief of the project's objectives, a description of the simulation and the types of impairments shown. With the first user of the VR HMD, which others could see on the mirrored screen or projection, the choice of choosing specific settings or using a demo was offered, with the demo option chosen primarily. The environments were not explored without impairments as it important for user to not mentally map the virtual space before attempting to navigate with impairments, as people with CVI do not have that option in reality. Medical professionals, therapists, special school teachers and parents used the settings to replicate a known person's impairments to visualise what that person may experience in similar real-world environments. Duration of single user engagement with the VR HMD ranged from 3–10 min. Users were observed and given support with instructions for use of hardware and basic interactivity with the virtual environment, but were not guided through a space or told what they were intending to see. After testing CVI-SIM, the questionnaire was given to the user. With larger audiences participating together at a single demonstration event the questionnaire was sent by email to be completed later. Follow up information and links to the project were supplied for further research after the demonstration event.

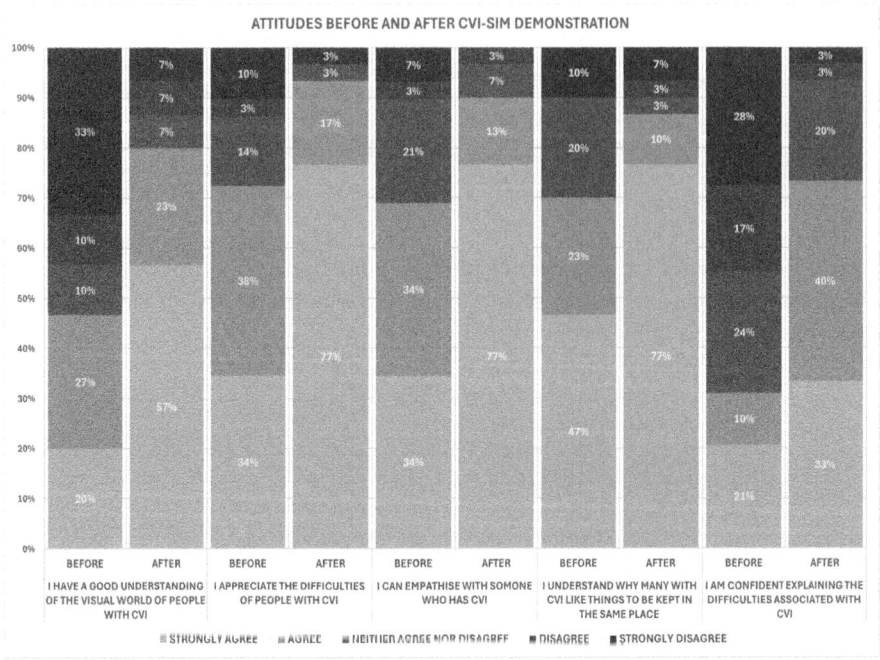

Fig. 6. Comparison of before and after results.

Questionnaires included demographic information, prior knowledge of CVI, use of VR HMD and virtual environments. As part of the comparative study, respondents were given identical Likert scale statements to rate before and after the CVI-SIM experience, to measure impact. At the point of writing, over 30 stakeholders have been evaluated, but evaluation is ongoing.

The before and after results are shown in Table 6 and suggest a strong transition to a better understanding and empathy towards CVI caused by engagement with CVI-SIM. For example those agreeing with the statement "I have good understanding or the visual world of CVI" rose from 46% to 80% those agreeing with the statement "I appreciate the difficulties of people with CVI" rose to 71% to 93%.

The questions and results shown in Table 7 show agreement and strong agreement with statements suggesting positive actions will be taken and appropriate measures made. For example in response to the statement "I will clear and declutter areas because of using CVI-SIM", 90% expressed agreement. In response

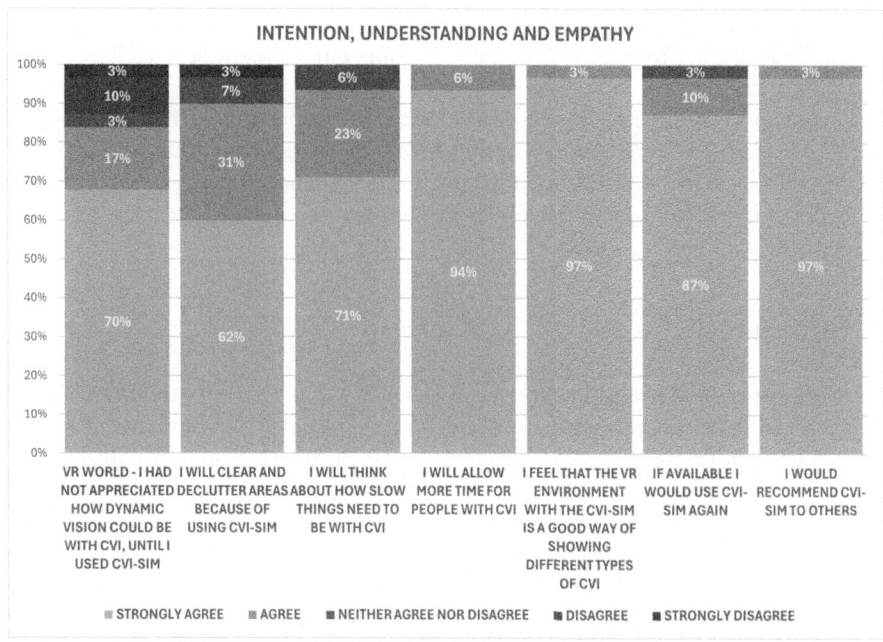

Fig. 7. Table of responses to questions on a Likert Scale.

to "I feel that the VR environment with the CVI simulator is a good way of showing different types of cerebral and visual impairments", 100% agreed, and in response to "I would recommend CVI-SIM to others", 100% also agreed.

These figures suggest that CVI-SIM enables people to better understand CVI. In doing so they are empowered to support measures that will improve the environment for people with the conditions, through actions such as decluttering, allowing more time and slowing things down.

8 Reflections and Future Work

VR simulations provide an immersive experience, showing a person not just the different visual world of a person with CVI, but a different experience, including feelings of vulnerability, confusion, stress and anxiety. The purpose of CVI-SIM is to show what has been very difficult to explain, so people will make changes to help those affected by CVI.

From testing to date the impact has been considerable, and CVI-SIM is useful not just as a simulator but also as a teaching resource, alternative to traditional teaching methods which are not accessible to many with literacy difficulties, making the VR simulator a more accessible resource.

CVI-SIM has also been a conduit to learn more about CVI, where theories can be tested and the simulations either improved or altered as we learn more.

The collaboration between Medicine & Computer Science has been key in the development of the programme, with the ongoing engagement and feedback from the CVI community.

There is potential for cross-sector learning, such as engaging with the museum sector. Through these activities, museums are reconsidering what accessibility means for their visitors who may have CVI, and looking at changes. Other areas for future developments could include further public spaces like train and bus terminals as well as airports.

9 Summary

This work proceeded from the observation that it was difficult to understand how the world looks to people with Cerebral Visual Impairment, but that if it was more widely understood, it would be possible to make relatively straightforward changes to environments to improve the wellbeing of people with CVI. Drawing on experience working with heritage exhibits where gaming technologies have been used to enable people to experience the past, we set out to develop simulations of CVI which would enable people to experience and consequently gain a better understanding of CVI. Meeting with enthusiastic support from stakeholders such as teachers, museum practitioners, parents and medical experts, it has been possible to test the simulations created within a range of environments. This has in turn enabled stakeholders to factor their new understanding into the design of new museum spaces, classrooms and the home environment.

References

1. Aballéa, S., Tsuchiya, A.: Seeing for yourself: feasibility study towards valuing visual impairment using simulation spectacles. Health Econ. **16** (2007)
2. Ada, C.B.: Virtual reality simulation of cerebral visual impairment. Master's thesis, University of St Andrews (2021)
3. Black, S.A., et al.: In-school eyecare in special education settings has measurable benefits for children's vision and behaviour. PLoS ONE **14**(8), e0220480 (2019)
4. Cassidy, C.A., Fabola, A., Oliver, I., Miller, A.: Time travel as a visitor experience: a virtual reality exhibit template for historical exploration. In: Communications in Computer and Information Science, vol. 1044 (2019)
5. Cassidy, C.A., Fabola, A., Rhodes, E., Miller, A.: The making and evaluation of picts and pixels: mixed exhibiting in the real and the unreal. In: Immersive Learning Research Network. Communications in Computer and Information Science. Springer (2018)
6. Chokron, S., Dutton, G.N.: From vision to cognition: potential contributions of cerebral visual impairment to neurodevelopmental disorders. J. Neural Transm. (Vienna) **130**(3), 409–424 (2023)
7. Dutton, G.N.: Cognitive visual dysfunction. Br. J. Ophthalmol. **78**(9), 723–726 (1994)
8. Edmans, J.A., Lincoln, N.B.: The frequency of perceptual deficits after stroke. Br. J. Occup. Ther. **52**(7), 266–270 (1989)

9. Jacobson, L., Flodmark, O., Martin, L.: Visual field defects in prematurely born patients with white matter damage of immaturity: a multiple-case study. Acta Ophthalmol. Scand. **84**(3), 357–362 (2006)
10. Kooiker, M.J.G., Swarte, R.M.C., Smit, L.S., Reiss, I.K.M.: Perinatal risk factors for visuospatial attention and processing dysfunctions at 1 year of age in children born between 26 and 32 weeks. Early Hum. Dev. **130**, 71–79 (2019)
11. Krösl, K., Medeiros, M.L., Huber, M., Feiner, S., Elvezio, C.: Exploring the educational value and impact of vision-impairment simulations on sympathy and empathy with XREye. Multimodal Technol. Interact. **7** (2023)
12. Lewis, J., Brown, D., Cranton, W., Mason, R.: Simulating visual impairments using the unreal engine 3 game engine. In: 2011 IEEE 1st International Conference on Serious Games and Applications for Health (SeGAH) (2011)
13. Little, S., Dutton, G.: Some children with multiple disabilities and cerebral visual impairment can engage when enclosed by a 'tent': is this due to Balint syndrome? Br. J. Vis. Impairment **33**, 66–73 (2015)
14. Lu, J.: Evaluating virtual reality simulation of cerebral visual imparment. Master's thesis, School of Computer Science (2023)
15. Manley, C.E., et al.: Object identification in cerebral visual impairment characterized by gaze behavior and image saliency analysis. Brain Develop. **45**(8), 432–444 (2023)
16. McCaffery, J., Miller, A., Vermehren, A., Fabola, A.: The virtual museums of Caen: a case study on modes of representation of digital historical content. In: 2015 Digital Heritage, vol. 2, pp. 541–548 (2015)
17. McDowell, N.: A review of the literature to inform the development of a practice framework for supporting children with cerebral visual impairment (CVI). Int. J. Incl. Educ. **27**(6), 718–738 (2023)
18. Nakayama, K.: Nakayama (2012)
19. Philip, S.S., Dutton, G.N.: Identifying and characterising cerebral visual impairment in children: a review. Clin. Exp. Optom. **97**(3), 196–208 (2014)
20. Ravenscroft, J., St Clair Tracy, H., Blaikie, A.: Cerebral visual impairment on the web: an exploration of an educational web resource as a bridge to public understanding. Front. Commun. **6** (2021)
21. Väyrynen, J., Colley, A., Häkkilä, J.: Head mounted display design tool for simulating visual disabilities. In: MUM 2016: Proceedings of the 15th International Conference on Mobile and Ubiquitous Multimedia (2016)
22. Williams, C., et al.: Cerebral visual impairment-related vision problems in primary school children: a cross-sectional survey. Dev. Med. Child Neurol. **63**(6), 683–689 (2021)
23. Wilson, C.: Virtual reality simulation of cerebral visual impairments. Master's thesis, University of St Andrews (2021)
24. Yang, J.: Evaluating virtual reality simulation of cerebral visual impairment. Master's thesis, University of St Andrews (2023)
25. Zagar, M., Baggarly, S.: Low vision simulator goggles in pharmacy education. Am. J. Pharmac. Educ. **74** (2010)

Design and Development of XR-Based Data Problem-Solving Content for Sustainable Development in Education

Suhyun Ki and Jeeheon Ryu(✉)

Chonnam National University, Gwangju, South Korea
{s.h.ki,jeeheon}@jnu.ac.kr

Abstract. The integration of education for sustainable development (ESD) into K-12 curriculum has become crucial in the global pursuit of a sustainable future. Education for climate change, one of the main ESD topics, needs to connect to student's real life and authentic learning. The objective of this study was to suggest the creation and advancement of climate change educational material utilizing eXtended reality (XR). The material was intended to utilize digital twin data related to carbon emissions and portray the level of carbon neutrality across the map of South Korea. The ESD content was crafted following the fundamental stages of the ADDIE instructional design model. Furthermore, this study provided a model for the development process of XR-based ESD content and explored its educational effectiveness.

Keywords: Education for Sustainable Development (ESD) · eXtended Reality (XR) · Data Problem-Solving · ADDIE · Design and Development Research

1 Introduction

Education for sustainable development (ESD) has become a crucial aspect of global educational initiatives, as highlighted by UNESCO, which underscores its role in equipping learners of all ages with the requisite knowledge, skills, values, and empowerment to tackle pressing global issues like climate change, biodiversity loss, resource depletion, and inequality [1]. Within K-12 education, ESD is integrated across various subjects such as mathematics, science, English, and social sciences, allowing students to grasp the intricate relationship between human activities and the natural world [2]. South Korea, for instance, is actively promoting ecological transition education through amendments to the Basic Education Act, encouraging experiential, hands-on learning activities that instill climate response and ESD principles among students [3].

To effectively advance ESD objectives, students must engage in self-regulated and self-directed learning, acquiring relevant knowledge and problem-solving skills in real-life contexts [4]. This pedagogical approach emphasizes contextual learning, aiming to connect students with authentic research inquiries and practical applications [5]. Given the urgency of climate change, integrating it into ESD curricula holds significant promise, as it is a pervasive global crisis with profound implications for students' lives [6].

The advent of readily accessible climate data, both local and global, underscores the importance of climate change literacy and numeracy in achieving cross-disciplinary educational goals [6]. Leveraging digital twin technology, which synchronizes real-world data into virtual models, offers a novel avenue for student-centered ESD learning, facilitating data-driven inquiry linked to real-life scenarios [7]. Furthermore, incorporating extended reality (XR) into digital twin environments enhances learning experiences by providing multisensory and immersive access to real-world information and data [7].

The integration of digital twin and XR technologies into ESD holds immense potential, enriching educational experiences by providing rich contextual information and fostering experiential learning activities [7]. This study aims to elucidate the design and development process employed to incorporate digital twin data and XR technology into K-12 ESD instructional content, defining digital twin data as real-world data synchronized within XR environments [7].

Research questions are as follows:

RQ1. What were the consideration of design and development of the ESD content?
RQ2. What was the process of design and development of the ESD content for climate change education?

2 Literature Review

2.1 ESD Related to K-12 Curriculum

Integrating ESD into K-12 curricula offers manifold benefits for enhancing the quality of school education [2]. ESD pedagogies, often grounded in specific locales or issues, foster critical thinking, social critique, and analysis of local contexts [8]. Various studies have explored the effects of integrating ESD into K-12 curricula. For example, Padmanabhan and Singh [9] devised science and social science curricula infused with ESD concepts, leading to heightened understanding of sustainable development. Similarly, Hopkinson and James [10] integrated ESD principles into STEM-related subjects, resulting in increased practical knowledge and skills among students.

When incorporating ESD into K-12 curricula, educators must consider effective strategies to enhance students' engagement and competence in ESD. Riess and colleagues [4], in their review of 17 scientific publications on ESD, identified two significant recommendations for achieving ESD objectives in teaching and learning. First, they advocate for a high degree of student self-direction, evidenced through self-reports and self-assessments in seminars and model projects. Second, they emphasize the importance of teacher guidance, supported by references to hypothesis-testing and quasi-experimental studies, to effectively implement methods and procedures. These recommendations underscore the need for teachers to provide opportunities for students to construct their own knowledge and develop problem-solving skills to effectively promote ESD goals. Thus, educators aiming to integrate ESD into K-12 curricula must adapt their teaching methods accordingly.

2.2 ESD with Digital Twinning Data in XR

The concept of the digital twin originated with Michael Grives' idea for Product Lifecycle Management (PLM) [11], envisioning a connection between virtual and real systems spanning from product design to disposal [12]. Digital twin technology encompasses various forms depending on the level of data integration, including representing physical reality as a virtual model (Digital Model), synchronizing real-world data into a virtual model (Digital Shadow), and facilitating bidirectional information exchange between physical reality and the virtual model (Digital Twin) [7].

The potential applications of digital twin technology in ESD education are multi-faceted. Firstly, the mirroring of information between physical and virtual realms opens up possibilities for blended learning [13]. Secondly, real-time data usage allows for learning processes and project prediction simulations [15]. Lastly, the technology acts as a test bed for exploratory learning, enabling hypothesis formulation, predictions, and exploration of What-If scenarios in conjunction with physical reality. This fosters opportunities for real-time data-driven experiments and hands-on experiences, aiding in establishing logical connections in conceptual and procedural learning [16].

Furthermore, eXtended Reality (XR) enhances and broadens learners' sensory perceptions and experiences through computer-generated virtual environments [17]. In XR environments, educational resources can be shared extensively [18], and immersive learning experiences are facilitated through interactive elements like movement, gestures, and gaze [19].

The combination of XR and digital twins holds significant potential in ESD, as XR technology provides informative and intuitive interfaces while digital twins offer a wealth of data, forming the basis for creating digital content in XR interfaces [16].

3 Methods

We adhered to the ADDIE model, as devised by Dick and Carey [20], for the design and development of ESD content. This model encompasses Analysis, Design, Development, Implementation, and Evaluation stages. Initially, we conducted an analysis phase focusing on ESD content, targeting students and aligning it with the ESD-integrated curriculum standards across various subjects. During the design phase, we outlined the objectives of the ESD content and devised a process based on a data problem-solving model. In the subsequent development phase, we detailed the tools used for development, the structure of the ESD content, and elucidated how to incorporate digital twin data into the content. The digital twin technology used in this content was, strictly speaking, similar to a digital shadow that synchronizes real-world data to a virtual model, but digital twin technology also includes such unidirectional shadowing [7].

Finally, we executed an evaluation through expert review, assessing both the advantages and areas for improvement of the ESD content during the implementation and Evaluation phases.

4 Results

4.1 Analysis

The increase in greenhouse gas emissions, such as carbon dioxide, significantly impacts climate change, prompting the international community to declare 'Carbon Neutrality' and pursue policies to reduce carbon emissions [21]. The government of South Korea announced its '2050 Carbon Neutrality' initiative in 2020 and is enforcing 'Mandatory Ecological Transition Education' through amendments to the Basic Education Act. Environmental education requires more than simple conceptual knowledge transfer; it necessitates understanding the concept of Carbon Neutrality based on real-world phenomena and exploring practical approaches to implement it. Therefore, there is a need for attempts in content design that leverage digital twin technology for accessing real-world data and augmented reality technology for experiencing real phenomena in virtual environments. The ESD content developed for climate change education targeting high school students (K10-12) in South Korea. The ESD content was developed for climate change education targeting high school students (K1012) in South Korea. The embedded ESD aligns with the Social Studies, Common Science, and Earth Science curricula within Korean K-12 education (see Table 1).

Table 1. ESD content align with K-12 curriculum.

Subject	Related Chapter and Standards	Learning Elements
Social Studies	Investigate diverse efforts by the government, civil society, businesses, etc., to address environmental issues, and explore personal strategies for practical implementation	Nature and Human/ Environmental Problem Solving
Common Science	Understand various natural phenomena as outcomes of the circulation of substances and the flow of energy within the Earth system, exemplifying interactions between the lithosphere and hydrosphere	Earth System/ Materials Circulation
Earth Science	Distinguish and explain the causes of climate change into natural and anthropogenic factors. Discuss the environmental, social, and economic impacts of climate change resulting from human activities and explore scientific approaches to resolving climate change issues	Changes in the Atmosphere and Oceans/Climate Change

4.2 Design

Objectives. Students will be able to identify regions in South Korea where carbon neutrality is not effectively achieved, thereby gaining insights into the concept and practical strategies for achieving carbon neutrality through investigative activities utilizing data.

Learning Activities. This ESD content focuses on guiding learners to develop carbon-neutral measures through learning activities that analyze actual carbon data according to inquiry questions and match it with regional information in Korea. Table 2 shows the content's data-driven inquiry activities and specific learning activities.

Table 2. Learning activities of ESD content

Data-Driven inquiry activities	Activities of ESD Content
Identification the specific question to solve	Conceptual learning on carbon neutrality Motivation for learning and presentation inquiry questions: "What are the regions in South Korea where carbon neutrality is not effectively achieved, and what are the reasons?"
Decision what data to collect on	Exploring the content freely and selecting the carbon emissions and absorption data necessary for problem-solving Organizing selected data in accordance with criteria
Preparation, manipulation, visualization data modelling and validation of findings	Contrasting the carbon data analysis results with actual information and drawing tentative conclusions
Summarization and communication	Developing practical measures for achieving carbon neutrality in the region based on learned information and data

4.3 Development

Development Tools. The principal development tool employed was Unity, which was utilized for creating the user interface (UI) of the content and designing eXtended Reality (XR) interactions for learners. Carbon-neutral-related data was stored in Google Sheets, with the Unity Web Request feature utilized to dynamically extract stored data in real-time. Furthermore, the Photon feature was leveraged to facilitate remote or collaborative learning among multiple users, providing methods to communicate with web servers. Learners interacted with the content using Microsoft HoloLens2 headsets. Figure 1 illustrates the development tools utilized.

Structure of Content. The structure of the ESD content included data, a data map, and pop-up windows, as illustrated in Fig. 3. At the top of the pop-up window (labeled as "a" in Fig. 2), the inquiry question related to ESD was displayed. Upon selecting the desired data (labeled as "c" in Fig. 2), students could observe the chosen data visualized in real-time on the map (labeled as "d" in Fig. 2). The pop-up window (labeled as "g" in Fig. 2) provided detailed learning instructions and activities (labeled as "f" in Fig. 3). Moreover, to enhance learners' comprehension of the acquired data within a socio-cultural context, information about the characteristics of the region was presented through videos and text

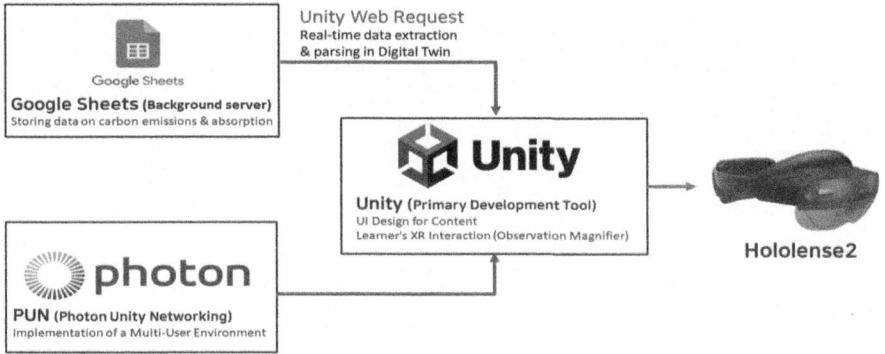

Fig. 1. Development tools.

(labeled as "d" in Fig. 2). Learners could hover over specific areas using a magnifying glass (labeled as "e" in Fig. 2) to access regional information (labeled as "b" in Fig. 2) within the pop-up window.

Utilization of Digital Twinning Data. The Digital Twin components integrated into the content comprised several key elements. Firstly, the content enabled the transmission of real-time data linked with Google Sheets. As depicted in Fig. 3, data on carbon emissions, carbon absorption, and the level of carbon neutrality for specific years across various regions of South Korea were retrieved from Google Sheets. The data utilized in this content adhered to the following formulas:

- Carbon Emissions ($tonCO^2eq$) = Regional total carbon emissions sum for each source (Electricity + Gas + Local Heating + Transportation)
- Carbon Absorption = Reginal total carbon absorption based on Forest Area
- Net Emissions = Carbon Emissions - Carbon Absorption ($\leq$ 0 means Carbon Neutrality)

Secondly, real-time visualization and monitoring of data on the virtual map were feasible. As depicted in Fig. 4, students had the ability to select and examine relevant data retrieved from Google Sheets, including metrics such as Electricity, Gas, Heating, Transportation, Carbon emissions, Carbon absorption, and Net emissions. This chosen data was visually depicted on the virtual map, with darker shades indicating higher numerical values.

Thirdly, students could derive crucial insights by analyzing and processing the monitored data. For instance, they could devise strategies to achieve carbon neutrality in their localities by understanding information such as regional carbon emission patterns and the current state of carbon neutrality through this content.

4.4 Implementation and Evaluation

This content underwent independent expert reviews to assess its suitability as an ESD content. Expert reviews involved analyzing a design by UX and K-12 education experts

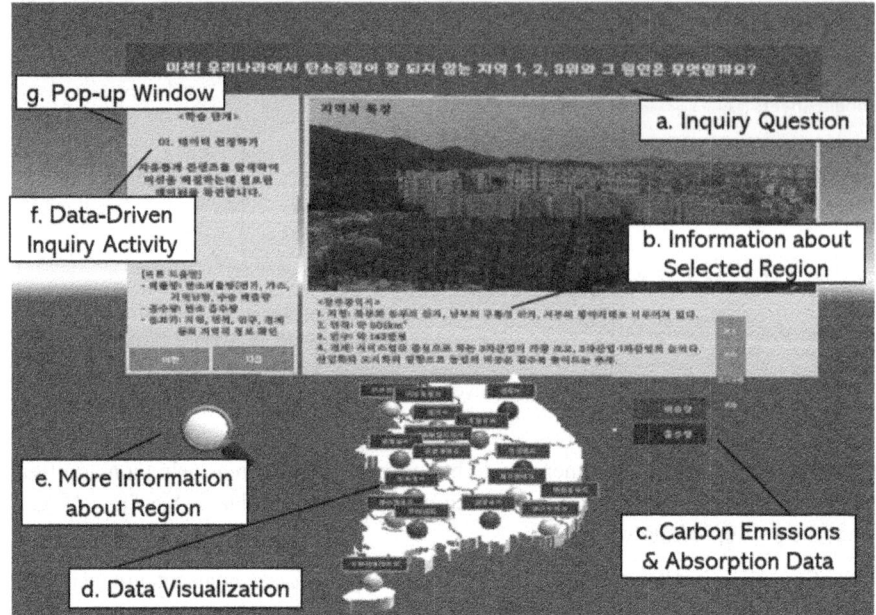

Fig. 2. Structure of content.

Index	location	electronic	gas	heat	transport	emission	absorption	mission-absorption
1	서울특별시	19,506,330	95,899	673,576	15,054,260	35,330,065	350,474	34,979,591
2	부산광역시	8,545,948	32,405	36,302	4,616,503	13,231,158	947,850	12,283,308
3	대구광역시	6,519,372	22,061	104,372	3,715,668	10,361,473	1,237,071	9,124,402
4	인천광역시	10,087,936	33,080	266,675	5,741,161	16,128,852	381,109	15,747,743
5	광주광역시	3,647,266	14,020	36,471	2,279,389	5,977,146	431,941	5,545,205
6	대전광역시	4,013,506	14,836	72,963	2,398,788	6,500,093	906,290	5,593,803
7	울산광역시	11,735,776	8,661	0	2,003,916	13,748,353	1,883,290	11,865,063
8	세종특별자치도	1,335,780	2,278	88,023	828,418	2,254,499	620,925	1,633,574
9	제주특별자치도	2,035,435	65,188	0	1,415,108	3,515,731	1,816,730	1,699,001
10	경기도	46,330,929	119,649	1,775,840	35,260,737	83,487,155	12,437,793	71,049,362
11	강원도	5,290,256	10,143	0	4,829,256	10,129,655	38,916,031	-28,786,376
12	충청북도	10,667,056	19,765	72,562	5,365,886	16,125,269	13,526,266	2,599,003
13	충청남도	15,957,886	38,094	41,996	7,120,279	23,158,255	8,654,792	14,503,463
14	전라북도	8,331,529	21,376	5,328	4,891,001	13,249,234	11,835,431	1,413,803
15	전라남도	10,067,416	18,105	14,254	4,973,957	15,073,732	15,106,834	-33,102
16	경상북도	16,540,254	100,351	11,909	8,187,801	24,840,315	35,136,783	-10,296,468
17	경상남도	13,629,742	26,573	71,158	7,335,279	21,082,752	20,260,859	801,893

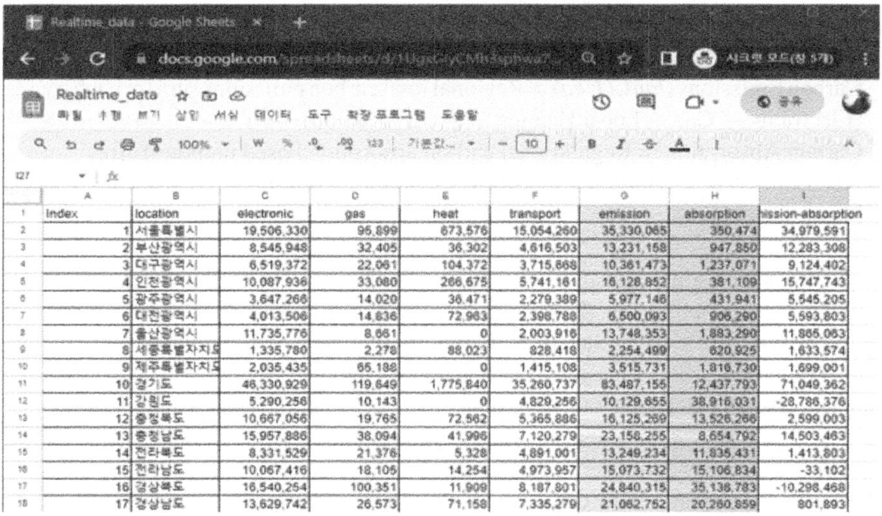

Fig. 3. Real-time data linked with Google Sheets.

to identify usability strengths and problems in the content. Table 3 shows the general characteristics of expert panels. The expert group were consisted with four panels, all of which were Korean. They had over 2 years of experience in UX design or research

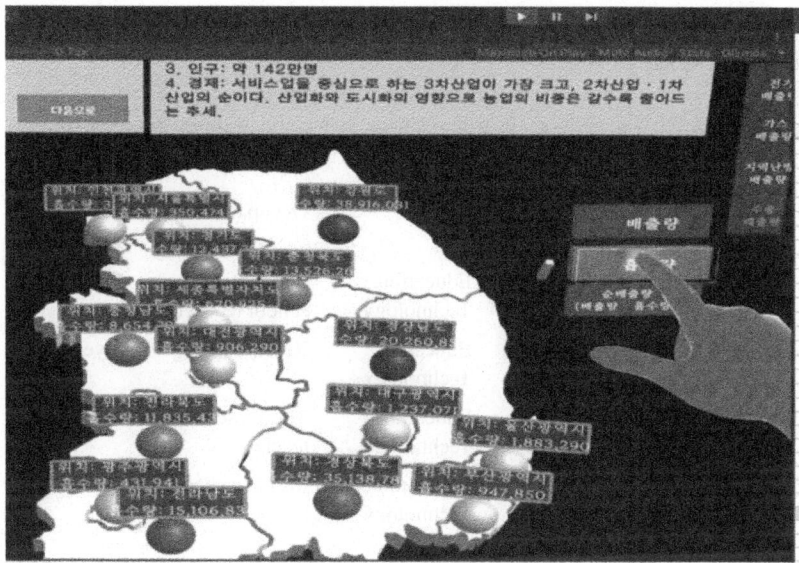

Fig. 4. Data visualization.

and over 10 years of experience in K-12 educational institutions. After personally experiencing the content, panels evaluated it independently based on the content quality certification evaluation criteria [14]. According to the panel's review, the strengths and improvements of the content are listed as follows.

Strengths

- Students can acquire data literacy and investigative skills through the experience of importing, processing, and analyzing real data in a virtual space.
- Students could implement real-world phenomena as virtual digital objects, thus promoting their immersion and agency.
- Students could grasp the close relationship between the geographical and industrial characteristics of South Korea's regions and carbon emissions.

Improvements

- It needs to be clarified which aspects of real-time application of real-world information are highlighted.
- Implementation of simulations using the latest data is required.
- It is necessary to ensure real-time integration with real-world information, including actual objects.
- It would be beneficial to validate the content provided in the study and expanding the learning content to cover recent social issues.
- Post-assignment content review, summarization, and clarification are needed.

- Intermediate learning steps should be incorporated to enable learners to contemplate solutions to the problems presented.

Table 3. Characteristics of expert panels

Panel	Gender	Degree	Major	Occupation	UX research experiences
A	Female	Ph.D.	Education Technology	Elementary school teacher	7 years
B	Male	Doctoral Candidate	Education Technology	Researcher	3 years
C	Female	Doctoral Candidate	Education Technology	Middle school teacher	3 years
D	Male	Master	Education Technology	Middle school teacher	2 years

5 Discussion

This study introduced a design and development process for XR-based content tailored for ESD, following the ADDIE model. In the Analysis phase, ESD was integrated into the standards and learning elements of Social Studies, Common Science, and Earth Science in the K-12 curriculum to facilitate effective teaching and learning. During the Design phase, the objectives of the ESD content were clarified. The content aimed to identify regions in South Korea where carbon neutrality was not effectively achieved and to hypothesize reasons related to industrial, demographic, and topographical features. Students engaged in investigating Net-zero regions using carbon data to solve the problem of certain regions. Expert reviews provided recommendations for improving the developed ESD content.

Design considerations were applied to both the design and development phases of the ESD content. Students were expected to conduct real-world data-based inquiry activities in an immersive environment implemented with XR and digital twin technologies. Carbon emissions and absorption data for each region of South Korea, sourced from the web, were imported into the XR environment. This data was visualized on a virtual map with varying colors, enabling students to immediately observe how Net-zero was realized. Additionally, multimedia presentations, including text and videos, provided information on the extent of achieving Net-zero. Students utilized this ESD content while wearing Hololens 2, an untethered mixed reality headset, and participated in problem-solving activities based on digital twinning data from real regions in South Korea.

6 Conclusion

This design and development study of the content holds several implications for immersive learning and education for sustainable development:

Firstly, integrating ESD content with digital twinning data can motivate students to enhance their problem-solving inquiry activities based on real data. This approach is closely linked to students' data literacy and self-regulated learning abilities.

Secondly, incorporating XR technology into ESD content increases student engagement and focus during learning. XR provides sensory-rich information and intensifies interaction with students, leading to a more immersive learning experience.

However, a limitation of this study is that usability testing of the developed ESD content with K-12 students was not conducted. Although expert reviews were obtained, whether their feedback would resonate with students remains uncertain. Therefore, in future research, we will validate the educational effectiveness of the content by integrating expert feedback with student testing.

Acknowledgments. This study was funded by Institute of Information & communications Technology Planning & Evaluation (IITP) grant funded by the Korea government (MSIT) (No. 2022-0-00137, XR User Interaction Evaluation and Employing Its Technology).

Disclosure of Interests. The authors have no competing interests to declare that are relevant to the content of this article.

References

1. UNESCO Homepage: https://www.unesco.org/en/education-sustainable-development/need-know (n.d.). Last accessed 29 Jan 2024
2. Zguir, M.F., Dubis, S., Koç, M.: Embedding education for sustainable development (ESD) and SDGs values in curriculum: a comparative review on Qatar, Singapore and New Zealand. J. Clean. Prod. **319**, 128534 (2021)
3. Min, Y.: KOFAC Issue paper 2022-7. Korea Foundation for the Advancement of Science & Creativity, Seoul (2023)
4. Riess, W., Martin, M., Mischo, C., Kotthoff, H.G., Waltner, E.M.: How can education for sustainable development (ESD) be effectively implemented in teaching and learning? an analysis of educational science recommendations of methods and procedures to promote ESD goals. Sustainability **14**(7), 3708 (2022)
5. National Research Council: A for K-12 Science Education: Practices, Crosscutting Concepts, and Core Ideas. National Academies Press, Washington DC (2012)
6. Prazian, M.V., Prykhodko, V.M.: High-quality education for better sustainability and resiliency. In: IOP Conference Series: Earth and Environmental Science, vol.1254, p. 012031. IOP Publishing (2023)
7. Kuehner, K.J., Scheer, R., Strassburger, S.: Digital twin: finding common ground–a meta-review. Procedia CIRP **104**, 1227–1232 (2021)
8. Laurie, R., Nonoyama-Tarumi, Y., Mckeown, R., Hopkins, C.: Contributions of education for sustainable development (ESD) to quality education: a synthesis of research. J. Educ. Sustain. Dev. **10**(2), 226–242 (2016)
9. Padmanabhan, J., Singh, S.P.: Integrated approach to ESD towards enhancing Knowledge on sustainable development. World Sci. News **26**, 50–60 (2016)
10. Hopkinson, P., James, P.: Practical pedagogy for embedding ESD in science, technology, engineering and mathematics curricula. Int. J. Sustain. High. Educ. **11**(4), 365–379 (2010)

11. Grieves, M., Vickers, J.: Digital twin: Mitigating unpredictable, undesirable emergent behavior in complex systems. In: Kahlen, F.-J., Flumerfelt, S., Alves, A. (eds.) Transdisciplinary perspectives on complex systems, pp. 85–113. Springer, Cham (2017). https://doi.org/10.1007/978-3-319-38756-7_4
12. Cimino, C., Negri, E., Fumagalli, L.: Review of digital twin applications in manufacturing. Comput. Ind. **113**, 103130 (2019)
13. Kartashova, L.A., Gurzhii, A.M., Zaichuk, V.O., Sorochan, T.M., Zhuravlev, F.M.: Digital twin of an educational institution: an innovative concept of blended learning. In: Proceedings of the 1st symposium on advances in educational technology (AET 2020), vol. 2, pp. 300–310. Scitepress (Science and Technology Publications), Setúbal (2020)
14. Korea Association of Consilience Education: The content quality certification evaluation criteria (n.d.). https://www.kaoce.org. Last accessed 29 Jan 2024
15. Bucchiarone, A.: Gamification and virtual reality for digital twins learning and training: architecture and challenges. Virtual Reality Intell. Hardware **4**(6), 471–486 (2022)
16. Madni, A.M., Madni, C.C., Lucero, S.D.: Leveraging digital twin technology in model-based systems engineering. Systems **7**(1), 1–13 (2019)
17. Reiners, D., Davahli, M.R., Karwowski, W., Cruz-Neira, C.: The combination of artificial intelligence and extended reality: a systematic review. Front. Virtual Reality **2**, 721933 (2021)
18. Bucea-Manea-Țoniș, R., Bucea-Manea-Țoniș, R., Simion, V.E., Ilic, D., Braicu, C., Manea, N.: Sustainability in higher education: the relationship between work-life balance and XR e-learning facilities. Sustainability **12**(14), 5872 (2020)
19. Coban, M., Bolat, Y.I., Goksu, I.: The potential of immersive virtual reality to enhance learning: a meta-analysis. Educ. Res. Rev. **36**, 100452 (2022)
20. Dick, W., Carey, L.M.: The systematic design of instruction. Scott, Foresman, Glenview, IL (1978)
21. Zhou, Y.: Worldwide carbon neutrality transition? Energy efficiency, renewable, carbon trading and advanced energy policies. Energy Rev. **2**(2), 100026 (2023)

Special Track 3: Literacy Equity and Immersive Learning

Outline of a Theoretical and Technological Approach for Reducing Inequalities in the Design of a 360 Synchronous Interactive Telepresence System

Andrea Garavaglia(✉) , Ilaria Terrenghi , and Maurizio De Nino

University of Milan, Via Festa del Perdono, 7, 20122 Milano, Italy
andrea.garavaglia@gmail.com

Abstract. The paper discusses the development of an immersive prototype for synchronous learning, emphasizing pedagogical and technological choices aimed at supporting equity and inclusion in an interdisciplinary perspective. Rooted in the pedagogical approach, it focuses on enhancing synchronous 360-degree video for interactive telepresence in higher education. Addressing the lack of immersive synchronous videoconferencing systems, the project aims to facilitate synchronous interaction between teachers, students, peers, and the learning environment, and to promote feedback loop. The prototype, called ISL360 (ImmerSyncLearn360), aims to promote equity and inclusion by creating student-centered post-pandemic educational pathways that are accessible to all. It ensures synchronous presence for those who experience various types of barriers to movement (physical, psychological, or otherwise) and enables everyone to reach spaces that would otherwise be inaccessible. Beginning with a review of the literature on equity and inclusion with immersive technologies, we will present some design choices, both pedagogical and technological.

Keywords: Telepresence · Immersive Education · Inclusive Technology

1 Introduction

This contribution was made to address the aspects of inclusivity that permeated the reasons that are leading our research group to implement and test an immersive telepresence device with adoption of 360 video. The research involves the development of a prototype technology solution, called ISL 360 (ImmerSyncLearn360), to test instructional design models in differentiated settings.

By proposing this research project, we want to achieve several objectives [1], one of which directly concerns the issue of equity and inclusion. Designing an innovative student centered "post covid" didactic paths, intentioned to develop skills in different subject areas and professional contexts, we aim at allowing the inclusion of students, trying to make immersive technology as inclusive as possible. This prototype could help those who cannot participate in face-to-face activities, such as those who have mobility impairments or disabilities, suffer from social anxieties, or have insufficient access to public transportation. The prototype is also functional for including the high number of students in learning environments that usually require little or fixed number access or that are not easily accessible by all.

In this project, teaching and educational needs drive technological development, and in a reciprocal logic, technological development brings suggestions and further guidance, as well as stimulating teachers' creativity. This aspect is crucial since the attempt is precisely to optimize the design process with a view to activating the best educational conditions obtained considering the maintenance of the best technological conditions.

2 Theoretical Framework: Inclusion and Equality in Immersive Education

Virtual Reality (VR) systems are learning environments that are increasingly used in educational settings, especially in higher education and universities. Although their use is still massive in the gaming and entertainment world, they are particularly functional in the world of education and training, especially because they can effectively provide immersive experiences and interactive learning environments that can be implemented in different aspects of our lives. Together with the very high potential that these systems bring to the world of education, VR has a crucial role to play in the field of human improvement from an ethical point of view. Taking into account some assumptions in this field, some of which claim that the development of recent technologies exacerbates inequalities [2], it is important to understand instead whether there may be features specific to VR or ways of using it in an inclusive way, or whether this can help to understand the phenomenon of inequalities and contribute to the development of inclusion and equality.

Indeed, there are several studies in the literature that argue the definition of immersive technologies as tools for equality. In particular, it has been pointed out that virtual reality can even be called a "force for equality" from several perspectives [3, 4].

In this article, the broad topic of immersive technologies as a medical tool that can support patients with serious physical and mental conditions will not be considered. This topic complains the use of VR for terminally ill or chronic pain patients, or those suffering from post-traumatic stress disorder, phantom limb syndrome, and phobias by offering them realistic simulations of adventures they cannot undertake in real life [5], which is also a recurring theme in the debate on equity and inclusion.

Instead, we will focus on the field of education by considering the factors that enable immersive technologies to break down barriers, both physical and social, and create interactive opportunities for students to learn, collaborate and empathize with others at a deeper level. We will discuss these issues by proposing arguments from a dual perspective, the first educational and the second technological.

From an educational point of view, one of the most functional perspectives for approaching the issue of inclusion and equity is that of Universal Design for Learning (UDL) [6]. The principles of this approach, which originated from a group of architects, product designers, engineers, and environmental design researchers working at the Center for Universal Design (CUD) at North Carolina State University, could be effectively applied to the overall design of instruction as well as immersive learning experiences [7].

According to Ciasullo [8], educational proposals in immersive format are very attractive and formative as privileged tools for Universal Design: they allow enormous modifiability and creation, offer multiple situations of representation, multiple opportunities for action and expression, and increase the possibilities for participation. When designers apply the principles of Universal Design, their products and environments can meet the needs of potential users with different characteristics.

Taking into account the principles of UDL [9], it is firstly crucial to provide a supportive learning environment using an inclusive, welcoming and encouraging approach: in addition to proposing a variety of online activities that facilitate and encourage all types of learning styles, it is important to foster an open environment where students can easily communicate with the teacher and peers and where all contact details are clearly shared (i.e. email and phone number). In addition, learning is most effective when it is multimodal and when students have multiple ways to access and interact with the material. For this reason, it is a good idea for the instructor to not only allow for active experimentation in addition to lecture, but also to use different teaching strategies (such as discussion, debate, think-pair-share) and mediators (verbal and visual). Exercises and final quizzes are also essential, as long as they provide timely and qualitative feedback to the student.

A second very interesting point of analysis is suggested by the Center for Information Technology and Innovative Foundations. In a recent report on the potential uses of augmented reality and virtual reality for equity [10], it shows how immersive technologies can support equity and inclusion if they are designed with these goals in mind. This first suggestion explains how, in order to design truly inclusive technologies, it is first essential to work on inclusive choices already in the design phase: an immersive technology can only be characterized as inclusive if it is conceived and designed by a qualified and heterogeneous team. In this way, VR solutions for learning can serve as a tool to combat implicit bias, improve access to opportunities, and create new channels for communication and collaboration across distance.

There are two other concepts that are particularly functional to enrich the discussion of these issues. The first is the idea that immersive technologies can make environments and experiences available to people who would otherwise be unable to access them because of geographic distance or physical/mental barriers. Efforts to create more inclusive spaces and learning environments are often constrained by physical limitations, from limited classroom capacity to proximity to public transportation. Individuals with mobility or other disabilities, social anxieties, or inadequate access to public transportation (or commuters who would have to travel long distances) may be at a disadvantage when physical presence is required. In these cases, immersive technology is uniquely positioned to overcome the limitations of physical space to create more accessible and equitable experiences. In addition, some evidence highlights access to previously inaccessible environments as a key potential benefit of the technology [11].

A second consideration of particular importance relates to the ability of immersive education to enhance person-to-person interactions across locations [11]. Immersive learning environments can ensure interactions between users when they occur in a synchronous mode. Multi-user experiences allow otherwise isolated users to form communities and support systems across the boundaries of physical distance. In this way, learning can take place in a shared environment where peers can observe, discuss, and work as if they were "really there," physically present in a virtual space [12], providing a more engaging, interactive, and individualized experience than similar audiovisual technologies.

Finally, from a purely pedagogical perspective, it is interesting to note the large body of research on how immersive experiences can be an important tool for raising awareness of issues of inclusion and equality. Some research suggests that the immersive environment can be effectively used to train the ability to evaluate unfair situations [13] or to foster compassion and empathy for the suffering of others [14, 15]. Other research instead focuses on using immersion to expose users to discriminatory firsthand experiences of physical, mental, class, race, and gender discrimination [16]. Although there is some evidence to support the negative effects of repeated exposure, such as a condition called secondary traumatization or "compassion fatigue" [17], research has shown that individuals feel a sense of embodiment with their virtual representation (avatar) in VR, whether or not the avatar reflects their physical appearance [18]. This significantly reduces the cognitive distance between the individual and the perceived "other," which is a key goal of empathy interventions.

The second key to discussing the issue of equity in immersive worlds, as we anticipated above, is related to the technological dimension.

To discuss this second part, it is functional to take up some principles of UDL, those that refer to the technical dimension of learning environments. We will then conclude with 3 additional considerations.

Regarding the UDL principles, it can be argued that some of them are reminiscent of technological implementations. The principle "Straightforward and consistent" suggests designing tools that are intuitive, avoiding unnecessary complexity or distraction, and ensuring that tests and quizzes relate directly to information covered in class or required material. The principle of "minimize unnecessary physical effort or requirements" suggests that the immersive learning situation should be accessible and minimize the amount of clicking, scrolling, or searching for information. In addition, it might be effective to use library online or WebCT features for reading materials that can be accessed from anywhere. Following the "Be Explicitly Presented and Readily Perceived" principle, the designer must carefully choose fonts, provide a choice of file formats, and ensure that Web pages coded in HTML use tags for graphics. Finally, according to the "Be Accessible and Fair" principle, it is very effective to arrange some graphic elements that can help the student to focus his attention on a specific point in the environment, and to place material such as organizers, lecture outlines, and key points [7].

There is also a large body of research discussing how the use of avatars in immersive experience situations can impact issues of equity and inclusion [3]. Perception-limiting technologies that also remove certain details and information about the user, the environment, and the people around the user can also address inequality by removing the identifying factors that often underlie racial, gender, and other biases, especially when these technologies are other-oriented [19].

The study by Creed et al. [19], which focuses primarily on disabilities, is very interesting as it discusses the key barriers to the use of AR/VR technologies for users with physical, visual, and hearing impairments. In summary, the research highlights the following considerations:

- For users with hearing impairments: There is currently a lack of adaptable AR/VR devices that are compatible with existing assistive technologies and tools used by users with hearing impairments. Results showed a lack of clarity in sounds and instructions in audio format, and difficulty in locating and navigating environments (in many immersive environments, sound sources are unknown or unclear). In terms of collaboration and interaction with peers during an immersive experience, the lack of synchronization in conversations and poor rendering of avatars that do not support lip reading are highlighted.
- for users with visual impairments: Creed et al. [20] first explain the lack of standardization, guidelines and protocols for the development of consumer products for users with visual impairments. In particular, the integration of audio description for environmental description, navigation, and interaction, voice activation, and accessible menus could be critical to avoid sensory and/or information overload.
- For users with physical impairments: The most recurring theme concerns the challenges of using AR/VR headsets and controllers that require users to move limbs with great dexterity and speed. Thinking about software usability, it is necessary to consider involuntary movements and fatigue (physical, mental, temporal), as well as the risks associated with losing track of physicality, balance, and perception of limbs in fully immersive environments. When thinking about hardware usability, it is necessary to consider primarily the challenges associated with the current lack of AR/VR support on wearable devices, navigating environments, menus, and buttons during (and before) AR/VR use.

It is undoubtedly important to continue to think about the issue of accessibility of technologies, ensuring that they become increasingly more user friendly, including for those who wear glasses, require hands-free controls, or need to use AR/VR in small spaces or while seated, while also making the technology more accessible to people with disabilities [21].

Finally, to support inclusion, it is important to design immersive learning experiences that can be enjoyed from a variety of devices, whether through desktops or head-mounted displays (HMDs), and allow students to experience learning with the tool they have at their disposal. According to some authors [22], a "good inequality" could be built in this way: one way to manage this is simply to familiarize students with each other's systems, to reduce misunderstandings about what the different systems can and cannot do, and perhaps even to take advantage of the system differences and distribute the work in a way that makes better use of the two or more VR systems.

3 The ISL360 Solution for Improve Equality

This research aims to test ways to enhance distance education through the adoption of 360-degree synchronous video streams for an interactive telepresence learning environment. The solution being developed, called ISL360 (ImmerSyncLearn360), is based on the synchronous distance education paradigm and considers the challenge of developing applications driven by educational needs [23] with a view to reducing inequalities.

The experimentation aims to reduce two limitations in particular: the first limitation concerns the difficulty of involving all students in the teaching and learning process [24] at all levels, regardless of the limitations of the environment or the learners' deficits, and of creating the right conditions for them to actively participate in all educational phases [25–27].

A second limitation concerns the complexity for teachers to propose situated learning experiences that have a clear contextual meaning and that support students not only in the theoretical acquisition of learning, but also in concrete involvement in learning situations.

Much importance, moreover, is placed on the interaction between teacher and learner, which in fact can take place effectively mainly in synchrony, a condition that poses greater guarantees to the effectiveness of the processes of regulating teaching action and aligning the teaching and learning process [23]. The interaction must also encourage the activation of two-way feedback [28], so as to engage students and improve their engagement and motivation.

3.1 Educational Choices for Reducing Inequalities

The aspects of educational inclusion that guide the development of the ISL360 solution relate in particular to a few aspects that are considered fundamental.

The first is the ability to overcome physical and social barriers to promote opportunities for interactive situational learning with the teacher and other students in environments that were previously inaccessible or very difficult to access.

On the one hand, the inclusion of environments is achieved by allowing students with disabilities, special deficits, or other issues that do not allow full access to the environment to participate in activities that are delivered within the actual physical environment by the teacher himself.

The study by Creed et al. [20] confirms and supports the importance of this aspect, making appropriate distinctions between physical, visual and auditory disabilities. Students with physical-motor disabilities should be given the opportunity to access using the compensatory devices and aids they already use on a daily basis. For visual and hearing disabilities, the discussion should be somewhat different in that, depending on the possibilities offered by technology (e.g., real-time captioning), the teacher should be alert to the way they are conducted, possibly introducing some ad hoc instructional steps to fully include students. In these cases, it is suggested that the activity be designed and carried out together with a specialist who has in-depth knowledge of the students or their disabilities.

On the other hand, inclusion is achieved by giving a large number of students access to educational activities that are delivered in settings where, for various reasons, access is limited to a very small number of people. These settings include laboratories with limited access, operating rooms, or outdoor spaces that are difficult to access, such as rural or mountainous areas.

As anticipated above, in these cases immersive technology can overcome the limitations of physical space to create more accessible and equitable experiences. This is a set of conditions addressed by Wong and Gillis [11], given the significant benefits that can be generated by the adoption of technologies that enhance access and inclusion.

A second aspect that receives strong attention concerns the interaction between teachers and students in the shared environment that is achieved by the solution being tested. The analysis of factors that can enhance and improve interactions between individuals [9] is particularly concerned with the conditions under which teachers and learners experience instruction in different contexts, taking into account the different educational goals. In terms of inclusiveness, the introduction of pointer tools and drawing lines or arrows on the screen by the teacher and students allows for enriching interaction phases by making communication intentions and explication of concepts clearer by taking advantage of tools that we generally do not have available to us in the real, physical setting (see the "Pointer" and "Line Drawing" tools in Sect. 3.2).

In this way, learning can take place in a shared environment where peers can observe, discuss, and work as if they were "really there," physically present in a virtual space [12], providing a more immersive, interactive, and personalized experience than similar audiovisual technologies.

In terms of the principles of UDL [9], we need to take a step back and try to understand which learning styles are preferred depending on the physical environments from which the activity is delivered and, most importantly, the educational and training purpose. When it comes to multimodality, it is important that the online environment is accessible both with HMD and on the desktop side, just as the material used during the synchronous activity must also be made available in the asynchronous environments (eg. LMS), where students generally have access to download files in different formats. If the ISL360 application does not allow for the integration of material in an accessible format, it is important that it is still present in the asynchronous learning environment so that students can still enjoy it in an alternative mode.

Multimodality should therefore not necessarily be considered at the level of individual technologies, but in the totality of the resources used during the learning journey. A more holistic view is needed, especially given the fact that one device alone cannot solve all problems, but it is at the level of instructional design that all aspects need to be considered. Multimodality, in fact, must be the result of a 360-degree attention, taking into account all educational phases, environments and tools used by teachers and students throughout. Therefore, following Dick [10], it is important that all decisions are made during the entire instructional design.

3.2 Technological Choices for Reducing Inequalities

Technology can be a powerful tool for improving education, teaching and learning, but it can also create or widen digital inequalities if it is not used equitably and inclusively. Therefore, technological choices should be guided by the principles of human rights, social justice and sustainable development.

Distance teaching and extended reality (XR) are two technological choices that have the potential to reduce inequalities in education, teaching and learning by widening access, improving quality and promoting inclusion. However, they also pose some challenges and risks that need to be addressed.

Distance learning is a mode of education that uses various technologies, such as online platforms or mobile phones, to deliver instruction and learning materials to learners who are physically separated from teachers and peers. Distance learning can increase access to education for learners who face barriers such as geographical distance, disability, conflict or health issues, and can also offer greater flexibility, personalization and collaboration for learners and teachers. However, distance learning also requires adequate infrastructure, devices and skills, which can create digital divides and inequalities among learners if its usability is too complex.

Extended Reality (XR) encompasses various technologies that combine or create digital and physical environments. XR includes: VR (virtual reality), AR (augmented reality), and MR (mixed reality), as well as other immersive technologies such as VR360 [29].

XR is a technology that can increase learner engagement, motivation, and retention, as well as provide opportunities for learners to experience different cultures, perspectives, and scenarios, which can foster intercultural competence, empathy, and critical thinking. However, XR also requires high-end equipment, Internet connectivity, and technical support, which can limit its availability and affordability for many learners, especially in resource-poor settings. In some cases, XR can also cause some negative effects, such as motion sickness, disorientation, and isolation, which can affect learners' well-being and performance.

XR and distance learning are therefore technological choices that can have both positive and negative impacts on reducing inequalities in education, teaching and learning. To maximize their benefits and minimize their risks, they need to be carefully designed, implemented, and evaluated, taking into account the needs, preferences, and contexts of learners and teachers.

VR, AR, MR, and VR360 are different types of technologies that can be used for distance learning, but they have different advantages and disadvantages. Here is a quick comparison:

- VR (Virtual Reality) creates a fully immersive and interactive digital environment that blocks out the real world. VR requires a headset and can provide a realistic and engaging learning experience, but it can also be expensive, isolating, and can cause motion sickness.
- Augmented Reality (AR) [29] adds digital elements to the real world, such as images, sounds, or text that can be viewed through a smartphone, tablet, or glasses. AR can enhance the real world with useful information, but it can also be distracting, intrusive, and device-dependent.
- MR (Mixed Reality) combines VR and AR, allowing physical and virtual elements to interact. MR typically requires a headset and can create a hybrid and dynamic learning environment, but it can also be complex and can create inequality because the learning environment is different for different learners,

- VR360 (Virtual Reality 360) is a technology that allows users to view and interact with 360-degree videos or images, which can create immersive and realistic experiences while maintaining comfort [30]. VR360 can be accessed through the web, a smartphone or a headset, and it can be interactive or passive, with high or low quality.

These are some of the main differences between VR, AR, MR and VR360 technologies for use in distance learning, but they are not the only ones. Each technology has its own strengths and weaknesses, and the best choice depends on the learning objectives, content, context, and budget.

Based on these issues and the objective of the research, we decided to use VR360 technology because it can be used with different levels of immersion and with different devices, and is less expensive. Each learner can choose what is best for them and their condition.

With these basic guidelines, the ISL360 architecture was defined as shown in Fig. 1 [1].

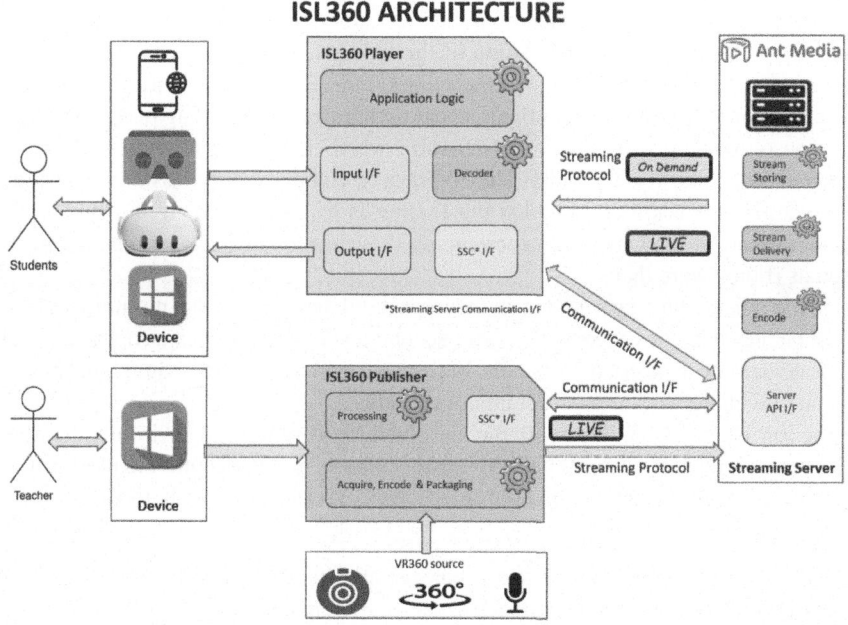

Fig. 1. ISL360 Architecture with the three main components of the platform: ISL360 Publisher, ISL360 Player and Streaming Server.

In this architecture, in addition to the VR360 camera and the device used by the teacher and student, there are three main components: ISL360 Player, ISL360 Publisher, and Streaming Server.

The Publisher component is a Windows-based PC application that allows the instructor to select the course and create a new live session (Fig. 2). Once the live session is created, the instructor has a set of tools (see later) that provide the ability to create a truly immersive and interactive lesson.

Fig. 2. On the left the course selection and on the right the live lesson creation or selection.

The player component can be used on either a Windows-based PC or a mobile phone, cardboard or HMD such as Meta Quest3 or compatible. This wide choice of devices reduces technological and economic unavailability and allows you to use the device you feel most comfortable with, thereby increasing comfort and well-being.

For distance learning, the perceptual aspects of user experience and interaction will be the fundamental guiding elements in the design and implementation of the ISL360 platform. In this context, the resolution of the video stream (number of megapixels of each frame) and the latency are extremely important. For these reasons, the streaming server component must allow continuous and uninterrupted streaming of VR 360 video with a resolution of at least 4k (3840x2160), which is the minimum resolution that guarantees adequate visual quality. The 360-degree video makes it possible to faithfully reproduce the environment in which the teacher is lecturing, making the student feel an integral part of the class and experiencing the learning environment chosen for the lesson as if they were there.

On the other hand, experiments on the impact of latency show that motion-to-photon (MTP) latency becomes acceptable at sub-second levels. Therefore, appropriate streaming strategies must be used to handle high-resolution video and reduce all latencies associated with network infrastructure components.

The low latency, combined with the use of a three-dimensional environment, allows for real-time interaction using specially designed tools integrated into the platform.

Some of the tools that can be used by teachers and students within the platform are described below:

- Chat: audio and text chat with text-to-speech and speech-to-text features that can be activated in case of limitations in hand use or writing ability.
- Spatial Sound: This is a work-in-progress whose goal is to evaluate and integrate the use of an ambisonic microphone to record a 360-degree audio field to provide a true audio perception that can help with some uneven conditions. This approach is being studied because it is difficult to use as it records an excessive amount of spatial information and includes a much larger amount of ambient noise and reverberation than the mono microphone.
- Pointer: a tool for pointing to objects in the displayed scene, thanks to the use of a three-dimensional arrow (Fig. 3) that can be placed on any point of the scene; the pointer can be added to the scene by both the teacher and the student and is visible to everyone, but can be removed only by the teacher or the owner.

- Line Drawing: a system for drawing lines of different thickness, following the outline of what is observed or writing in the air as if everything were a virtual blackboard (Fig. 3).
- Zoom: a magnifying glass that allows you to enlarge an area of the displayed screen or to move your point of view closer to a point of interest. This tool is very useful if you have poor eyesight or a loss of concentration when you are distracted by elements in your environment.
- Captioning: Using a speech recognition system and a real-time cloud-based translation service, everything explained during the lesson is recognized, translated into the desired language and displayed at the bottom of the HMD screen or display. This mechanism makes it possible to improve learning for those with both hearing and language disabilities.

Other tools can only be used by the teacher, such as

- 3D Tools: a tool that allows you to upload 3D models (of different formats) and insert and place them within the lesson set (Fig. 3), with the ability to move, rotate, resize, hide and remove the object at any time; showing and manipulating the lesson object increases the learning rate and attracts the attention of even easily distracted students.
- Teleport: An interesting tool that allows you to upload a still image or VR360 video and use this content as a new lesson setting. All connected students will be teleported into this new environment, giving them the ability to change settings in less than a second while staying in the same place, depending on the topic of the lesson.
- PiP: Picture in Picture, a feature that allows images or videos to be viewed in a three-dimensional window positioned by the teacher at the desired location, so that additional multimedia content can be used to promote inclusion and reduce the comprehension gap.

Fig. 3. Pointer, Line Drawing and 3D tools (the ancient amphora).

4 Conclusions

The presented project, whose inclusive potential was discussed, has three main phases: 1) preliminary analysis of application requirements; 2) development of the technology platform; and 3) pilot study.

The first two parts have been substantially completed.

During the design, a preliminary risk analysis was performed on the possibility of technical problems that could lead to inadequate implementation of the solution. Some of the risks highlighted were: risks related to insufficient bandwidth resources, complexity of developing an easy-to-use user interface for students, complexity of interactions, and audio-video synchronization.

During the development of the prototype, all of the preliminarily identified risks were mitigated, although other unforeseen problems emerged, such as the implementation of two-way multichannel audio and the complexity of implementing educational activities with advanced technologies. The first of these points was overcome by using a lecture hall approach, while the second can be circumvented by providing video tutorials or preset materials (e.g., 360 videos and ready-to-use 3D models).

The third phase, the start of which is imminent, involves the pilot study of a small sample consisting of 6 teaching activities with different characteristics and different disciplinary objects, mostly from laboratory activities of universities. The lab activities from the universities will be selected and assigned to experimental and control groups with about 8–10 participating students each. Among which there will be at least one student with classroom accessibility problems. Each lab session will be videotaped. At the end of each session, participating students will be asked to fill out a survey on the quality of teaching interaction and feedback received. At the end of the experimental sessions, a focus group will be offered to the teachers involved to obtain useful information about the technological solution and validation of the paradigm.

In conclusion, the technological solution was created taking into account the inclusion of those students who cannot access the real environment in which teaching activities are transmitted and delivered. The present work has addressed from both educational and technological perspectives the ways of this inclusion, taking into account the specificities of different students.

The technological results obtained so far are a solid basis for the continuation of the project and the implementation of the pilot study.

Acknowledgments. This research was funded by the University of Milan under the Project "Piano di sviluppo di ricerca – Grandi Sfide di Ateneo – Linea 6" and by the Department of Philosophy "Piero Martinetti" of the University of Milan under the Project "Departments of Excellence 2023–2027".

Attributions. The article is the result of the authors' comparisons and reflections, who shared the entire structure. According to the author declaration system CRediT: Andrea Garavaglia: Conceptualization, methodology, writing original draft & review, visualization (par. 1, 3.1, 4). Ilaria Terrenghi: writing original draft & review, Investigation (par. 2). Maurizio De Nino: Software, writing original draft & review (par. 3.2, 4).

References

1. Garavaglia, A., Terrenghi, I., De Nino, M.: Development of a first draft prototype of 360 Synchronous interactive telepresence. In: Minerva, T., De Santis, A. (eds.) Innovating Teaching & Learning. Inclusion and Wellbeing for the Data Society, pp. 76–85. Isyde 2023 Conference Proceedigns (2024)
2. Suvalescu, J.: How far could gene editing go? https://www.bbc.co.uk/sounds/play/w3ct3j6s. Last accessed 14 Feb 2024
3. Franks, M.A.: The desert of the unreal: Inequality in virtual and augmented reality. UCDL Rev. **51**, 499 (2017)
4. Dowell, S., et al.: Principles of justice, equity, diversity, and inclusion in health care distance simulation education: consensus building via the nominal group technique. Acad. Med. **98**(12), 1443–1450 (2023)
5. Matchar, E.: Instead of Painkillers, Some Doctors Are Prescribing Virtual Reality, SMITHSONIAN (2016). http://www.smithsonianmag.com/innovation/instead-painkillers-some-doctors-are-prescribing-virtual-reality-180959866
6. Burgstahler, S.: Universal Design of Instruction (UDI): Definition, Principles, Guidelines, and Examples. Do-It. ERIC Number: ED506547 (2009)
7. Rutherfoord, R.H., Rutherfoord, J.K.: Universal instructional design for learning how to apply in a virtual world. In: Proceedings of the 8th ACM SIGITE Conference on Information Technology Education, pp. 141–146 (2007)
8. Ciasullo, A.: Universal design for learning: the relationship between subjective simulation, virtual environments, and inclusive education. Res. Educ. Media **10**(1), 42–48 (2018)
9. Burgstahler, S.E., Cory, R.C.: Universal Design in Higher Education: From Principles to Practice. Education Press, Harvard (2010)
10. Dick, E.: Current and potential uses of AR/VR for equity and inclusion. Information Technology and Innovation Foundation (2021). https://itif.org/publications/2021/06/01/current-and-potential-uses-arvr-equity-and-inclusion/
11. Wong, A., Gillis, H., Peck, B.: VR accessibility: Survey for people with disabilities. (2017). https://www.ben-peck.com/papers/VR_Accessibility_Survey.pdf
12. Witmer, B.G., Singer, M.J.: Measuring presence in virtual environments: a presence questionnaire. Presence **7**(3), 225–240 (1998). https://doi.org/10.1162/105474698565686
13. Chen, J.A., Tutwiler, M.S., Jackson, J.F.: Mixed-reality simulations to build capacity for advocating for diversity, equity, and inclusion in the geosciences. J. Diversity Higher Educ. **14**(4), 557 (2021)
14. Zahiu, A., Mihailov, E., Earp, B.D., Francis, K.B., Savulescu, J.: Empathy training through virtual reality: moral enhancement with the freedom to fall? Ethics Inf. Technol. **25**(4), 50 (2023)
15. Jason, G.: Virtual Reality Is the Global Empathy Machine, MEDIUM (2017). https://medium.com/singularityu/virtual-reality-is-the-global-empathymachine-283b1ee4192
16. Georgiadou, A.: Equality inclusion and diversity through virtual reality. In: Park, S.H., Gonzalez-Perez, M.A., Floriani, D.E. (eds.) The Palgrave Handbook of Corporate Sustainability in the Digital Era, pp. 181–193. Springer, Cham (2021). https://doi.org/10.1007/978-3-030-42412-1_10
17. Bloom, P.: It's Ridiculous to Use Virtual Reality to Empathize with Refugees, ATLANTIC (2017), https://www.theatlantic.com/technology/archive/2017/02/virtual-reality-wont-make-you-more-empathetic/515511
18. Bertrand, P., Guegan, J., Robieux, L., McCall, C.A., Zenasni, F.: Learning empathy through virtual reality: multiple strategies for training empathy-related abilities using body ownership illusions in embodied virtual reality. Front. Robot. AI **5**, 26 (2018). https://doi.org/10.3389/frobt.2018.00026

19. Kuchera, B.: Being Someone Else: How Virtual Reality Is Allowing Men and Women to Swap Bodies, POLYGON (2014). https://www.polygon.com/2014/3/4/5423330/oculus-rift-vr-gender-swap-girl-mirror-look
20. Creed, C., Al-Kalbani, M., Theil, A.: Inclusive AR/VR: accessibility barriers for immersive technologies. Univ. Access Inf. Soc. (2023). https://doi.org/10.1007/s10209-023-00969-0
21. Mott, M., Cutrell, E., Franco, M.G., Holz, C., Ofek, E., Stoakley, R., Morris, M.R.: Accessible by design: An opportunity for virtual reality. In 2019 IEEE International Symposium on Mixed and Augmented Reality Adjunct (ISMAR-Adjunct), pp. 451–454. IEEE (2019)
22. Spante, M., Axelsson, A.S., Schroeder, R.: The good inequality: Supporting group-work in shared virtual environments. In: Schroeder, R., Axelsson, A. (eds.) Avatars at Work and Play: Collaboration and Interaction in Shared Virtual Environments, pp. 151–166. Springer Netherlands, Dordrecht (2006)
23. Laurillard, D.: Teaching as a Design Science. Building Pedagogical Patterns for Learning and Technology. Routledge, London (2012)
24. Bucholz, J.L., Sheffler, J.L.: Creating a warm and inclusive classroom environment: planning for all children to feel welcome. Electro. J. Inclusive Educ. **2**(4) (2009)
25. Garavaglia, A., Terrenghi, I.: Analisi dell'esperienza formativa universitaria prima e dopo la pandemia: Il caso di un corso di laurea triennale in area umanistica. In: Apprendere con le tecnologie tra presenza e distanza. Brescia: Scholé, Brescia (2022)
26. Carenzio, A., Ferrari, S.: Situazioni didattiche non standard. In: Rivoltella, P.C. (a cura di), Apprendere a distanza. Teorie e metodi, pp. 68–75. Raffaello Cortina Editore, Milano (2021)
27. Trentin, G.: Tecnologie e inclusione: come fare di necessità virtù. In Dal mito di Theuth alla DaD. Per una storia della formazione a distanza. In: Rivoltella, P.C., Rossi, G. (a cura di), Tecnologie per l'educazione, pp. 57–68. Pearson, Italia Milano (2019)
28. Hattie, J., Timperley, H.: The power of feedback. Rev. Educ. Res. **77**(1), 81–112 (2007). https://doi.org/10.3102/003465430298487
29. Vertucci, R., D'Onofrio, S., Ricciardi, S., De Nino, M.: History of augmented reality. In: Nee, A.Y.C., Ong, S.K. (eds.) Springer Handbook of Augmented Reality, pp. 35–50. Springer International Publishing, Cham (2023). https://doi.org/10.1007/978-3-030-67822-7_2
30. Popolo, V., Di Nardo, M., De Nino, M., Di Leo, R., De Cristofaro, A.: Wellbeing and Smart Working in the new industry era. XXV Summer School "Francesco Turco" – Industrial Systems Engineering (2020)

Mind Perception of Avatars: A Focus Group Study

Komala Mazerant[1](✉), Alexander P. Schouten[2], Sanne B. T. Smit[1], Zeph M. C. van Berlo[3], and Lotte M. Willemsen[1]

[1] Rotterdam University of Applied Sciences, Wijnhaven 99, 3011 WN Rotterdam, The Netherlands
dubok@hr.nl
[2] Department of Communication and Cognition, Tilburg University, PO. Box 90153, 5000 LE Tilburg, The Netherlands
[3] Amsterdam School of Communication Research, University of Amsterdam, Nieuwe Achtergracht 166, 1018 WV Amsterdam, The Netherlands

Abstract. Virtual Reality (VR) is increasingly used for collaborative learning in education. To navigate these virtual learning environments, people use avatars. Understanding how people perceive avatars, and treat them humanly, is crucial for designing inclusive virtual learning environments. This study examines the ways in which students attribute and detract mental states to avatars based on their characteristics, through the process of mind perception. To do so, six focus groups were conducted, during which students designed avatars that varied on two dimensions of mind perception: (1) agency or (2) experience. This was followed by group discussions on the characteristics of these avatars associated with agency and experience. Avatars were attributed low experience and agency, when designed as nonhuman entities (e.g., robots or animals), depicted with incomplete bodies, unrealistic appearances, negative appearances, and suggested side character roles. Conversely, avatars attributed with high experience and agency typically showcased human-like figures with unique personal styles, realistic representations, positive appearances, and convey a strong sense of individual identity and storyline centrality. This implies that VR developers, teachers and educationalists should take these characteristics into account to design inclusive collaborative learning environments.

Keywords: Avatars · Mind Perception · Agency · Experience · Collaborative Learning

1 Introduction

In education, the use of virtual reality (VR) for collaborative learning is increasing, fueled by the forced transition to online education during the COVID-19 pandemic [1]. Applications vary from virtual onboarding programs (e.g., www.rbs-hubs.nl), training for soft skills such as communication, empathy, and cooperation (e.g., https://thesimulationcrew.nl/), to holographic teachers in the classroom [2]. VR has been shown to increase engagement [3], spatial learning [4], and experiential learning [5]. As such, VR can be a valuable means of facilitating and enhancing collaborative learning [6].

To navigate these virtual learning environments, people use avatars [7]. These are visual representations of individuals used to represent their identity and to enable interactions [8]. An avatar serves as the representation of an online user's physical self, enabling them to engage in the activities of the virtual world by crafting, personalizing and manipulating the 'self' [9]. Avatars are formed through a combination of conscious personal choices and the technological affordances of virtual worlds. Apart from customizable features like hair color, clothing and body type, virtual environments provide users a wide range of options to represent themselves, ranging from more to less realistic avatars (e.g., abstract characters such as a cartoon or block-like figure versus photorealistic characters), as well as options that allow users to represent themselves as entities beyond human appearance [10]. Examples include the choice to be represented by non-human forms such as an animal, a robot, or fantasy figure. As such, digital spaces afford the experimentation of completely new identities [11].

Being represented by an avatar can potentially dehumanize the person behind the avatar, leading to adverse effects on communication and collaboration. Such negative downstream consequences are likely to arise, when people project non-human characteristics of the avatar onto the avatar owner. Initial evidence for such a process is provided in a recent study by Schouten and colleagues [12]. The study shows that when a person communicates through a non-human avatar, such as a telepresence robot, their communication partner has been shown to project more robot-like characteristics onto that person [12]. Broader research on dehumanization also shows that when human attributes are detracted and individuals are reduced to objects, they are denied humanness [13]. Dehumanization has negative consequences, such as reduced pro-social behavior (e.g., helping others) and increased anti-social behavior (e.g., aggression) (for an overview [14]. Therefore, reducing dehumanization is pivotal for designing an inclusive virtual learning environment [15].

How and why certain entities are perceived as more or less human is explained by mind perception theory. This theoretical framework explains how people attribute mental states and capacities, including emotions, intentions, desires, knowledge, and the ability to think and feel, to others—whether they are real people, fictional characters, or digital entities like avatars [16]. These attributes can be categorized along two dimensions: experience and agency. Experience is defined as "the perceived capacity for sensation and feelings" [17]. This dimension encompasses a broad spectrum of states that enables one to feel or sense, including the ability to experience bodily sensations like hunger and pain but also more complex emotional states such as pleasure and consciousness. Agency is defined as the perceived capacity for "intentional action" [18]. This includes a wide range of qualities that enables one to act and intend, like self-control, judgment, moral reflection and the ability to communicate and remember.

According to mind perception theory, people can perceive agency and experience in human but also non-human entities, albeit with noticeable variations in the extent of agency and experience ascribed. Some entities are ascribed little agency and experience (e.g., a dead person), others little agency but high levels of experience (e.g., certain animals such as chimpanzees and pets), high agency but little experience (e.g., supernatural entities with power, such as God), or high scores on both agency and experience (e.g., an adult human [16]). The conclusion of this research is that people need to attribute both agency and experience for something or someone to be perceived human.

How people perceive avatars in terms of experience and agency is not yet fully understood. Avatars are represented by human beings, but can take any form: human and non-human. Hence, it is imperative to understand the exact characteristics that contribute to these perceptions of experience and agency, especially in light of prior research showing that (de)humanization carry significant ramifications for interpersonal interaction. Individuals employ perceptions of agency and experience to comprehend or engage with entities, demonstrating a greater inclination to establish social bonds when they can ascribe specific characteristics of a human mind to someone or something [17]. With the increasing importance of virtual environments, understanding mind perception of avatars is thus crucial to understand how users interact with and respond to these digital representations.

Based on mind perception theory, the aim of our study is to explore how students perceive and attribute mental states of experience and agency to avatars, and what role avatar characteristics play. To systematically explore these dynamics, we conducted 6 focus groups involving university students. Through qualitative analysis, we seek to uncover nuanced insights into participants' perceptions, shedding light on the nuanced interplay between avatar characteristics and mind perception in virtual environments. This research contributes to a deeper understanding of the psychological processes underlying avatar-mediated communication, with potential implications for the design and optimization of virtual learning environments to enhance user experience and social interaction. The lack of comprehensive research in this area highlights a significant gap in our knowledge. To address this gap, we formulated the following research questions:

RQ1: What characteristics of avatars do students associate with experience?
RQ2: What characteristics of avatars do students associate with agency?

2 Methodology

The goal of our study is to investigate which avatar characteristics students associate with agency and experience. To attain this goal, we used a qualitative focus group design which consisted of two stages. First, students designed an avatar that varied in level of agency or experience. Second, students discussed the characteristics of these avatars that were associated with agency and experience. We conducted six focus groups, each comprising six to nine participants, in December 2023, following ethical approval from the local Institutional Review Board. Each focus group was moderated by a researcher. These six researchers underwent training, consisting of two meetings, to familiarize themselves with the study's objective and the focus group guide (see Appendix A).

2.1 Participants

All participants were third-year Communication Studies students of the Rotterdam University of Applied Sciences. At the beginning of the three-week course on Immersive Content, 85 students were invited to participate in a workshop on avatar creation and evaluation. Every student involved in the course took part in the workshop, but only those who consented to participate in the study had their data included. Forty-nine participants were recruited for the focus groups (Age $M = 21.4$, $SD = 0.21$; min: 19, max: 26; Female $= 83.7\%$, Male $= 16.3\%$) by giving their informed consent. These participants were divided into six groups, moderated by a trained researcher. All participants knew each other by name, allowing them to easily respond to each other.

2.2 Procedure

The procedure consisted of two stages: an avatar-creation stage, and the focus group discussion. The first (plenary) stage started with an explanation of the theoretical conceptualization of mind perception theory, and students were provided with the definitions of agency and experience. Subsequently, students were introduced to three avatar creator tools, each varying technological affordances, namely Heroforge, ReadyPlayerMe and Reblium. Next, participants were asked to design different avatars for one of four different possibilities: an avatar that was (1) low on agency and low on experience, (2) high on agency and low on experience, (3) high on agency and low on experience, and (4) high on agency and high on experience. Participants were randomly assigned to two of the possibilities. After designing avatars for the two assigned possibilities in 40 min time, each participant received a printed screenshot of their avatars (total avatars $N = 98$) and was invited to bring these to the group discussion.

In the second stage, participants discussed the avatars in six different focus groups. Participants were randomly assigned to a focus group. After informing participants that the focus groups would be audio recorded, the facilitator introduced the study aim and explained the protocol for the focus group. On the table, the two axes of agency and experience were laid out. Then, participants were asked to collectively position the avatars they brought along on the two axes, aiming for the greatest possible consensus. Participants were asked to think out loud and discuss the reasons for placing each of the avatars along the axes. The facilitators used directed follow-up questions to ask for clarification or to discuss certain choices. As soon as a consensus was reached, a picture was taken of the positioning of all avatars on the axes. Afterwards, digital audio recordings were immediately reviewed for compliance with the protocol and completeness, and then transcribed verbatim by trained researchers.

2.3 Data Analysis

The transcripts were analyzed by conventional content analysis [19], also described as inductive category development [20]. Three of the authors coded the focus group transcripts, and each focus group was coded by two coders. Disagreements were resolved through discussions. Data was coded in Atlas.ti version 24.0. Pertaining to the goal of the paper, we coded the transcripts to identify avatar characteristics that were related to low or high agency or experience. We coded whether the quote discussed low experience (E−), high experience (E+), low agency (A−) or high agency (A+).

In the inductive code category development process, we discovered a distinction between participants' comments on observable avatar characteristics and perceptions regarding the avatar design. Therefore, we coded observable characteristics referring to a property of the avatar that can be identified by looking at the avatar with a code that started with "Pr:", followed by the (observable) property. Examples are hair, clothing, entity, form and size. We coded participants' perceptions of the avatar using "Pe:" followed by the perception. Perceptions are impressions of the beliefs, attitudes and personality of the avatar that cannot objectively be identified from the avatar's characteristics. Examples are "has its own identity", "has a negative appearance", "is going on an adventure", "seems like a side character".

We used open coding to code the properties and perceptions of the avatars [20]. That is, other than the above rules, we had no predetermined codes related to properties and perceptions of the avatars. In the first stage, we identified 153 codes for properties and 234 codes for perceptions. Through discussion, we classified these different codes in 8 overarching themes related to the properties of the avatars and 9 themes related to perceptions of the avatars (see Table 1). We then conducted a co-occurrence analysis to identify which themes were associated with low or high agency or experience.

Table 1. Overarching themes for properties and perceptions, derived from open coding.

Characteristics	Overarching themes	Examples codes
Properties	*Entity*	
	Human	*real person, human body, human*
	Robot	*robot, robot bunny*
	Animal	*rabbit, ape, bear, teddy bear*
	Fantasy	*centaur, mermaid, mutated animal*
	Body detail	
	Incomplete body	*body absent, face covered, no hands*
	Eyes	*non-human eyes, strange eyes*
	Personal style	
	Fashion	*fashionable clothing, accessories,*
	Beauty	*make-up, purple hair, hair in a bun*
Perceptions	*Realism*	
	Unrealistic	*not credible, non-visible in daily life*
	Realistic	*looks real, resemblance to real person*
	Image	
	Positive appearance	*confidence, friendly appearance*
	Basic appearance	*standard look, basic, standard pose*

(continued)

Table 1. (*continued*)

Characteristics	Overarching themes	Examples codes
	Negative appearance	*no appearance, looks angry*
	Identity	*personality, can identify with*
	Character	
	Main character	*main character, movie character*
	Side character	*side character, non-playing character*
	Story	*shopping, part of a gang, goes to festival*

3 Results

Based on the analysis of the transcripts of the focus groups, conceptual indicator models have been constructed to answer the research questions regarding what characteristics of avatars do students associate with experience (**RQ1**; see Fig. 1) and what characteristics of avatars do students associate with agency (**RQ2**; see Fig. 2).

3.1 Experience

As shown in Fig. 1, participants attributed avatars less capacity (i.e., low experience) or more capacity (i.e., high experience) for sensation and feelings, based on entity, detail, personal style, realism, image, and character.

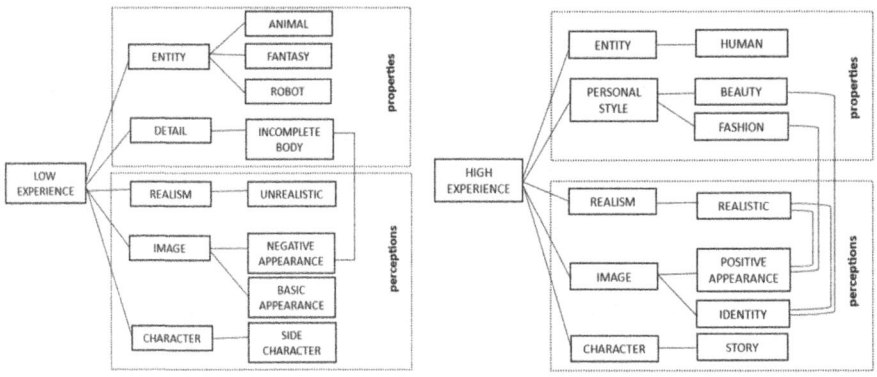

Fig. 1. Conceptual indicator model, linking experience to avatar characteristics.

Entity. Entity can be categorized into avatars represented as a) a human, b) a robot, c) an animal, and d) a fantasy figure (e.g., a centaur or mermaid). The degree of experience that participants attributed to avatars as animals and avatars as fantasy figures seemed to be depending how it relates to other avatar entities. Human-like avatars were attributed more experience, as those avatars were inherently seen as related to the human ability to have feelings, while animals and fantasy figures were attributed to a lesser extent.

RX[1]: I would also slightly lower the experience for that centaur; it never surpasses a virtual human. However, a robot was consistently attributed low experience. Robots were seen as entities that cannot feel emotions.
RX: A human has flesh and blood. You can see that, but this [robot] is actually just a piece of metal. You can't feel anything with it. It's just cold.

Detail. Avatars varied in the extent to which details of the body are visible. For example, an avatar might only have a head and no body, or the face might be partially covered by a mask, obscuring details of the mouth or eyes. Participants saw the absence of body details as a signal of low experience.

RX: You don't see the whole body. For all you know, she could be standing like this or like that. Or, I don't know, very insecure. You just don't know. You can't judge based on something you don't see. Moreover, the absence of body details was linked to negative appearance.
RX: Simply because he doesn't have eyebrows. Well, I might find him looking even dumber.

Personal Style. Avatars represented in fashionable clothing, colorful hair, or makeup, with accessories, were attributed high experience, far more than avatars with a basic outfit. The expression "clothes make the man" also seemed to be applicable in the virtual context, since the way an avatar was styled affected how participants attributed the extent to which an avatar had the capacity for sensation and feelings. Moreover, participants linked fashion to having an identity and positive appearance.

RX: It's more of a pronounced character. There's really a personality behind it. Self-expression, wanting to show oneself and maybe not wanting to go along with everything that's normally seen as normal. I[2]: And where do you derive that from?
RX: Hair color, size, striking clothes, colors. That's what I think.

Realism. Participants indicated that the degree of realism is an important aspect of whether an avatar is attributed experience. If an avatar was realistic, closely resembling how things appear in the real world, it was linked to the capability to have feelings. As opposed to lesser realistic avatars, such as more fantasy or cartoonish avatars, which were attributed low experience. More realistic avatars were also assigned to have some kind of individual identity.

RX: Because it's still more human-like. And I do feel that with the face, you already have an idea of how someone is. For example, when I see this character, I would feel less... I find this one more cartoonish.

---

[1] RX stands for a quote of one of the 49 focus group participants.
[2] I stands for one of the six interviewing researchers.

Image. Participants frequently mentioned the appearance of the avatars in relation to experience. Avatars could have a negative appearance (e.g., "she doesn't look very smart"), a basic appearance (e.g., "very neutral, simple avatar"), or a positive appearance (e.g., "she looks hip"). Participants linked negative and basic appearances to a lesser capacity for sensation or feelings, while linking positive appearance with a greater capacity for sensation or feelings. Besides a positive appearance, participants repeatedly mentioned that an avatar seems to have its own identity. This was mostly linked to fashion and realism.

RX: And then that cheerleader [avatar] also has her own, pronounced... Yeah, also her own personality when you look like that. I: And what characteristics do you derive that from, that own personality?
RX: Well, her outfit and what she's wearing. Also, a bit how she stands, I think.

Character. Last, participants connected experience to the avatar being a story character. Avatars with low experience were often characterized as "side characters" or non-playing characters with no feelings.

RX: This resembles one of those characters that just follow along in a game, you know. You can tease them a bit. Like, you can just give them a shove or something. There's little emotion in them, and they don't mind if you do.

Participants often perceived a narrative behind avatars with high experience, envisioning them engaged in activities like working, shopping, or going on an adventure.

RX: Because it [the avatar] is a kind of festival-goer. It really gives character. And at a festival, of course, a lot of emotions come out.

3.2 Agency

As demonstrated in Fig. 2, participants attributed avatars less capacity (i.e., low agency) or more capacity (i.e., high agency) to intend and to act, based on entity, detail, personal style, realism, image, and character.

Entity. Participants regarded human-like avatars highly capable of acting and intending, as they often ascribed human capabilities such as free will and making your own choices to avatars who resembled human entities. Avatars represented as robots, animals and fantasy figures were regarded those abilities to a much lesser extent. Similar to experience, participants regarded human-like avatars highly capable of acting and intending.

I: Why do these avatars score high on agency?
RX: I think because they look the most human and well-groomed.

Furthermore, avatars as robots were experienced low in agency. Although participants perceived robot avatars capable to act, it is not based on free will.

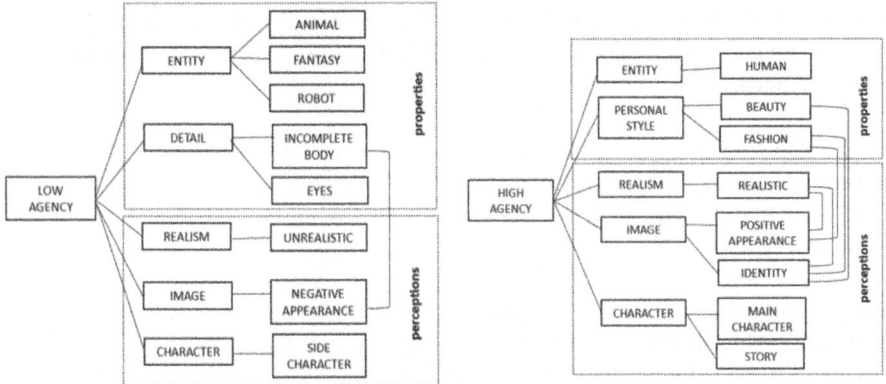

Fig. 2. Conceptual indicator model, linking agency to avatar characteristics.

RX: He has little arms that just do this and that's it, but he doesn't have free will, he's just programmed. He's just programmed to do things, he won't do things on his own.

Detail. Just as mentioned by experience, the degree to which details of the body were visible, seemed to matter in the attribution of agency. Participants saw the absence of body parts quite literally as the absence of possibilities to act.

RX: Because he doesn't really have hands to speak of. Or anything he can really do things with. Maybe he can walk, but that's about it.

The details of the avatars' eyes were not mentioned in relation to experience, but only in relation to agency. According to the participants, the gaze of an avatar made the avatar less capable of acting independently. For example, these avatars had a deviant eye color, or an empty stare.

RX: This avatar doesn't have its own will anymore and such. And also doesn't really have the choice to do things on its own. But it is still a human. But... From the inside, it's not human.
I: And are there specific character traits that indicate that?
RX: She has white eyes and also that strange robot thing on her head. A human that's been a little taken over by a robot.

Personal style. Like experience, agency was attributed to avatars represented in fashionable clothing, colorful hair, or makeup, with accessories, far more than avatars with a basic outfit. Participants indicated that with pronounced outfits, the avatar appeared to have been thinking about its way of dressing by itself.

RX: Because he's wearing sunglasses. You can also tell from his clothing that he's capable of making choices. You see a man with glasses, clearly someone who loves fashion. His opinion is clearly expressed.

Realism. Participants mentioned realism in the context of high experience, but even more prominently when they were discussing which avatars they evaluated high in the context of agency.

RX: You can see that it's not a realistic avatar, you can still see that it's not a real person. So I would place it high [on agency], but not at the extreme point. Yeah, I think if there was a picture of a completely real person, that would be all the way at the top right [on agency].

Image. Similar to low and high experience, participants linked negative and positive appearance to low respectively high agency. Different from experience, basic appearance was not mentioned frequently in the context of agency.

RX: Because she walks confidently, it seems like she's heading towards a goal. And so she must have thought about that. And you can't have a goal without thoughts.

Identity was also repeatedly mentioned by the participants in relation to high agency—similar to high experience—which was mostly linked to beauty and fashion.

RX: And I also think this one really has character with the purple hair and the makeup as well. It seems to be a somewhat powerful character who also knows what they want, I think. And who embarks on their own adventure.

Characters. Similar to low and high experience, side characters were frequently mentioned regarding low agency, and perceived narratives behind the avatars was connected with high agency. Different from experience, agency also involved discussions about avatars as main characters.

RX: He does seem like a main character.
RX: Yeah, he looks like the savior of the community. He can do multiple things. He can fly and run. This one does have a spear or something.
I: And why would you then place him higher on the agency ladder?
RX: Because that kind of radiates... Yeah, radiates power. Victory.

In all, the overarching themes were fairly consistent between agency and experience (see Fig. 3), with a few exceptions (i.e., basic appearance only linked to low experience, eyes only linked to low agency, main character only linked to high agency).

4 Discussion

The aim of the study was to explore which avatar characteristics students associate with agency and experience. The results show that avatars were attributed low experience and agency, when designed as nonhuman entities (e.g., robots or animals), depicted with incomplete bodies, unrealistic appearances, negative appearances, and suggested side

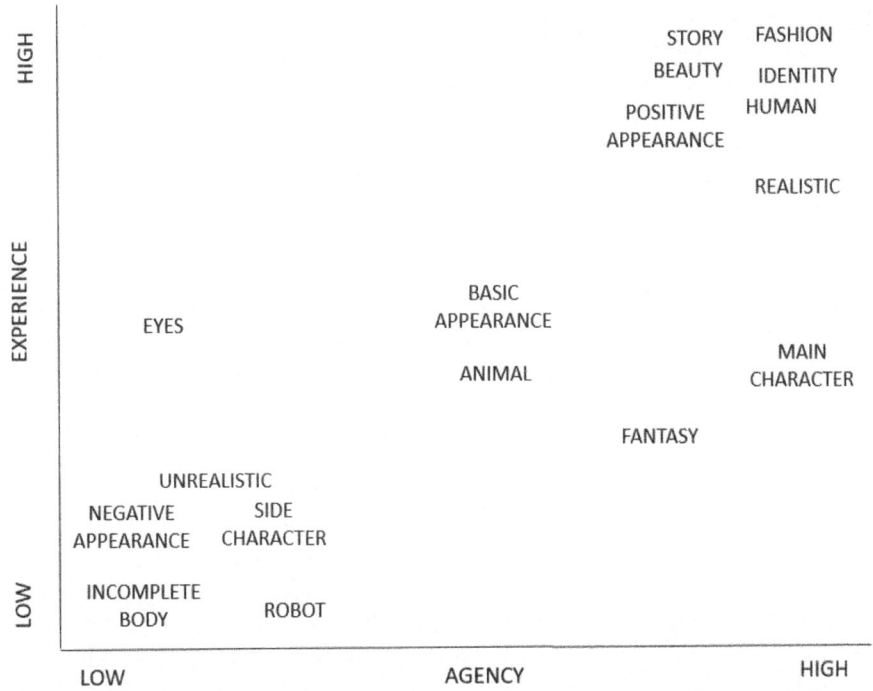

Fig. 3. Characteristics linked to experience and agency, based on the focus groups' transcripts, also including the pictures taken of the plotting schemes of each focus groups.

character roles. Conversely, avatars attributed with high experience and agency typically showcased human-like figures with unique personal styles, realistic representations, positive appearances, and convey a strong sense of individual identity and storyline centrality. As such, we make several contributions.

First, we contribute to the literature about the ethics of VR design by demonstrating that avatar characteristics do matter for facilitating an inclusive learning environment. Based on the basic principles of psychology and sociology, social relationships are reserved only for those to whom we ascribe human characteristics [21]. This study shows that a full and visible body is a rather essential condition in this perspective, according to students. This adds to prior research, already showing that co-presence (i.e., psychological connection of the mind, the sense of being together [22]) is lower when participants saw their partner with incomplete body parts [23, 24]. Furthermore, the results emphasize the significance of self-expression and projecting one's own identity. However, there are limitations concerning the extent to which this expression should occur in virtual learning environments. While VR provides opportunities for the exploration of entirely new identities [11], avatars should be realistic and human-like instead of representing a non-human race (e.g., fantasy character, alien or a white cube) to be perceived as capable of independent action and emotional experience. This is in line with the literature on anthropomorphism (i.e., the assignment of human traits to entities that may or may not be human [8]), indicating that looking human (i.e., high form of anthropomorphism) is judged more favorably (e.g., more credible and competent [8]). As such, these findings provide ethical guiding principles for designing inclusive VR environments taking students' perceptions into account.

Second, this study enhances the literature on mind perception theory by identifying specific characteristics related to experience and agency. While prior work on mind perception theory compares 13 different characters, such as a baby, a dead woman, a robot, oneself, and God [16], this study goes further by examining the common characteristics of 98 avatars. In addition to comparing entities, this study also evaluates characteristics such as clothing, realism, and the degree of visible body detail. More specifically, we discovered that characteristics associated with experience are largely consistent with those associated with agency, although the reasoning is slightly different (e.g., fashionable clothing is linked to high experience because it is a form of self-expression, and it is linked to high agency because it suggests that the avatar can make its own choices). By doing so, our findings contribute to the solidification of the model proposed by Gray and colleagues [16, 17].

Although this study sheds light on mind perception of avatars, this study comes with limitations as well. First, the participants of the focus groups were limited to Communication students, predominantly women (83.7%), with little to no experience with VR prior to the course on Immersive Content, from Western Europe. This could yield several biases. For instance, prior research indicates intercultural differences regarding to the extent to which people appreciate customized (versus uniform) avatars [25]. Moreover, also gaming experience appears to affect avatar choice [25]. Thus, the generalizability of the results is limited to students with similar background characteristics (i.e., West-European, female students, little to no VR experience). To strengthen the external validity of the results, future research should replicate this research design, using a more diverse student sample regarding gender, cultural background, and familiarity with VR. We suggest that future researchers conduct a comparative analysis using quantitative measures to examine the extent to which students' background characteristics affect the perceived agency and experience of avatars and their characteristics.

Second, this study was exploratory in nature, aiming to map out the characteristics of avatars associated with agency and experience. For this purpose, focus groups were a suitable method. However, to test causal relationships, future researchers should examine some of these characteristics in an experiment. In addition, it would be a valuable future research endeavor to further strengthen the literature on immersive learning by examining the extent to which differences in perceived agency and experience influence learning outcomes. This would build upon prior research regarding avatar representation and collaboration outcomes in virtual learning environments, comparing robot avatars with videocall [12], comparing photorealistic avatars with animated and no avatars [26], and comparing self-avatars with uniform avatars [27].

Limitations aside, this study provides a comprehensive view of how students perceive avatar characteristics in relation to experience and agency. As such, it gives guidance for VR developers, teachers and educationalists to give shape to collaborative learning environments with a human touch.

Acknowledgments. We would like to thank Raul Martinez-Orozco and Kim Stolk for assisting in running the focus groups.

Disclosure of Interests. The authors have no competing interests to declare that are relevant to the content of this article.

Appendix

Discussion Guide.
  Instructions:

1. Turn on the voice recorder.
2. Place the various avatars (12 to 20 pieces) created by the students printed on the table. Place the paper with two axes (experience – agency) on the table. Ask the students to collectively place the avatars on the two axes, aiming for the greatest possible consensus. Then, the discussion leader poses the following questions.

  Follow up questions:

1. Which avatar do you believe scores very high on agency? In other words, an avatar that can think logically, act based on free will, make moral judgments, remember things, and have memories. What characteristics contribute to this? To what extent does the degree of detail (body type, height, skin color, hairstyle, facial features, body characteristics, gender, ethnicity, race (non-human/aliens), clothing, shoes, accessories, realism (abstract-cartoonish-photorealistic) play a role?
2. Which avatar do you believe scores very low on agency? In other words, an avatar that cannot think logically, does not act based on free will, cannot make moral judgments, does not remember things, and has no memories. What characteristics contribute to this? To what extent does the degree of detail (body type, height, skin color, hairstyle, facial features, body characteristics, gender, ethnicity, race (non-human/aliens), clothing, shoes, accessories, realism (abstract-cartoonish-photorealistic) play a role?
3. Which avatar do you believe scores very high on experience? In other words, an avatar that has awareness, the ability to feel and experience, such as sensory experiences (e.g., enjoying something or feeling pain) and emotions, and seems to have its own personality.
What characteristics contribute to this? To what extent does the degree of detail (body type, height, skin color, hairstyle, facial features, body characteristics, gender, ethnicity, race (non-human/aliens), clothing, shoes, accessories, realism (abstract-cartoonish-photorealistic) play a role?
4. Which avatar do you believe scores very low on experience? In other words, an avatar that has no awareness, no ability to feel and experience, such as sensory experiences (e.g., enjoying something or feeling pain) and emotions, and does not seem to have its own personality. What characteristics contribute to this? To what extent does the degree of detail (body type, height, skin color, hairstyle, facial features, body characteristics, gender, ethnicity, race (non-human/aliens), clothing, shoes, accessories, realism (abstract-cartoonish-photorealistic) play a role?

  Take a photo of the final result of the avatars plotted on the two axes.

References

1. Ball, M.: The Metaverse: And How it Will Revolutionize Everything. Liveright Publishing, New York City (2022)
2. Limbu, B., van Roijen, R., Beerens, M., Specht, M.: HoloLearn: towards a hologram mediated hybrid education. In: Dascalu, M., Mealha, Ó., Virkus, S. (eds.) Smart Learning Ecosystems as Engines of the Green and Digital Transition, pp. 117–132. Springer, New York City (2023)
3. Nur Affendy, M.N., Wanis, A.I.: A review on collaborative learning environment across virtual and augmented reality technology. In: IOP Conference Series: Materials Science and Engineering, Article 012050. IOP Publishing, Bristol (2019)
4. Chavez, B., Bayona, S.: Virtual reality in the learning process. In: Rocha, Á., Adeli, H., Reis, L., Costanzo, S. (eds.) Trends and Advances in Information Systems and Technologies, pp. 1345–1356. Springer, New York City (2018)
5. Kwon, C.: Verification of the possibility and effectiveness of experiential learning using HMD-based immersive VR technologies. Virtual Reality 23(1), 101–118 (2019)
6. Van der Meer, N., Van der Werf, V., Brinkman, W.P., Specht, M.: Virtual reality and collaborative learning: a systematic literature review. Front. Virtual Reality 4, 1159905 (2023)
7. Lan, X., van Berlo, Z.M.C.: Can non-humanlike avatars induce the Proteus effect? The roles of avatar identification and embodiment in influencing social participation. Computers in Human Behavior: Artificial Humans 1(2), 100020 (2023). https://doi.org/10.1016/j.chbah.2023.100020
8. Nowak, K.L., Fox, J.: Avatars and computer-mediated communication: a review of the definitions, uses, and effects of digital representations. Rev. Commun. Res. 6, 30–53 (2018)
9. Ducheneaut, N., Wen, M. H., Yee, N., Wadley, G.: Body and mind: a study of avatar personalization in three virtual worlds. In: Greenberg, S., Hudson, S.E., Hinckley, K., Morris, M.R., Olsen, D.R. (eds.) Proceedings of the SIGCHI Conference on Human Factors in Computing Systems, pp. 1151–1160 (2009)
10. Pakanen, M., Alavesa, P., Van Berkel, N., Koskela, T., Ojala, T.: "Nice to see you virtually": thoughtful design and evaluation of virtual avatar of the other user in AR and VR based telexistence systems. Entertainment Comput. 40, 100457 (2022)
11. Freeman, G., Maloney, D.: Body, avatar, and me: The presentation and perception of self in social virtual reality. In: Nichols, J. (eds.) Proceedings of the ACM conference on human-computer interaction, article 239 (2021)
12. Schouten, A.P., Portegies, T.C., Withuis, I., Willemsen, L.M., Mazerant-Dubois, K.: Robomorphism: examining the effects of telepresence robots on between-student cooperation. Comput. Hum. Behav. 126, 106980 (2022)
13. Haslam, N.: Dehumanization: an integrative review. Pers. Soc. Psychol. Rev. 10(3), 252–264 (2006)
14. Haslam, N., Loughnan, S.: Dehumanization and infrahumanization. Annu. Rev. Psychol. 65, 399–423 (2014)
15. Bastian, B., Haslam, N.: Experiencing dehumanization: cognitive and emotional effects of everyday dehumanization. Basic Appl. Soc. Psychol. 33(4), 295–303 (2011)
16. Gray, H.M., Gray, K., Wegner, D.M.: Dimensions of mind perception. Science 315, 619 (2007)
17. Gray, K., Young, L., Waytz, A.: Mind perception is the essence of morality. Psychol. Inq. 23(2), 101–124 (2012)
18. Epley, N., Waytz, A.: Mind perception. Handbook Soc. Psychol. 1(5), 498–541 (2010)
19. Hsieh, H.F., Shannon, S.E.: Three approaches to qualitative content analysis. Qual. Health Res. 15(9), 1277–1288 (2005)
20. Mayring, P.: Qualitative content analysis. In: Flick, U., von Kardoff, E., Steinke, I. (eds.) A companion to qualitative research, pp. 266–269. Sage Publications, Thousand Oaks (2004)

21. Harth, J.: Empathy with non-player characters? An empirical approach to the foundations of human/non-human relationships. J. Virtual Worlds Res. **10**(2) (2017).
22. Nowak, K.: Defining and differentiating copresence, social presence and presence as transportation. In: Presence 2001 Conference, Philadelphia, vol. 2, pp. 686–710 (2001)
23. Heidicker, P., Langbehn, E., Steinicke, F.: Influence of avatar appearance on presence in social VR. In: 2017 IEEE Symposium on 3D User Interfaces (3DUI), pp. 233–234. IEEE: New York City (2017)
24. Yoon, B., Kim, H.I., Lee, G.A., Billinghurst, M., Woo, W.: The effect of avatar appearance on social presence in an augmented reality remote collaboration. In: 2019 IEEE Conference on Virtual Reality and 3D User Interfaces (VR), pp. 547–556. IEEE, New York City (2019)
25. Corneliussen, H., Rettberg, J.W.: Digital Culture, Play, and Identity: A World of Warcraft reader. MIT Press, Cambridge (2008)
26. Aseeri, S., Interrante, V.: The influence of avatar representation on interpersonal communication in virtual social environments. IEEE Trans. Visual Comput. Graphics **27**(5), 2608–2617 (2021)
27. Han, E., et al.: People, places, and time: a large-scale, longitudinal study of transformed avatars and environmental context in group interaction in the metaverse. J. Comput.-Mediated Commun. **28**(2), zmac031 (2023)

Author Index

A
Abrantes, Eduarda I-201
Andrei, Maria II-37
Arya, Ali I-272
Arztmann, Michaela I-302

B
Bailenson, Jeremy I-65
Balamurugan, Neha I-187
Bates, Richard II-37
Beams, Brian I-65
Beck, Dennis I-112
Bento, Marco I-460
Blaikie, Andrew II-81
Boel, Carl I-142
Bonfim, Cristiane Jorge I-471
Brenner, Corinne I-386
Buchner, Josef I-363
Burnett, Gary I-80, I-167

C
Calyam, Prasad I-261
Cassese, Francesco Peluso I-49
Cassidy, Catherine Anne II-37, II-81
Chen, TzuChin I-386
Christopoulos, Athanasios I-317
Cipollone, Elèna I-49
Comanici, Mario I-363

D
De Nino, Maurizio II-109
Dengel, Andreas I-363
Domínguez Alfaro, Jessica Lizeth I-302
Duan, Yupei I-261

E
Economides, Anastasios A. I-130
Etemadi, Ashley I-417

F
Fabregat, Ramon II-19
Fernandes, Filipe II-3
Frazier, Kai I-65
Freytag, Sarah-Christin I-18
Froehlich, Fabian I-3, I-348

G
Galaup, Michel I-201
Garavaglia, Andrea II-109
Gauen, Sarah I-272
Glaser, Noah I-249, I-261
Goggins, Sean I-329
Gonzalez Martinez, Maria I-201
Griffin, Joseph I-329
Gross, Benedikt I-217
Gütl, Christian I-363

H
Haddad, Hana I-386
Han, Eugy I-65
Hancock, Jeff I-65
He, Hao I-329
Heinrich, Sonja II-37
Hildebrandt, Jannik I-287
Holford, Mandë I-386
Holly, Michael I-287
Homer, Bruce D. I-3, I-348

J
Jeong, Yuseon I-446
Jeuring, Johan I-302
Joshi, Amogh Chetankumar I-261

K
Kambhampati, Anirudh I-261
Kaye, Rachael I-187
Khaleghian, Hanieh I-187
Ki, Suhyun II-96

Kim, Kukhyeon I-446
Koutromanos, George I-399
Krüger, Jule M. I-156

L
Laffey, James I-329
Lagarrigue, Pierre I-201
Lembo, Luna I-49
Lencastre, José Alberto I-460
Li, Shangman I-249, I-261
LiKamWa, Robert I-187
Liu, Sunny I-65
Lu, Jie I-249
Lu, Wenyi I-329

M
Magalhães, Celestino I-460
Mazerant, Komala II-123
McCann, Julie I-272
McGivney, Eileen I-65
Memminger, Josef I-363
Mikropoulos, Tassos I-399
Miller, Alan I-232, II-37, II-52, II-81
Miller, Mark Roman I-65
Moore, Christine I-187
Morgado, Leonel I-112, I-471
Morsanuto, Stefania I-49
Moustakas, Konstantinos I-317
Mozelius, Peter I-177
Mulders, Miriam II-68
Mystakidis, Stylianos I-317

N
Nacke, Lennart I-95
Nikou, Stavros A. I-130
Nuguri, Sai Shreya I-261
Nyman, Perin Joy Westerhof I-232
Nyman, Perin Westerhof II-52

O
Ochoa Hendrix, Jessica I-386
Oles, Kamila II-81
Oliver, Iain I-232, II-37, II-81
Ousley, Cannon I-261

P
Panzoli, David I-201
Parishani, Zeinab I-261

Pedrosa, Daniela I-471
Perifanou, Maria I-130
Petersen, Xander I-65
Pirker, Johanna I-95, I-217, I-287
Pisani, Sharon II-37
Plass, Jan L. I-3, I-348
Porter, Austin I-187

Q
Queiroz, Anna C. M. I-65

R
Reis, Gustavo dos I-201
Riener, Andreas I-375, I-431
Ryu, Jeeheon I-446, II-96

S
Sadler, Troy D. I-329
Safikhani, Saeed I-95, I-217
Sanchez-Holguin, Kilian I-18
Scanlon, Eileen I-34
Scavarelli, Anthony I-272
Schmidt, Matthew I-249
Schouten, Alexander P. II-123
Schreiber, Luca I-431
Serrano-Ausejo, Elisa I-177
Shah, Tanmesh I-375
Smit, Sanne B. T. II-123
Spangenberger, Pia I-18
Steinmaurer, Alexander I-363
Suzuki, Yuko I-34

T
Teather, Robert J. I-272
Terrenghi, Ilaria II-109
Thivet, Judicaël I-201
Tracy, Helen St Clair II-81
Träg, Kristian H. II-68

U
Urban, Alex I-329

V
van Berlo, Zeph M. C. II-123
Vontzalidis, Georgios I-317
Vrellis, Ioannis I-399

W

Wakelin, Rebecca I-272
Weißenberger, Markus I-431
Weng, Yueqi I-249
Werner, Cláudia II-3
Wild, Fridolin I-34
Willemsen, Lotte M. II-123
Woolsey, Erika S. I-65

Y

Yang, Mohan I-261
Yu, Fan I-329
Yuan, Victor I-232

Z

Zhang, Junyu II-52
Zúniga-Solórzano, Marcos E. II-19

The manufacturer's authorised representative in the EU is Springer Nature Customer Service Centre GmbH, Europaplatz 3, 69115 Heidelberg, Germany. If you have any concerns regarding our products, please contact ProductSafety@springernature.com

Printed and bound by CPI Group (UK) Ltd, Croydon, CR0 4YY

25/03/2026

02078191-0020